Indoor Gardening

BY DOROTHY AND THOMAS HOOBLER
WILLIAM C. MULLIGAN
ELVIN McDONALD

A compilation of *House Plants, Cacti & Succulents, Miniature Gardens* and *Gardening in Containers*

D1511847

A GROSSET SUPER GOOD LIFE BOOK

PUBLISHERS · GROSSET & DUNLAP · NEW YORK
A FILMWAYS COMPANY

Copyright © 1975, 1976 by Grosset & Dunlap, Inc.
All rights reserved
Published simultaneously in Canada
Library of Congress catalog card number: 76-1615
ISBN 0-448-12477-7
Printed in the United States of America

Contents

PART IV: GARDENING IN CONTAINERS

Part I
House Plants

BY DOROTHY and THOMAS HOOBLER

1
Basics

In all likelihood, you already have tried growing plants indoors or you wouldn't have picked up this book. Maybe you had some success, and are interested in finding out more about plants. You might have had little success, or not as much as you liked, and hope to find out why. In either case, you probably liked the idea of adding life, color, and beauty to your house or apartment by growing plants. The first step toward success with house plants has already been taken: you like having them around.

The second step is finding out whether they like having you around. The idea that some people have a green thumb that guarantees they can grow practically anything is widespread. The corollary, of course, is that if you are not the lucky possessor of a green thumb, you will be a failure as a gardener. This isn't true. We strongly believe that the most important factor in growing indoor plants is choosing the right plants — plants that are right for you and for your environment.

As you look over this Part, you'll find that the chapters on specific plants deal first with plants that require next to no care, then plants that require routine care, and finally plants that require real devotion. This division shouldn't necessarily be taken to mean "easy," "medium-hard," and "very difficult" plants, although we may slip and call them that in passing. For some people, the most difficult plants are those that require little or no care, and the easiest will be those that need a lot of care.

Read the chapter on basic needs and care, chapter one, to see if you really know how to treat your plants well. People are often surprised to find that the cause of their failures with plants is too much water or fertilizer or sunlight. Remember: if your plants are doing well, you don't need any help from us, though you may enjoy learning about other plants you are not familiar with. If they're not doing as well as you'd like, use this Part to find out why.

Bright places are not necessarily windowsills. Look around your home or office for other places to keep plants. A table out in a bright part of a room is a good possibility, bookshelves are another, and if you are short on surfaces, turn your eyes to the ceiling and see if hanging pots could be the answer for you.

Environment

Wherever the place you envision plants in your home or office, that place is an environment. It has, as much as woodland, jungle or desert, an average temperature, a certain humidity, an amount of light. It also has a changing climate — perhaps no heat over the weekend, or extreme dryness during the winter, or sun only when the leaves are off the trees outside. No doubt there are plants that will thrive in any environment you have, but to choose the ones that will, you must find out more about the environment you can offer.

Light

When considering what kinds of plants you can suitably grow indoors, the plant's need for light is the first thing to consider. The measurement of light is technically expressed in foot-candles; few of us, however, have the scientific equipment necessary for measuring the number of foot-candles of light a plant will receive in an average day in a certain spot indoors.

The kind of advice that says, "This plant will do well in a window with a southern exposure," also fails to take into account what the conditions are outside that window. If your south-facing window in the city looks out on a tall building that blocks the sun and sky, it's not as bright as a north window in the suburbs where nothing blocks the view.

We'll call on you to use your judgment, even though estimating light intensity is a tricky process. When we talk about a sunny window, we mean one where a plant will be exposed to the direct rays of the sun for at least two hours a day. A bright window is one that gets a little

At the first sign of spring weather, novice plant-owners often rush their plants out on the patio or fire escape to enjoy the bright sun and fresh air. This is a case of killing with kindness. Plants that have spent the winter in a relatively dark room are easily burned by exposure to full sun.
Moving plants outside for the summer is an excellent idea if you can manage it. But you should accustom them to full sun by starting with 15 minutes of it and working up. The same thing goes for outside air. If the temperature is lower than what your plants are used to, it isn't a good idea to expose them to it, no matter how sunny the day. Wait until the weather is dependably warm.

direct sun, and has reflected sunlight for most of the day. An ordinary window is one where all light is reflected off the ground or other buildings, but where the light is bright enough most of the day to do reading or close work like sewing. A shady window is one where you would not find reading or sewing comfortable for long periods without an artificial light. There are some lightless windows, such as those facing on an airshaft or in a below-ground room. Finally, there are rooms or offices where there are no windows, and all the light is artificial.

Humidity

Humidity, of the three environmental basics, is probably the one we are least aware of; most of the time, the air in our homes feels comfortable to us. Yet humidity is easily as important as light and heat to the well-being of our plants.

Although the humidity outdoors changes daily with the weather, most homes are fairly dry places. A relative humidity of 15 to 25 per cent is not unusual in most apartments or homes. Winter can be particularly dry. Contrast that with, for example the natural environment of the African violet, where the humidity is normally above 60 per cent, and often much higher.

We can say with certainty that the number one cause of house plants failing to flower is low humidity. Dry air can also be the cause of the leaf browning that many people find so bothersome in their plants. In extreme cases, entire leaves can shrivel.

Humidity is measured by *relative* humidity measurements, determined by the ratio between the amount of moisture in the air and the amount that the air could hold at a given temperature. Since warm air can hold more moisture than cold air, relative humidity drops in warmer rooms. Particularly low in humidity are rooms heated by artificial heat in the winter. In summer, when the air is naturally moist, it also holds a lot of moisture. That's why you're so uncomfortable in the summer. When you are, remember that your house plants that came from jungle-type environments are very happy.

Fortunately, there are ways of raising the humidity around your plants while leaving it comfortably low for you and your family in the rest of the room. We'll discuss these methods on page 17.

The basic idea in raising humidity is to keep extra water in the vicinity of your plants. As it evaporates, it adds water to the air in the local environment of your plant. The easiest way of all to keep humidity high for plants that don't require very high humidity is to keep a lot of plants together in one spot. Moisture from the soil itself will be enough to raise the local humidity to the level most plants will need.

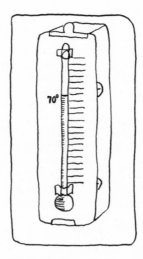

To get some idea of the average day and night temperature of your home or office, invest in an ordinary household thermometer. Leave it in exactly the place you want to put your plant (not just in the same room, because temperatures 4 feet off the floor are different from those at the floor, and a spot near the window is different from a spot in the middle of the room). Check the temperature a few times a day, and late at night as well as early in the morning. Make a note of the averages as well as the extremes, and buy your plants accordingly.

Putting your plants on the windowsill is a good idea, from the standpoint of getting the most light possible for them. But on cold winter nights, the temperature next to a window can be a lot lower than in the rest of the room. If your plants are drooping in the winter mornings, try moving them farther away from the windows. Another good solution is to draw a blind or curtain between the plant and the window. Particularly in offices, where the night temperatures are likely to be cold, closing the venetian blinds can make all the difference for your plants.

Warmth

If you lack light in your apartment, and want to grow plants that require a lot of light, it is easy to set up an artificial lighting system. Likewise, you can find easy ways of increasing the humidity in the vicinity of your plants. Heat, however, is a more difficult problem.

The solution to the problem is to make an accurate assessment of the usual temperature in your apartment, house, or office. Pick the kinds of plants that like that temperature. It's a lot easier to do that than to bring home a plant because you like its leaves or flowers, and then find that it likes night temperatures below 55° or above 75°. If you have your own thermostat, live alone, or are willing to change the conditions in your apartment, your choice of plants will be that much larger.

Most houses and apartments have temperatures above 70° in the daytime and below 65° at night during the winter months. In the summertime, of course, temperatures can go above 90° and stay above 80° at night. Take that into account, too, because there are a lot of plants that don't tolerate too-hot weather.

If you're planning to start a garden in your office, get plants that are able to withstand drastic swings in temperature. Many landlords turn the heat way down at night and on weekends. You might come back some Monday morning to find your prized plant drooping or all but killed from a bout with near-freezing temperatures.

Air conditioning can be harmful to plants placed near a window unit or the open duct of a central system. A steady blast of that cold air can be as damaging to your plants as putting them out for the first frost. In the same way, temperatures near a heating duct and especially a steam-heat radiator can be far higher than the normal temperature in the room. Be careful about setting plants too close to these.

Finally, a word about drafts. In the spring or summer, the temptation is to raise the windows high and give our plants a nice dose of that fine outside air. In most cases, this is fine, but certain plants, in particular African violets and codiaeum (croton) don't take to cool breezes at all.

Evaluating Your Environment

Now you are aware of the four most important elements in the health of your indoor plants: light, humidity, heat, and yourself. The most important of these is yourself, because it is how you will be taking care of the plant in its day-to-day needs that will overcome deficiencies or advantages in the other three basic needs.

How to use this information? First, evaluate the area in which you will be growing plants. If you want to grow plants in your office, you may find that there are no windows, a dry atmosphere, and a very cool night or weekend temperature. These are handicaps, but they only limit your choice of plants to those that can cope with the office conditions. Kalanchoe and Sansevieria are only two of the plants that will grow in such circumstances. Use the sections on individual plants on pages 34 to 89 to find some others.

Suppose you like flowering plants, and have a vision of your small apartment filled with color and beauty practically year-round. Should you go out and buy plants that show off their blooms well in the florists? If you do, you're likely to bring them home and watch them wilt, unless you've checked out the conditions at home beforehand, and made sure that the plants will grow under those conditions. If the conditions are wrong, you may be prepared to install artificial lights or bring up the humidity to accommodate your plants. Planning and evaluating beforehand will save you a lot of trouble and disappointment later on.

Finally, what kind of person are you? What do you hope to get from growing plants, and how much work do you want to put into the job? If you're the sort that always is into everything, and you know you're going to make a fuss over your plants — watering daily with a thermometer in hand, repotting, mixing just the right soil blend — then don't pick out one of the plants that needs little care. About the only thing that will kill some of these plants is too much attention.

On the other hand, if you're basically carefree, slightly absent-minded, and don't find yourself at home on any kind of regular basis, pick out plants that will do well on your schedule. Pick your plants, like your friends, with care.

When the plant you buy has grown in different conditions from those it will face in your home, it may temporarily go into shock. The leaves may droop, and the whole plant can look bad for several weeks. This is not necessarily due to disease or insect pests — though it might be.

Properly treated, most plants recover if given the right shock care. First, do not water it for at least two or three days. Plants in shock don't absorb water, and all you'll do is risk root rot.

Don't put your new plant in the sunniest window you've got, even if this book says it needs direct sunlight. Let it get accustomed to conditions in your house. When and if you do put a new plant in a sunny window for the first time, watch it closely. Dry spots and patches are signs of scorching, and mean you should move the plant to a shadier spot.

Don't fertilize new plants for six months after you've bought them. The only exceptions are those plants that this book specifically recommends be given fertilizer.

Finally, it is always a good idea to segregate new plants from your other plants for at least two weeks and up to six weeks, if convenient for you. Then, if anything is wrong with your new plant, it won't affect your entire collection.

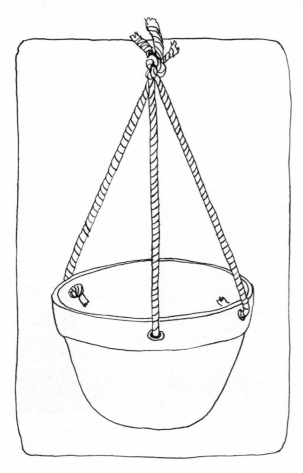

Hanging pots do a lot to beautify an otherwise bare window. The pots can be made of any material, but before you buy, check carefully to see what the hanging rope is made of. If it's a picturesque fiber material, and it loops inside the pot, it will very quickly rot through (from being being watered), dumping plant and soil all over your floor. Get hanging pots with wire, leather, or nylon hangers.

Because they're up in the air, hanging pots seem to need watering more often. And because the soil is often up out of your sight, you can easily forget. Choose the kinds of plants that can go neglected for a time without wilting for your hanging pots.

Containers

Clay

The red clay pot is still the most common type of indoor plant container. The porous clay lets the pot "breathe," and the soil inside thus has less of a tendency to pack tightly and become too wet. Packed soil keeps roots from growing freely and causes the tips of leaves to yellow and dry up. Soil that stays too wet can cause roots to rot. Because a new clay pot will absorb moisture, it's a good idea to soak it in water for half an hour or so before putting a plant in it. Otherwise, the pot can take the water away from the plant. Clay pots develop whitish stains on the outside after being used for awhile. These are salts from the soil leaching through. They are unsightly, but harmless, except if they collect on the rim of the pot where plant stems or leaves can touch and be burned by them. Wash them off the sides with a wire brush if they become too unsightly.

Ceramic

The glazed ceramic pots that are sold in many stores are fine for your plants, though they seem wildly overpriced to us. If they have no drainage hole in the bottom, you'll have to be very careful not to overwater. See page 16 for watering instructions. The glazed pots don't breathe as well as clay pots, but water won't seep through the ones without holes, so they are safer for furniture.

Plastic

Plastic pots don't breathe at all, but that's not necessarily a disadvantage. You will have to water a plant in a plastic pot less often than a plant in a clay pot, so plants in plastic pots require less care. Every so often, though, you should check with your finger or a fork to see if the soil is becoming too packed, and loosen it if it is. Don't use the transparent kinds of plastic pots, whether they're tinted or not. It's not good for roots to be exposed to light. A plastic dish to collect water under the pot won't let water through onto a table.

Foam

The newest kind of pot is made of foam bubbles, that have dried into a semi-hard plastic, usually colored a pale orange to resemble clay. These have the advantage of breathing better than ordinary plastic. However the pots are so light that they tend to tip over easily. And the prices charged for them are so outrageously high where we live that we refuse to buy them.

Besides their porosity and pleasing color, clay pots have the advantage of coming in various proportions to suit the shape of different plants. Short wide pots look better with short plants, and tall pots are a necessity with deeply rooted plants.

Ceramic pots can add color and texture, not to mention pattern, to your plantings. They are especially useful when you are using a particular plant as a decorative accent in a room. Ceramic pots come in many shapes for hanging.

These days, most of the plants you buy will come in plastic pots. There is no problem in using them permanently for plants like these succulents that require infrequent watering. Repotting may be necessary if frequently-watered soil tends to pack hard.

Foam pots, though they are light and tend to tip, do "breathe," and therefore there is little problem with soil packing. Other than that, they seem to have no particular advantage that would cause us to recommend them, unless the lightness itself appeals to you.

Repotting

If you buy a young plant for a dollar or so at a plant shop, it will likely come in a small, squarish plastic pot about 2 inches across the top. Very soon you will have to repot it, because the young cuttings sold this way grow quickly.

Plants purchased for more substantial sums, or that you have grown yourself, probably have a more commodious pot, 4 to 6 inches or more, depending on the type of plant. Eventually, however, even these plants will have to be repotted. How long they can stay in their old pots depends on the growth habit of the particular plant.

Signs to look for that indicate a plant has become "pot bound," or too large for its pot, include: roots starting to grow out of the bottom drainage hole, a general tightening of the top of the soil that is caused by roots bunching up there, rapid drying out of the soil and wilting of the plant between waterings, and, after several years, a hardening and packing of the soil that cultivation with a fork fails to remedy.

The sure check is to remove the plant from the pot, and look at the root ball. If the entire outside of the soil is covered with a network of crowded, tangled roots so that soil is hardly visible, your plant needs more space in which to grow. If the roots do not seem overcrowded, you can simply replace the plant in its pot with no harm done.

The number one mistake of novices in repotting is to repot in a pot that's much too big, thinking to save themselves the trouble of repotting again soon. Unfortunately, plants growing in pots that are too big can develop troubles. The soil can pack too tightly and choke off new root growth. Moisture remains in the soil and stagnates, encouraging root rot.

Pick a pot for repotting whose top diameter is between 2 and 4 inches larger than the present pot, depending on how big the plant is and how fast it grows. Larger plants and very fast growers can safely be replanted into a pot that's 4 inches larger.

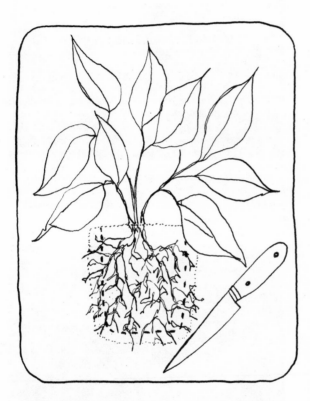

There are alternatives to repotting, if you have a fairly good-sized plant that you don't want to grow any larger. Remove the plant from its pot and trim off the outer layer of roots all around sides and bottom with a very sharp knife, as if you were giving the plant a haircut. Put the plant back in its original pot with extra soil around sides and bottom to replace the area from which you cut roots. Then dig up the top 2 inches of soil, discard it, and replace with fresh potting soil. This is called "top dressing."

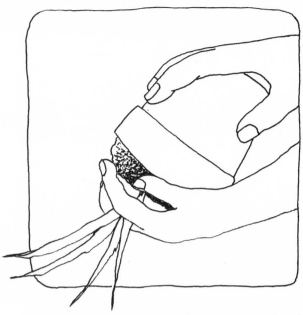

Water your plants a short time before you repot, so the soil won't crumble away when you remove it from the pot. Hold the plant with its stem between the fingers of your hand, spreading your hand over the surface of the soil. Turn the plant over (or, if it's very large, on its side) and give the rim of the pot a sharp tap. The pot can now be lifted off easily.

The new pot should be ready and waiting. Cover the bottom drainage hole with broken shards of an old pot or ½ to 1 inch of gravel to allow water, but not soil, to escape. Then fill the bottom with 2 to 3 inches of soil. Place the root ball and plant inside. There should be about ½ to 1 inch of clearance between the top of the soil and the rim of the new pot. If necessary, take the root ball out and add or subtract soil from the bottom to bring the root ball to its proper level.

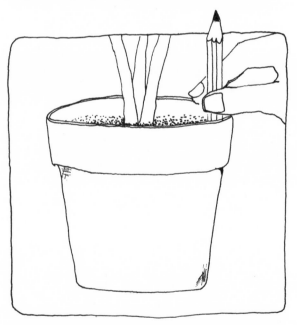

Holding the plant level, fill in the sides of the pot with slightly moist soil. Tuck it down carefully with a long implement (a pencil will do, eraser end down) and press it firmly with your fingers. Replace the pot in its dish and water again until water runs out the drainage hole at the bottom. If you're repotting into a pot with no drainage hole, water only enough to make sure the new soil is moist, not soaking wet.

The plant can be put back in its usual place in your house. It may go into shock for a few days, but this is not likely. Do not water again until the soil is dry. This may be a longer period than usual. If the plant droops for a few days, don't worry. It may take several weeks to resume its normal growth.

There are many styles of watering cans, but most people will find those with long spouts the easiest to handle. The stream of water is under control so you won't overflow your pots, and the spout will fit nicely underneath the foliage of plants like succulents which don't like their leaves wet.

When watering large pots, be sure to direct the stream of water around the edges of the pot, not just into the center. This method will assure that roots near the perimeter of the pot get even distribution of water.
Some people like to water by filling the dish underneath the plant with water and letting the plant absorb it. This is fine as long as the plant is given enough water so that the top of the soil becomes moist too.

Watering

Proper watering of your plants is one of the keys to successful indoor plant growing. One of the most-asked questions by new plant owners is: "How often should I water my plant?" The answer is very simple: let the plant tell you how often.

The idea that there is a proper time for watering plants, like once a week or once every two days, is false. We can say that a coleus, for instance, will need more frequent watering than a sansevieria, but we can't tell you a definite time for watering. Why not? Because the proper time depends on the environment within your home — how dry, how much sunlight, how warm it is.

Actually, knowing the proper time to water is much simpler than that. First, know your plant. The sections of this book that discuss individual plants will tell you whether your plants are water-lovers or plants that should be kept fairly dry. Using that knowledge, you will also have to observe the condition of the soil.

First rule: Don't water your plant when the soil is still damp from a preceding watering. Keeping the soil moist at all times is the surest way of starting the roots to rotting. If the soil on top is slightly dry, it may still not be time to water. If your plant is in a large pot, the soil underneath may still be moist. Put your finger in the soil and find out.

Second rule: When you water, don't water half way. Give your plant enough water so that the excess runs out of the drainage hole. For large plants, this is especially necessary. The habit of giving a little water a few times a week, will keep the roots at the bottom of the plant dry and rot the roots in the upper part of the soil. Make sure the plant has been well saturated.

If the plant is very dry, and the soil has lost some of its porous quality, the water may run quickly through and out the bottom without being absorbed by the soil. If you let the water stay in the dish underneath the plant for an hour or so, the plant will reabsorb the water it needs. Any remaining water in the dish should be poured off so it won't stagnate and cause root-rot.

Third rule: Never, never water your plants with cold water. It can kill them or put them into shock. Test the water with your hand to see that it is tepid or mildly warm.

Humidifying

There are many plants that will grow very easily in the condition of low humidity that is common to most homes. Some of the plants in this book that we think need extra attention or even devotion, however, will require extra humidity to grow well.

Some of the signs that a plant is calling for more humidity are: dark, dry patches around the edges of the leaves, leaves that otherwise appear healthy dropping off the plant, buds appearing and then "blasting" (drying up and failing to open or blossom).

One of the simplest methods of raising the humidity around your plants is to mist them. This can be done with an old plunger-type window-cleaner bottle or one of the inexpensive metal or glass containers sold by garden shops. Spray a fine cloud of lukewarm water all over the tops and bottoms of the leaves. As it evaporates the plant luxuriates in a cloud of welcome humidity.

Drawbacks of misting are that it can't be used for plants such as African violets that may rot or spot as a result of water on their leaves. Also, misting is a bit sloppy, and you are likely to mist your windows and furniture at the same time you mist your plants.

We think a better method of raising the humidity is putting the plants in dishes, window boxes, trays, or even larger pots that are filled with moisture-retaining substances that will slowly release additional humidity.

Sponging off your leaves with a damp sponge is a good idea, not only to raise the humidity, but to clean the leaves of dust and dirt that can foul their pores. Plants with hairy leaves, such as African violets and gynuras, and cacti and succulents cannot be sponged. Some other plants have leaves that are too numerous or too delicate to be sponged. Brushing these leaves with a small paintbrush is a good way to remove any unsightly and unhealthy dirt or dust that has collected.

Both pet and garden stores sell pebbles that can be used as a floor for water trays. The water level should be below, not above, the pebble surface. Plant stores sell trays, or use your own choice of ceramic dishes.

Misting not only increases humidity, but helps to keep leaves clean too. Light misting is unlikely to hurt furniture, but do segregate those plants which can be damaged by having their foliage wet.

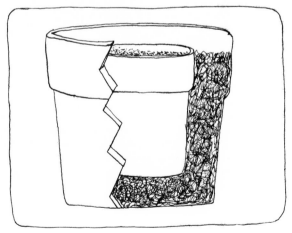

A pot within a pot makes sense for small plants in particular. The "stuffing" can be damp peat, sphagnum, or even vermiculite. Put a layer in the bottom of the pot first, put the smaller pot inside, and stuff the sides firmly.

What about digging your own potting soil right out of the back yard? The trouble with this method is that backyard soil is unlikely to have the qualities needed for indoor plants. "But you can grow flowers in it," you reply. Yes, but outdoor plants are stronger than indoor plants, and ordinary soils tend to pack tightly and not drain easily in pots.

Some people recommend sterilizing outdoor soil yourself, to rid it of spores, insects, and bacteria that are liable to attack tender indoor plants. The method for sterilization is to bake the soil at a high temperature in your oven. Somehow the people who give this advice never get around to telling you how to get rid of the horrible smell that permeates oven and kitchen for days afterward.

An ordinary plastic pail is invaluable for mixing small amounts of soil. What becomes a great nuisance is the plastic and paper bags soil, sand and other components come in. They break after a while, and everything spills. The large gallon-size freezer containers with screw-on lids might come in handy for storing soil.

Soil

There is no need to worry about soil for your plants; a bag of commercial potting soil can be purchased at any variety store, plant store, or other garden outlet. This packaged soil will have the proper nutrients for indoor plants, will be sterilized and free from disease, and will be of the right consistency to absorb and hold water.

You should know about some of the components of good potting soil, because any one of them can be useful as a growing medium for specialized gardening.

Peat moss, as sold for indoor plants, is the ragged, spongy, brown, almost flaky kind. Sometimes it will be available in brick form. The bricks should be broken up before you use the material in pots. Peat moss absorbs and holds water, but is hard to get wet the first time you use it. If you're mixing it in your own soil to increase its absorbency, make sure the peat is moist before you add it to the pot. Peat moss also contributes nutrients to the soil.

Sand is used in soils for plants that need good drainage, such as cactus. Some people start seedlings in sand, but since it has no nutrients, it's not good for growing mature plants. Don't use sand from the beach, even if it's a fresh-water beach. Builder's sand, from a construction site, or the sand sold for aquariums in pet stores is the right consistency and type for mixing in soil.

Vermiculite and perlite are the white or metallic-looking crumbs that you see dotting potting soils like little white rocks. Neither has any nutrient value, but are put in the soil to help keep it from packing too tightly. Potting mix sold for starting seedlings has more vermiculite in it than ordinary soil, and some people choose to start seedlings entirely in vermiculite or perlite. Older plants grown in straight vermiculite or perlite must have fertilizers regularly added to the mix.

Sphagnum moss is yellowish, and looks like a tangled mass of threads and seeds. It is sometimes called sphagnum peat moss, but it shouldn't be confused with the brown peat moss. Used by itself, sphagnum moss can be a medium for growing orchids, or in air-layering plants (see page 30). It's loaded with nutrients.

Humus is the primary component of very good soil. You can grow plants in pure humus, if you can get it. If the soil you buy stays crumbly and absorbent in its pot without needing to be broken up by hand from time to time it has plenty of humus in it. If you live outside the city you can make your own humus by starting a compost pile.

Fertilizer

There are many methods of growing plants indoors successfully. The rule for you ought to be: if it works, keep doing it. Some people insist on fertilizing each and every plant at regular intervals, and swear that the luxuriant growth that results is due to the heavy fertilization. Others pot their plants in good, rich soil and depend successfully on the soil to provide proper nutrients — which it does, for them.

Let's start with a warning: you can hurt a plant by over-fertilizing. More is not better, in this case. Some plants have dormant periods. The novice, seeing that his plant has stopped its formerly rapid growth, immediately begins fertilizing heavily. The plant responds by turning its leaves brown, which brings on increasingly heavy doses of fertilizer from the alarmed gardener. The plant dies.

Used properly, artificial fertilizers can be an aid to rapid, strong growth of plants. Signs of trouble or plant distress, however, are not a signal to fertilize. In 95 per cent of cases, plant troubles are caused by too much or too little of the three basic needs, or by insects and disease. Fertilizer helps none of these conditions.

The best way to fertilize is to mix in with the potting soil some compost, dried and rotted animal manure, or bone meal. One part of these to 10 parts of your regular potting soil is sufficient.

As for the pills, pellets, capsules, liquids, and powders that are sold for fertilizing plants, you can judge their strength by the three numbers you find on the label. The first number is the percentage of nitrogen in the fertilizer. Nitrogen aids in leaf growth. The second number is the percentage of phosphoric acid, which aids flower growth. The third number is the percentage of potash, which is necessary for root growth. Adding those three numbers up and subtracting the total from 100 will give you the percentage of inert ingredients in the product. A fertilizer marked "2-2-2," then, is very weak compared with one marked, "7-6-19," for example. You may prefer the weak one, however, if you're trying to just give your plants a little boost and not over-fertilize them.

Follow the directions on the plant food labels to the letter. Don't increase the dosages or frequency of use. If a white crust forms on the top of your soil or the outside of the pot, you're probably over-fertilizing. Water with plain water till the soil crust disappears.

Lovely little sets of potting tools are sold in most garden stores, but the thrift-minded potter will find a good kitchen spoon and a plain old table fork will work fine for moving soil around and for breaking up the surface soil in pots.

Fertilizer companies now sell fertilizer that is absorbed directly by the leaves of a plant. Mixed with water in proper proportion and applied with your misting bottle, it is a convenient way to fertilize.

You can use fruit and vegetable peels and other vegetable waste from the kitchen to produce your own compost pile, which will give you humus for your indoor plants.
If you have access to an open spot outdoors, pile up alternating 3" layers of garden soil and vegetable waste, including waste paper and newspapers, keeping the pile well watered. When you have enough for your needs, keep the pile moist, and turn the materials often – as frequently as every two or three days. Heat from bacterial decomposition will build up, and when the heat dies down, the compost is finished decomposing and ready to use.
A bucket of the same material set on a terrace or fire escape will have the same results on a smaller scale. But compost made in a closed container takes longer, and should be turned every day to hasten the process.

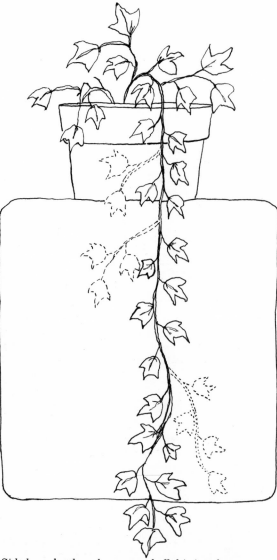

Side branches have been pruned off this ivy plant to encourage a single long trailing stem. If only the tips of the side branches had been pinched, the plant would simply have become more bushy. Instead, branches were cut off with scissors at the point where they grew from the main stem, thus encouraging the terminal growth at the end of the stem itself.

Pinching And Pruning

When to Pinch

When a plant's growth is well established, and it has accustomed itself to conditions in your house, it may need to be pinched. Not all plants benefit from this treatment, but for many it is almost essential.

Pinching is simply cutting off the growing tip of the plant — with fingers if the tips are tender, with scissors if the tips are harder. For most plants, this is done to encourage branching or growth on a lower part of the plant. You're telling the plant it can't go any higher, that it's time to branch out a little. Some plants will cooperate; others will send out another shoot or two and climb upwards with them. If this happens, pinch them off too; the plant may not be listening.

Don't be afraid to pinch; you're not hurting the plant. With plants like iresine and coleus, you'll notice the plant's growth doubling each time you pinch. In the end you'll have a fuller, healthier plant than if you let it grow long and scraggly.

With some kinds of hanging plants, you want to encourage growth along one stem, rather than several, to get a long, hanging shoot. Pinching is the solution here too, but you pinch off any stems that branch away from the main stem, letting the main stem grow with the full strength of the plant.

When to Prune

Pruning is a bigger job than pinching, and you may have to prune if you didn't pinch ruthlessly enough before. What pruning involves is cutting off unwanted branches, because the plant is too large or misshapen. Some flowering plants, of which the best known is the pelargonium or geranium, only flower on new growth. At the end of a season, then, they need to have most of their old branches cut back to make room for the next year's new growth.

Any dead or diseased branches, stems and leaves should be pruned off as soon as they are found. This is particularly true of plants that are succulents, like the African violets, because they rot easily. The rotting leaf, with stem, should be cut off at the base.

You should be a little more cautious about pruning than you were about pinching, although most house plants in good condition will take pruning in stride. If cutting from the top, try not to cut off more than a third of the plant. Trim the side branches accordingly so the plant is as balanced in shape as when it was full grown.

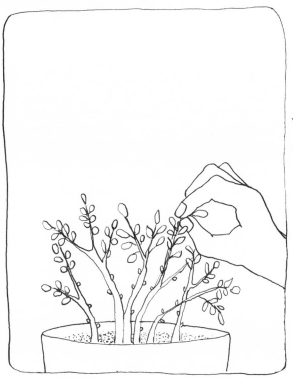 

Dormancy

Certain plants stop putting out new growth at certain times of the year, usually winter. (See pages 34–35 for which ones.) Don't be alarmed, and don't start taking corrective measures. The plant wants you to leave it alone so it can rest. Cut down on watering, and above all don't try to fertilize the plant out of its dormancy state. Some plants will maintain the growth they have started; their dormancy will usually be short. Other plants appear to die out completely, browning and dropping all their foliage. Don't be alarmed at this, either. With proper care they can be brought back when they're ready. (See Plants That Need Devotion, pages 66–75.)

Basically, pinching is done evenly all over the plant. The growing tips of plants contain a hormone that inhibits the growth of all the buds and branches behind the tip. When the tip is removed, so is that inhibiting hormone, and the buds to the inside of the plant have a chance to grow more quickly into new leaves and branches. Pruning, on the other hand, is used to get rid of old, unwanted branches, ones that spoil the shape of a plant, or crowded ones that hurt an open, airy effect. Pruning is selective, whereas pinching is wholesale.

Insecticides are often mixed with water to be sprayed on a plant with a mister. One can buy special plant misters such as the one in the illustration, or use an empty window-cleaner bottle. But the mister is less tiring to use, and its fine mist reaches undersides of leaves more efficiently.

Aerosol cans are a popular way to spray insecticide on plants. Their convenience is offset by the latest news that the supposedly inert gas used as a propellent in such cans in fact destroys ozone, the special form of oxygen in our upper atmosphere that protects us all from deadly cosmic rays. Don't use aerosols too close to the leaves; the freon gas used as a propellant can freeze them.

Cardboard dusters contain insecticide that can be used dry, pumped directly onto foliage from the duster itself, or mixed with water and sprayed on.

Pests and Diseases

"What's wrong with my plant?" You'll be less likely to ask that if you treat your plants right, because the answer is often that it's getting too much or too little light, water, heat, or humidity. Most people can recognize the drooping, dry look that results from not enough watering. It's not as easy, apparently, to realize that browning and drying of leaves can be the result of too much watering or too much sun. A window left open on a cold day can produce leaf dropping in a number of plants too. The activation of a steam radiator can increase a plant's need for water or cause the leaves to turn dark brown at the tips and edges. Any sudden sharp change in the conditions in which it lives, even if the change is brief, can adversely affect a plant. Plant diseases are relatively rare; check out what you've been doing to your plants before you start treating the plants for nonexistent pests and diseases.

As for pests themselves, most of the time they come into your home with the plants. If you are fortunate enough to have an indoor garden that has not been troubled by insects, take precautions. When you buy or receive a new plant, check it over carefully for insects. If at all possible, the new plant should be segregated — quarantined — from your other plants for two to three weeks, to give any dormant insect life a chance to make itself apparent.

Another good precaution is to follow the advice we gave in the "Soil" section on page 18, and leave backyard soil in the backyard. Potting your house plants in ordinary soil can bring pests and diseases into the house, where they can thrive. Commercial potting soil is sterlized.

Remember, too, that for many plants, particularly those that grow rapidly, it is normal to lose a few leaves from age from time to time. Check the sections on specific plants in the back of this Part to see if your plant's "illness" might just be a natural dormancy or shedding.

If you decide that your plant is suffering from

a disease or is being attacked by pests, get it away from other plants that it might infect. Sometimes the best procedure is to get rid of the plant entirely. You have to be the judge of how much the plant means to you, and how easily you can replace it.

White Flies

The white fly may be the most common pest the house plant gardener has to deal with. It's about ⅛ inch long, and as its name implies, is a white-winged insect. White flies roost on the underside of leaves, sucking sap. You will only notice them if you go over your plants pretty carefully, at least until they are numerous enough to cause serious damage. When leaves start turning yellow and dropping off the plant, you may have a white fly infestation. Shake the plant a little; if you have white flies, they'll fly off the leaves and cruise around before settling back into place.

If the white fly problem isn't too severe, you can kill them off by pinching them flat against the leaves with your thumb and forefinger. White flies aren't easily scared off from their meals, so they're easy to kill in this way. For more severe infestations, a malathion spray may have to be used.

Mealybugs

These tiny creatures resemble the white fly in that they are the same white color. Mealybugs, however, don't fly or move around. They look like tiny wisps of cotton on the bottoms of leaves or in the joints between leaves and branches. Since they also live by sucking the sap from the leaves or stems, their effect is the same as the white fly.

Dipping a Q-Tip in rubbing alcohol and touching the mealybugs with it is the quickest and easiest way to kill them off. Sprays are not as sure, because the cottony substance protects the mealybug underneath. Keep an eye out for more mealybugs after you've killed a few, because their numerous eggs are almost invisible.

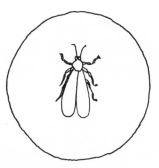

The white fly, considerably enlarged.

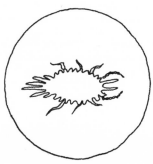

The mealybug, considerably enlarged. You will more likely see the white webbing of this insect than the insect itself.

Pesticides should be used with caution. Malathion is deadly to insects, but fairly harmful to people, too. It is commonly sold in a "50%" solution. A teaspoonful of it mixed with a gallon of water will be more than sufficient for spraying your plants. Move the plants outside for spraying if you can. If you can't, laundry room, basement or bathtub are all preferable to the kitchen.

Pyrethrum is sold in powder form and is often sold in a cardboard cylinder duster. It can be dusted lightly on the plants, or mixed with water according to the directions on the label. Use it soon after mixing with water, as it loses its potency quickly. It dries on the leaves and is a stomach poison to insects. So far, it seems to be harmless to humans.

Rotenone is available as a spray or dust. The dust is sometimes known as "derris dust." It is the key ingredient in many commercially-packaged "spray bombs." It is also harmless to man, but will kill fish, so don't use it if there are tanks of tropical fish in the room.

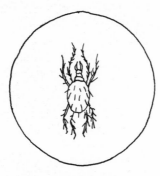

Spider mites, considerably enlarged. You can usually only see these if you shake them onto white paper.

Identifying the scale insect is impossible for you – look only for the hard "scale," which is a shell the insect secretes around itself.

Spider Mites

Some people call these red spider mites, but there are many different kinds and colors of mites — their chief characteristic being that they are almost too small to see anyway. Even if you inspect your plants carefully on a regular basis, you're liable to miss these tiny creatures, unless you notice the tiny, almost dust-like webs that they spin in hollows formed by the curve in a leaf. One way to spot spider mites is by holding the plant up to a light. If it is infested you should see a swarming colony of spider mites. Another way of spotting them is to hold a sheet of white paper under a branch, and shake the branch gently. The moving specks that fall onto the paper are spider mites.

If a plant is attacked by spider mites, its leaves take on a gray-green or yellow green color with an overall spotty or mottled look. Eventually the leaves fall off.

We have found it very difficult to completely get rid of spider mites, short of throwing out the plant altogether. Liquid sprays, such as malathion, tend to miss many of the tiny pests. A powder insecticide, such as derris dust, is better. If you can take your plant outdoors and give it a good spraying with the garden hose (without, of course, damaging the plant), you can wash away many of the mites. Repeating this process once a week for several weeks is recommended. The most effective method we've used is a complete immersion of the plant in a deep sink full of water. Leave it under for at least five minutes.

Scale

Scale is an insect that builds a hard shell around itself, sheds its legs, and stays where it is for the rest of its life — living off your plant. The shell of a scale insect can be gray, brown, yellow, black, or reddish, and they can be up to ½ inch in size, although the most common ones indoors will be closer to ⅛ inch long. Scale that feeds off the stems and trunks of trees can be mistaken for bark. On the other hand, normal parts of plants, such as the spores a palm forms on its leaves, can be mistaken for scale.

Your best guide is that if you can scrape it off easily with your fingernail, it's probably scale. Scraping them off is the surest way of removing them, along with a good scrubbing, because their shells protect scales from pesticides.

Aphids

Aphids are about ⅛ inch long and come in a variety of colors, from very pale green and white through red and black. What's important is that they also survive by sucking the juices from your plants. Signs of an aphid attack include stunted or misshaped leaves, as well as the familiar yellowing of healthy foliage. Aphids secrete a shiny, clear, sticky substance called honeydew. (So do scale and white flies and mealybugs, but not in the quantity aphids do; if there's enough honeydew for you to notice, you've probably encountered aphids.) Ants carry aphids around with them to "milk" them of the honeydew; the ants won't damage the plants, but the aphids will. The honeydew is also a good breeding ground for funguses which will discolor and even kill your plants.

Rotenone, pyrethrum, and malathion will kill aphids. Another solution is to give your plants a bath in soapy water. Soaking the entire plant in detergent and warm water for 10 minutes is one way; if your plant is too large for this kind of treatment, use a sponge to go over all the leaves, top and bottom, with soap and water. Rinse excess soap off with plain water.

Root aphids are harder to diagnose and to cure than leaf-sucking aphids, but if your plants seem to be oddly misshapen, remove them from their pots and see if you can spot some long-legged, crawling aphids deep beneath the surface. If you encounter this trouble, your only real hope is to water the plant with a nicotine solution or some other systemic poison. Consult your plant store.

Soil Pests

Various types of insects can live in the moist soil of your plants. They often appear when you water the plant. Little black fleas that crawl over the surface and fly in the vicinity of the plant are fungus gnats. These are annoying to people, and are only rarely harmful to plants. Malathion sprayed on the soil will kill them.

If your African violets, or any plant, appear stunted and misshapen, and you find the roots are knotted and gnarled, you may have nematodes. These are microscopic wire-worms that spread plant diseases. Our advice: throw the plant out, and hope the worms haven't spread to your other plants.

There are other insects that can be crawling around your soil. Specialized books list thousands of possible invaders. On the theory that they're living off something down there, you can try a home-brew method of control. Soak pipe tobacco in a pint of water overnight. Strain off the tobacco the next day, and pour the solution into the pot.

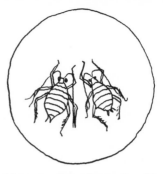

These are aphids, also shown larger than life, though they come in different sizes and many colors.

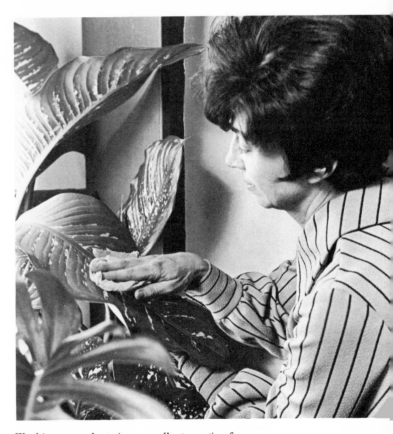

Washing your plants is an excellent practice, for many reasons. It helps raise the humidity around them, if only for a short time. It makes them look better and helps them "breathe" without interference from dust and dirt. Finally, many pests and diseases can be gotten rid of before they gain a foothold.
One method of washing your plants is to sponge both top and bottom of leaves gently with a wet sponge or cloth, or spray them in the kitchen sink with a hand spray. A mild detergent can also be used if desired. If the plant is large, or has many leaves, a bath under the bathroom shower or outside with a garden hose can be of help.

Artificial Light

There are a few plants that will grow with only the light in a windowless office or a one-room apartment whose single window faces onto an air shaft. However, people living in places without much natural light often want other kinds of plants, like colorful African violets, gesneriads, tuberous begonias, and cattleya orchids. Artificial lighting is the answer, for almost any kind of plant can be grown if enough artificial light is provided, even in situations where no other light is available.

First of all, remember that any light you can offer is helpful as a supplement to the natural light the plant gets. Even an ordinary lamp with a 40-watt bulb in it, burning on the same table with your plant, will be of help.

Fluorescent lights are the best kind of artificial lamp for your plants, because they emit a great deal of light with little heat. Burning enough incandescent bulbs to raise, say, African violets in your basement would create enough heat to damage the plants. Incandescent light also uses more electricity, and is therefore more expensive than fluorescent light.

Ordinary fluorescent lamps are sufficient for plants, but there are special lamps whose light spectrum is balanced especially for growing plants indoors. These include Gro-Lux by Sylvania, Plant-Gro by Westinghouse, and Natur-Escent by Duro-lite.

Fixtures to hold fluorescent tubes come in various sizes. Your choice will depend on how many plants you want to grow. If you're planning on African violets, we recommend you get a bigger fixture than you think you need. Innocent growers of one or two plants soon discover the pleasures of propagating and hybridizing. You'll be glad you have the room for a tableful of plants.

Actually, if you're going to the trouble of installing a fluorescent fixture, you might as well get one of the large kind that can accommodate two or four 48-inch tubes. Many artificial-light gardeners recommend combining fluorescent and incandescent lights; there are fixtures that have receptacles for both kinds of lamps. Any fixture you buy for using fluorescent lamps should have a white-painted reflector. If you install the fixture, make sure you can easily raise or lower it later, when you find out how much light your plants need. If the fixture can't be easily raised or lowered, set your plants about 11 inches under it.

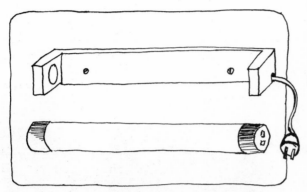

The shape of a fluorescent tube is to your advantage because it fits so easily in hard to light spots like inside bookshelves, over a high cabinet or under a stairwell where little natural light can reach. Although special plant stands are sold to hold these tubes, look first at the slim fixtures you will find in lighting stores that can simply be screwed into wall or shelf.

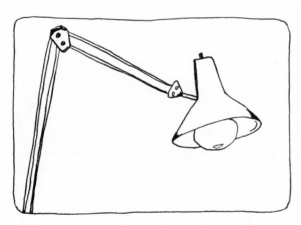

The advantage of incandescent bulbs is that they fit any regular fixture – for instance, a gooseneck light or those jointed lamps that clamp to the side of a table. This sort of fixture is directional, and especially useful for a single plant or small group kept in a dark part of the room.

If you don't plan to install a fluorescent bulb fixture, manufacturers also sell special incandescent plant lights that are about the intensity of 150-watt floodlights. These have the advantage of installing easily, because any fixture that will accommodate a screw-in bulb can be used. (Caution: don't exceed the wattage recommended for the fixture. Fires or melted fixtures can result.) As with the other incandescent bulbs, heat is a problem here, but this type of lamp is useful if you have a single plant in a dark corner that you want to give a boost to. We recommend you keep the plant at least 4 feet from the bulb.

Don't use spotlights for your plants at all. The heat generated by them is enough to fry any plant in a short time. Floodlights, ordinary lightbulbs, and incandescent plant bulbs are all fine.

Remember that plants have to have a daily dormant period in your home, as they have in nature. Don't keep your lights burning all the time. This isn't to say you should worry if you have the house lights on till late. We're talking about strong artificial light specially set up for plants to grow by.

If you have the plants in a place with no natural light, or almost none, such as a basement, you can let them stay in the dark all day, and turn on the lights when you get home so you can work with and enjoy them. But make sure they get some darkness on a regular basis so that they can rest.

Artificial light allows you to plant whole gardens in places where no plant would ordinarily grow. Here what might have been a useless area at the bottom of a flight of stairs becomes instead a year-round garden.

Plant Propagation

Cuttings

If a friend admires one of your plants, you can give him the plant — and keep it yourself. How? By reproducing the plant through cuttings. Taking a cutting is a very simple and easy way of propagating your plants. Be warned, however, that it is not possible to take cuttings of every plant. Some plants are propagated differently. Check the sections of individual plants on pages 34 to 73 to see if your plant is suitable for cuttings.

Taking a cutting is not a confusing or difficult process. Simply snip off cleanly a short, young branch that is growing vigorously. Good sharp scissors will work, but if in doubt use a razor blade. Depending on the size of your plant, a branch from 3 to 6 inches long will be fine. You can now put the branch in a glass of water and wait for roots to develop. A piece of charcoal in the glass will keep the water fresh. When roots have nicely started, which should be in one to six weeks, put the young plant in a pot with soil. Be careful in the transplanting not to break the new roots. Hold the cutting by its stem and fill in gently around the roots with a digging tool or spoon. Fill the pot to within an inch of the top, pat the soil down firmly, and add soil to bring the level to within an inch of the top again.

With many plants, the root system of cuttings develops quickly enough so that you can dispense with the water. Simply take the cutting, strip off any leaves along the bottom third of it, and put it in soil up to the level of the first leaf left on. It can also be started in sand or vermiculite. Keep the pot well watered, but not soppy, until the plant has perked up and shows new growth. Then water as you would any plant. Dipping the cutting in Rootone, which controls fungus diseases and contains a hormone that encourages rooting, is a good idea before planting a cutting directly in soil.

Leaf cutting is another method of propagation that will work for some plants. Take a large leaf from the plant and cut thin slits across the veins of the leaf in several places with a razor blade or sharp knife. Then place the leaf flat against a bed of moist sand or potting soil. Weight the leaf down with pebbles or sand so it stays flat. Keep the soil mixture moist and eventually small plantlets will spring up from

A plant can be propagated from cuttings taken from different parts: the drawing indicates where cuttings are taken for 1) propagating from a branch, 2) propagating from a leaf, 3) propagating from a stem.

the cuts in the leaves. When these grow several inches high, remove them carefully, keeping the sand or soil around the roots, and put them in their own pots.

Some plants such as philodendrons, scindapsus, zebrinas, and tradescantias seem to have no branches but are all stem and leaves. Just take the cutting a few inches down from the top of the stem. This won't harm the plant and will in fact encourage it to put out more stems or branches. Treat the cutting as any other cutting. Some people replant this type of cutting in the same pot with the original plant, to encourage a bushy look to the plant.

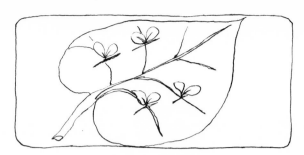

When a cutting is taken from a leaf, the plantlets will sprout, and later root, from locations along the veins in the leaf that have been cleanly slit. A clean slit that does not damage cells by crushing them must be made with a new razor blade, straight across a vein.

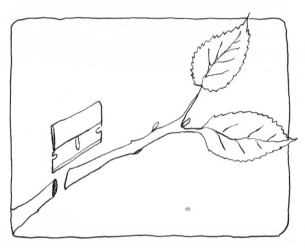

The first step in taking a cutting is to cut. Use a fresh razor blade, cutting diagonally across the stem of a healthy-looking branch.

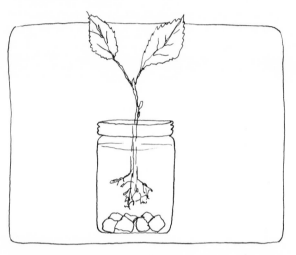

Cuttings can be rooted directly in moist sand or a starter like vermiculite. It is more fun however, to start a cutting in water so you can see the roots grow. The charcoal will help prevent decay.

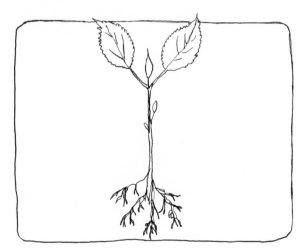

The roots on this cutting are developed enough to transplant it into potting soil.

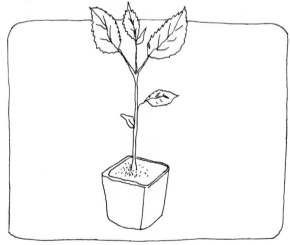

If you transplant into a peat pot now, you will be able to move the plant, pot and all, into a larger pot later – a space saving method if you are starting many cuttings.

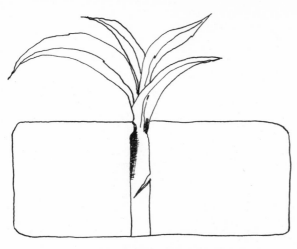

To air layer, cut diagonally part-way through the stem. A razor blade does the best job.

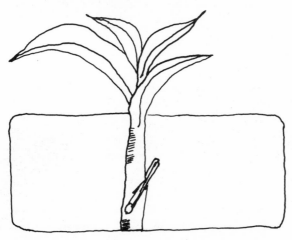

A matchstick or similar sliver of wood holds the cut apart so roots will grow from it.

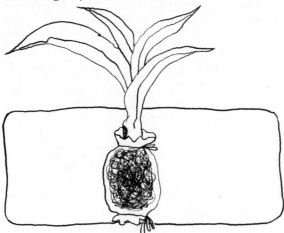

Moist sphagnum moss is bunched around the cut section, and held in place with plastic wrap tied at both ends so the sphagnum won't dry out.

Air Layering

Air layering is a good method of replanting large plants that have gotten "leggy." For one reason or another, their lower leaves have dropped off, and the plant now resembles a small palm tree with a long stalk and a bunch of leaves at the top. Air layering lets you get rid of the long stalk and start over with a bushy plant that will grow vigorously upward again.

Air layering is a method that encourages roots to grow from the stalk of the plant just below the growth of leaves. With a sharp knife, make a diagonal cut half-way through the stem. Be careful not to cut entirely through the stem. If you strip off some of the outer covering of the stalk, be sure not to completely strip it all the way around, or nourishment from the roots will not get to the leaves.

Place a matchstick or peg in the diagonal cut you have made so the two sections cannot grow back together. Then take some sphagnum moss which has been soaked in water and pack it around the stem, forming a ball around the place where the stem is cut. Wrap plastic kitchen wrap securely around the ball and tightly fasten it to the stalk at top and bottom. In a month or two, roots will have filled the ball of sphagnum moss. At that time, cut the stem completely through below the ball of moss, remove the wrap, and plant in a new container.

The plant stalk that remains after the top of the plant has been cut off can be used to propagate new plants. Cut it into 2 or 3-inch sections, and plant them on their sides half-buried in potting soil. New shoots will grow out of the stem; when they are 2 or 3 inches tall, cut each shoot off, along with its root, from the rest of the stem. Plant them as you would cuttings.

Division

Plants that grow without a central stem, but have many stems growing out of the ground in a clump, can be divided to make two or more plants. Propagate by division in the spring or early summer when a plant is growing vigorously. Simply unpot the plant and slice through the root system with a sharp knife, vertically dividing the plant. Plant each half in its own pot and water sparingly until growth resumes.

Propagating From Seeds

Many houseplants can be grown from seed,

and more and more mail-order catalogs and garden stores are offering them. The easiest technique for propagating from seed is to plant the seeds in peat pots or pellets. Pellets are flat peat discs that expand when placed in water; they are a good medium for starting seeds. Of course any ordinary small pot filled with peat moss, potting soil, or vermiculite will also do the job.

Terrarium-like cases for sprouting seedlings are on the market. These create a highly humid atmosphere that encourages sprouting and rapid growth. You can create the same "greenhouse" conditions by placing a plastic bag over your pot and securing it with a rubber band. There will be no need to water the soil until the bag is removed after the seedling is 2 to 3 inches high. Make sure the seedlings get proper drainage. Over-watering can cause a fungus disease, called "damping-off" that will kill the seedlings.

Seedlings should be placed in good light, but not direct sunlight. Temperature control is particularly important with seedlings. Make sure there are no rapid changes in temperature. Don't open windows near your seedlings if the temperature outside is much cooler than indoors. Don't put seedlings near (or on!) working radiators. Fumes from a gas stove can kill seedlings too.

When the seedlings have two sets of leaves, it is time to thin them. Use scissors to cut off the stems of those you don't want at soil level. Usually you will want to leave only the one strongest seedling in a peat pellet or peat pot. If you have planted seeds in larger containers, thin enough space between seedlings to allow you to dig out and handle each plant separately when you transplant.

If you planted seedlings in peat pots or pellets, they'll let you know when they're ready for a bigger pot by poking their roots through the sides of the pot. Repot container and all into ordinary potting soil. For repotting seedlings grown in other kinds of pots, you should let them grow in the original container as long as possible. The stronger they are when you transplant, the better. Cut through the root systems with a sharp knife to separate plants if the roots of separate seedlings have become intertwined. Follow repotting instructions on page 14.

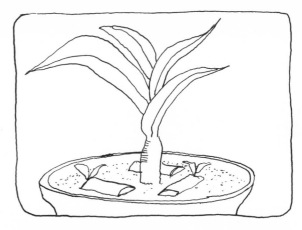

The top of the plant is repotted when it has rooted well into the sphagnum moss. The remaining stem of the original plant has here been sliced and planted into the same pot, where it will produce new plantlets. The result will be a full planting of new growth to replace the single spindly plant on the preceding page.

The multipurpose plastic food bag is here put to a new use. Plant seeds have been sown in moist soil directly in the bag. With the top tied, it becomes a perfect greenhouse in which seedlings can grow large enough to transplant into permanent pots.

Plants On Vacation

It's you that's on vacation, actually, and you're wondering how to provide care for your plants when you're gone. The major problem is, of course, watering. Before we get to that, however, a word about fresh air. Plants appreciate it as much as you do, and even if you keep your windows closed all day in winter, there is still more circulation of air with people coming and going than there is when everybody's gone. If possible, leave one window open if only a tiny bit while you're away. Better to leave it open in a room where there are no plants so there won't be any cold drafts directly on a plant.

Plant Sitters

The watering problem can be solved by persuading a friend to come in on a regular basis while you're gone. The trouble with that is, you'll find that even the most well-intentioned of friends don't water plants the way you do. If you know someone who's very good with plants, and knows their needs and foibles well, you're in luck. Otherwise, you run the risk that they will water too much or too little. Try to explain nicely just how much water you give plants, emphasizing the need to water until a little comes out of the drainage hole in the bottom and not watering at all if the soil is still moist from a previous watering. With these cautions, it's not necessary to have a friend who's an expert with plants. If you're only going away for two or three days, it may be possible to get along without extra plant-watering help at all. In the week or two before you leave, notice how long it is between times when your plants dry out. Many plants, particularly those in large containers, don't need to be watered that often, depending on the time of year and how dry it is in your home.

Watering Wicks

There are some plant-watering schemes that you can use in case you're going away for a week or two. One is the use of wicks. Plant stores and mail-order suppliers sell plant wicks, one end of which is placed in the soil of the plant, the other end in a bottle or jar of water. Capillary action transfers the water to the plant as the soil dries out.

Plastic Wrapping

Another possibility is to cover the soil of each

Plant wicks are a good vacation solution for plants that can stay moist all the time. Water in a narrow necked bottle will be depleted less from evaporation than water in, say, a wide-mouthed jar.

plant with plastic after watering, just before you leave on vacation. The plastic keeps the moisture from evaporating quickly, and should keep most plants healthy for a week or two. Experiment with this method while you're still at home, to see how long it is before the soil dries out enough to need a new watering. Moving the plants out of direct sunlight helps when using this method. They can stand low-light conditions longer than they can dry soil.

Bathtubs

One of the best methods, though a little more trouble, for taking care of your plants for a one or two-week vacation period is putting them in the bathtub. No, not filled with water. Start by placing some plastic cleaning bags or plastic sheeting on the bottom of the tub. Put several layers of newspaper on top of that. The more newspaper the better because the wet newspaper will hold a lot of moisture. Put your plants in the tub and water them thoroughly. If you have a shower, turn it on to water the plants and wet down the leaves. Then seal off the enclosure as best you can by pulling the shower curtain and putting more plastic over the top of the enclosure. If your plants are small and don't stick up above the rim of the tub, you can put plastic over the rim. This all forms a greenhouse effect and should give plenty of moisture for a couple of weeks. If your bathroom is dark — and most are — turn on the light while you are gone.

None of this advice, of course, applies to plants that can go for a week or two without water. Plants like sansevieria, cacti and succulents, peperomia, would suffer under very moist, humid conditions. And your African violets and gesneriads would never stand for having their leaves wetted down in the bathtub. Wick watering will do for plants whose leaves rot easily. If your job or life-style takes you away from home often, choose plants that can be left without water for long periods.

Starting Anew

If you have only a few plants, you can take cuttings from them just before going away, put the cuttings in a large bottle of water, and replant the cuttings when you return. Most people aren't heartless enough to leave the old plants to dry out, however. But with some plants, like coleus, that should be started anew each year anyway, it's possible to time their rebirth with your vacation.

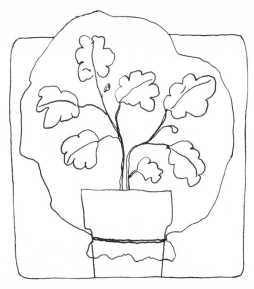

Rubber bands hold plastic wrap snugly around this pot. Wrapping a pot with plastic is less effective with plants whose stems arise from all over the pot surface. It works best with those plants that arise from a few stems only or from a narrow crown, like a fern or a jade plant.

Although taller plants than these would have prevented the vacationer from covering his whole bathtub like this illustration, they would most likely be in larger pots which would hold moisture for longer anyhow. Masking tape is the best bet to hold plastic wrap against wall and tub.

Care Chart

Name	Minimum Light Required	Extra Humidity Required For House Growth	Watering	Dormant Period In Which Care Requirements Change	Methods Of Propagation
Achimenes hybrids (nut orchid)	ordinary	yes	heavy	yes	cuttings
Adiantum tenerum (maidenhair fern)	shady	yes	heavy	no	division
Aechmea fasciata (urn plant)	ordinary	yes	moderate	yes	sends out shoot with plantlet
Ananas comosus (pineapple)	bright	yes	moderate	yes	sends out shoot with plantlet
Aphelandra squarrosa (zebra plant)	bright	yes	moderate	yes	cuttings
Araucaria excelsa (Norfolk Island pine)	bright	yes	moderate	no	cuttings
Asparagus sprengeri (asparagus fern)	shady	no	moderate	no	division
Aspidistra elatior (cast-iron plant)	shady	no	light	no	division
Beaucarnea recurvata (elephant's foot tree)	bright	no	moderate	no	seeds, bulbs or spores only
Begonia corolicta (stem begonia, angel-wing begonia)	bright	no	moderate	no	cuttings
B. masoniana (iron cross begonia)	ordinary	yes	moderate	yes	division
B. rex (rex begonia)	ordinary	yes	moderate	yes	division
B. semperflorens (wax begonia)	ordinary	no	moderate	no	cuttings
B. sutherlandii (tuberous begonia)	bright	no	heavy	yes	cuttings
Billbergia (bromeliad)	bright	yes	moderate	yes	sends out shoot with plantlet
Caladium hybrids (calamity plant)	ordinary	yes	heavy	yes	division
Calathea (maranta)	ordinary	no	moderate	yes	division
Caryota mitis (fishtail palm)	shady	no	moderate	no	sends out shoot with plantlet
Cattleya (orchid)	sunny	yes	moderate	yes	division
Chamaedorea elegans (parlor palm)	shady	no	moderate	no	seeds, bulbs or spores only
Chlorophytum comosum (spider plant)	shady	no	moderate	no	sends out shoot with plantlets
Cissus antarctica (kangaroo vine)	ordinary	no	moderate	no	cuttings
C. discolor (begonia treebine)	ordinary	yes	moderate	no	cuttings
C. rhombifolia (grape ivy)	ordinary	no	moderate	no	cuttings
Codiaeum variegatum pictum (croton)	bright	yes	moderate	no	cuttings, air layering
Coleus blumei (coleus)	bright	no	heavy	no	cuttings
Columnea (goldfish plant)	bright	yes	heavy	no	cuttings
Cordyline terminalis (flaming dragon tree, Hawaiian ti plant)	ordinary	yes	moderate	no	air layering
Cyclamen persicum (cyclamen)	ordinary	no	moderate	yes	division
Cymbalaria muralis (kenilworth ivy)	ordinary	no	moderate	no	cuttings
Cyrtomium falcatum (holly fern)	shady	no	moderate	no	division
Davallia fijiensis (rabbit's foot fern)	shady	no	heavy	yes	division
Dionaea muscipula	shady	no	heavy	no	seeds, bulbs or spores only
Dizygotheca elegantissima (false aralia)	ordinary	no	moderate	no	cuttings
Dracaena fragrans massangeana (corn plant)	shady	no	moderate	no	air layering
D. godseffiana (gold dust dracaena)	ordinary	no	moderate	no	air layering
D. marginata (dragon plant)	ordinary	no	moderate	no	air layering
D. sanderiana (corn plant)	shady	no	moderate	no	air layering
Euphorbia pulcherrima	ordinary	no	heavy	yes	cuttings
Fatshedera lizei (tree ivy)	ordinary	no	moderate	no	cuttings
Fatsia japonica (Japanese aralia)	ordinary	no	moderate	no	cuttings
Ficus benjamina (Benjamin fig)	ordinary	yes	moderate	no	cuttings, air layering
F. elastica (rubber tree)	ordinary	yes	moderate	no	air layering
F. lyrata (fiddle-leaf fig)	ordinary	yes	moderate	no	air layering
Fittonia argyroneura (silver-veined fittonia)	shady	yes	moderate	no	cuttings
F. verschaffeltia (pink-veined fittonia)	shady	yes	moderate	no	cuttings
Gynura aurantiaca (purple passion plant)	bright	no	heavy	no	cuttings
Hedera helix (English ivy)	ordinary	no	moderate	no	cuttings
Helxine soleirolii (baby's tears)	shady	no	heavy	no	division, cuttings
Hemigraphis colorata (flame ivy)	ordinary	yes	moderate	no	cuttings

Name	Minimum Light Required	Extra Humidity Required For House Growth	Watering	Dormant Period In Which Care Requirements Change	Methods Of Propagation
Howea fosteriana (parlor palm, kentia palm)	shady	no	moderate	no	seeds, bulbs or spores only
Hydrosme rivieri (voodoo plant)	bright	yes	heavy	yes	seeds, bulbs or spores only
Hypoestes sanguinolenta (freckle face)	ordinary	yes	moderate	no	cuttings
Impatiens (Patient Lucy)	bright	yes	moderate	no	cuttings
Iresine herbstii (bloodleaf)	ordinary	no	heavy	no	cuttings
Livistona chinensis (Chinese fan palm)	shady	no	moderate	no	seeds, bulbs or spores only
Maranta leuconeura (prayer plant)	ordinary	no	moderate	yes	division
Mimosa pudica (sensitive plant)	ordinary	yes	moderate	yes	seeds, bulbs or spores only
Monstera deliciosa (Swiss cheese plant)	shady	no	light	no	air layering
Neanthe elegans (parlor palm)	shady	no	moderate	no	seeds, bulbs or spores only
Nephrolepsis (Boston fern)	ordinary	yes	moderate	no	division, sends out shoot with plantlet
Nidularium (flame-center bromeliad)	bright	yes	moderate	yes	sends out shoot with plantlet
Paphiopedilum maudiae (orchid)	shady	yes	moderate	no	division
Pelargonium domesticum (Martha Washington geranium)	sunny	no	heavy	yes	cuttings
P. hortorum (zonal geranium)	sunny	no	moderate	no	cuttings
P. tomentosum (scented-leaf geranium)	ordinary	no	moderate	no	cuttings
Peperomia caperata (emerald ripple peperomia)	shady	no	light	no	cuttings
P. obtusifolia (blunt-leafed peperomia)	shady	no	light	no	cuttings
P. sandersii (watermelon peperomia)	shady	no	light	no	cuttings
Philodendron oxycardium (heart-leafed philodendron)	shady	no	light	no	cuttings
P. selloum (saddle-leafed philodendron)	shady	no	light	no	cuttings
Phoenix roebelanii (Phoenix palm, miniature date palm)	shady	no	moderate	no	seeds, bulbs or spores only
Pilea cadieri (aluminum plant)	bright	yes	moderate	no	cuttings
Platycerium bifurcatum (staghorn fern)	ordinary	yes	moderate	no	division
Plectranthus australis (Swedish ivy)	ordinary	no	heavy	no	cuttings
Podocarpus macrophylla maki (Chinese podocarpus)	shady	no	light	no	cuttings
Polystichum setiferum (English hedge fern)	shady	yes	moderate	no	division
P. tsus-simense (Japanese hedge fern, holly fern)	shady	yes	moderate	no	division
Pteris cretica (brake fern)	ordinary	yes	heavy	no	division
Rhapis humilis (lady palm)	shady	no	moderate	no	cuttings
Saintpaulia (African violet)	bright	yes	moderate	no	cuttings, division
Sansevieria trifasciata (snake plant)	shady	no	very light	no	cuttings, division
Schefflera actinophylla (umbrella tree)	ordinary	yes	moderate	no	cuttings
Schlumbergera bridgesii (Christmas cactus)	ordinary	yes	moderate	yes	cuttings
S. gaertneri (Easter cactus)	ordinary	yes	moderate	yes	cuttings
Scindapsus aureus (pothos, devil's ivy)	shady	no	light	no	cuttings
Senecio mikanioides (German ivy)	ordinary	no	moderate	no	cuttings
Setcreasea purpurea (purple heart plant)	ordinary	no	moderate	no	cuttings
Sinningia concinna (miniature sinningia)	ordinary	yes	moderate	no	division
S. pusilla (miniature sinningia)	ordinary	yes	moderate	no	division
S. x-varieties (miniature sinningia)	ordinary	yes	moderate	no	division
S. speciosa (gloxinia)	ordinary	yes	moderate	yes	cuttings, division
Spathiphyllum cannaefolium	ordinary	yes	moderate	no	division
Syngonium podophyllum (arrowhead plant, nephthytis)	shady	no	light	no	division
Tolmiea menziesii (piggy-back plant)	shady	no	heavy	no	sends out shoot with plantlet
Tradescantia fluminensis variegata (wandering jew)	shady	no	moderate	no	cuttings
Zebrina pendula (wandering jew)	shady	no	moderate	no	cuttings
Zygocactus truncatus (Thanksgiving cactus)	ordinary	yes	moderate	yes	cuttings

2
Easiest Plants

The plants in this chapter are "easy" to care for because they require little active attention. Some have light requirements that are low; others need somewhat more light. Almost any of them can be kept someplace in your home and will survive. One thing we want to stress again: if you can't restrain yourself from watering every day, spraying, fussing repotting, and giving a lot of care to your plants, then choose plants from another section of the book. About the only thing that can hurt some of these plants is too much attention. They like to be admired, but from a distance. For more information refer to Part II.

Sansevieria

Sanseviera trifasciata
(snake plant)

This is also called the snake plant, mother-in-law's tongue, and other names descriptive of the long, pointed strap-like leaves rising from a central crown. Sometimes the leaves are all green, with deeper green stripes running horizontally across the leaf; other varieties have a yellow edge running all around the leaf. These two kinds will grow in some case almost 3 feet high, but more commonly, 2 feet high.

All the sansevierias are, for our money the easiest house plants to grow. They tolerate almost all light situations, from sunny windows to only artificial light. They don't need, or want, frequent watering. If you water too much, they can become flabby, rot, or even burst. We have never heard of anybody underwatering a sansevieria.

If you have an old sansevieria, repot it, and give it fairly good light — it may send out several more central crowns which will grow quickly. You can grow these all together in the same pot, or divide the plant and pot each crown individually.

Chlorophytum

Chlorophytum comosum
(spider plant)

Everybody knows this as the spider plant, and it seems to be one of the most enjoyable plants for children to grow — not to mention adults.

There are two types of chlorphytum commonly sold. One has long thin grasslike leaves with a creamy-white center and green borders. The other has longer leaves, usually somewhat thicker, that are all green. Both of these grow out and upward from a central crown.

The real popularity of the chlorophytums comes from their unusual method of propagation. A mature plant (about one year old) sends out one or more stalks from the central crown, and several small plantlets grow along the stem.

The plantlets can be cut off the stalk when their leaves are 3 inches long and rooted in potting soil or a glass of water.

People seem to feel that the plantlets of chlorophytums must eventually be cut free, and find themselves with a houseful of growing chlorphytums that will, in turn, send out new shoots with more plantlets. This results in a sorceror's apprentice situation, with more and more chlorophytums reproducing constantly.

As a matter of fact, if you leave the plantlets attached to the original plant, they will thrive for several years. The large $20 plants in florist shops that have many stalks of plantlets were grown in this way. Unless you have many friends clamoring for plantlets, it's better to leave them growing on the main plant.

Chlorophytums need slightly more light than the sansevierias, though they will do well anywhere in a room that has ordinary or shady windows. A sunny window may be too bright for them. They can go for some time without water, and seem to resent being watered too often. Let the soil dry out between waterings. If you're not watering enough, the tips of the leaves may begin to turn brown. This condition also occurs if the room is too low in humidity, and can be corrected by spraying the plant with water every two or three days.

Sansevieria trifasciata

Sansevieria trifasciata Laurentii (the tall snake plant with a yellow border) will not reproduce this way. The cuttings will sprout, but the new plants won't have the yellow border of the parents.

Besides dividing plants that have sprouted new crowns, you can also propagate sansevierias by a variation of the leaf-cutting method. Trim off a 2-inch piece of one of the leaves and place it in wet sand. Place it upright, like a small tombstone, and a new plant will begin growing from a corner of the leaf cutting. When the new plant is 4 inches tall or larger, cut it off from the leaf cutting and repot it with ordinary potting soil.

All the plants on these two pages, as well as other philodendrons, like to have their glossy leaves washed with a moist sponge from time to time. Misting, or spraying with lukewarm water, is also welcome, though not necessary. This care will make the plants look better and contribute to their health.

However, there are preparations sold for shining your leaves. These we emphatically do not recommend. They make the leaves shiny, but our experience is that they make them sticky and less healthy as well. Don't wax your plants as you would your floors. Just keep them clean.

Philodendron oxycardium

Scindapsus aureus

Philodendrons And Relatives

Philodendron oxycardium (heart-leafed philodendron)

There are many varieties of philodendron. The most popular, and in fact the most popular of all house plants, is scandens, the heart-leafed philodendron. This modest little climbing plant, with its many 1 or 2-inch deep green leaves, is found in offices and homes all over the United States. Its modesty is counterbalanced by its hardiness in all kinds of light, humidity and attention or inattention. It's better off if you give it some ordinary window light — though not direct sunlight — and let it dry out thoroughly between waterings. But it thrives even in artificial light conditions.

Propagation of the heart-leafed philodendron is just as easy as its care. We know people who just snip off the ends of the plant when it grows too long, stick the end of the cutting back in the same pot, and before long the cutting has sprouted roots and is growing merrily away. You can get quite a bushy pot of philodendron by propagating them this way.

Scindapsus aureus (pothos, devil's ivy, marble queen)

A relative of the common philodendron is the scindapsus, sometimes called pothos, devil's ivy or marble queen. The scindapsus has slightly larger leaves and thicker stems than the ordinary philodendron, but its distinctive feature is the creamy yellow streaks that mark the heart-shaped leaves. This plant is just about as hardy as the philodendron.

For some reason people like to grow scindapsus in water. We prefer potting them in regular potting soil and using them as hanging plants. Like the philodendron, scindapsus prefers to dry out between waterings.

Syngonium podophyllum (arrowhead plant, nephthytis)

Syngoniums, often incorrectly called nephthytis, are another relative of the philodendrons. Syngoniums are not climbing vines, however. They have 3 or 4-inch long leaves, shaped like arrowheads, at the end of a leaf stalk. Typically, a syngonium plant consists of a clump of several leaf stalks. The leaves are basically green, although several varieties are shaded with a lighter green, white, yellow, or even silver. The light and watering requirements for syngoniums are the same as for

Syngonium podophyllum atrovirens

Monstera deliciosa

philodendrons. Let them dry out before watering again. Syngoniums seem to prefer dim light to very bright light. These plants are propagated by root division only. As the leaves mature, they will divide into three distinct sections, and later into still more sections.

Monstera deliciosa
(Swiss cheese plant)

There are many larger relatives of the philodendron. One of the most popular is the monstera deliciosa, or Swiss cheese plant. Monsteras grow from a single stalk. Mature leaves are 10 to 12 inches, and "lobed" or divided into individual sections, though young leaves are less dramatic, both in size and shape. Eventually, the monstera can outgrow your house. But well before that happens, a support of bark-covered wood in the pot will help it stand. The stem will send out roots to penetrate the bark, and eventually the roots will make their way back to the soil for extra nourishment. Monstera care is the same as for philodendrons. If you are giving it too much or too little water, its leaves will begin to yellow at the tips.

Philodendron selloum
(saddle-leafed philodendron)

The saddle-leafed philodendron resembles the monstera somewhat, in that its leaves are equally large and lobed, and it grows on a short stalk from which many leaf stalks grow. The saddle-leafed philodendron, however, has more and thinner lobes on each leaf than the monstera. It likes the same care as the other philodendrons. It won't respond as well as the monstera to staking onto bark. Let the leaf stalks spread around.

Aspidistra

Aspidistra elatior
(cast-iron plant)

We don't feel this is as pretty a plant as the sansevieria, but if you want some live green around your home without worrying about it, the aspidistra will do as well as anything you can find. Hence its name: the "cast-iron plant." The aspidistra has long, full blackish-green leaves growing at the end of leaf stalks that grow out of the soil in groups. Another variety of aspidistra has leaves colored with green and white stripes. At maturity, the leaves can be up to 2 feet long.

Aspidistra will tolerate any kind of low or artificial light and lack of water. Bright light won't hurt it, though. If you're not watering it enough, it will let you know by the way its leaves begin to crack. On the other hand, if you give it good light and water it whenever the soil dries out, it will sometimes reward you by shooting up purple flowers from the base of the plant.

This plant grows very slowly, but seldom wilts. If you want to propagate it, divide it by cutting through the roots and repotting the two sets of stalks in two pots.

Spathiphyllum

Spathiphyllum cannaefolium

This plant resembles aspidistra except that its leaves are entirely green, and it shoots up long stems with white flower clusters shielded against a leaf. Both plants have 2-foot leaves on stems at maturity. Spathiphyllum needs more water than aspidistra, and won't tolerate total neglect. Don't put it in direct sunlight. Spathiphyllum is part of the same family of plants as philodendrons. When its soil dries out, you should water it until the water comes out of the drainage hole at the bottom.

Unfortunately, neither spathiphyllum nor aspidistra are as commonly available as some other plants that are harder to grow. People just don't seem to think they're spectacular enough. They are rewarding plants, however, in that both will flower with good care and light. Spathiphyllum can be propagated by division.

If you want your spathiphyllum to flower, it can be encouraged by good humidity and temperatures above 70°.

Aspidistra elatior

Spathiphyllum

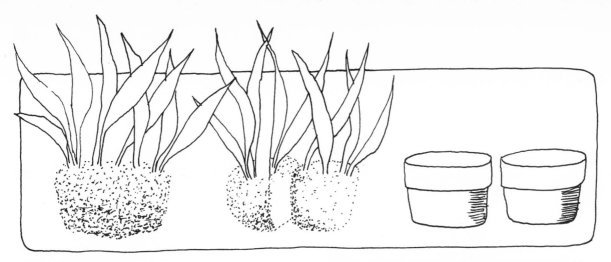

Peperomias

Peperomia caperata
(emerald ripple peperomia)

P. sandersii
(watermelon peperomia)

P. obtusifolia
(blunt-leafed peperomia)

There are three types of peperomias commonly sold. One has deep green leaves, with deep ridges. This is the "Emerald Ripple" variety. Another, the "Watermelon" type, has creamy white and green ridges on its leaves; its stems are bright red. A third type has blunter leaves with green centers and broad white or cream outer edges. All three have heart-shaped leaves from ¾ to 1½ inches across. Typically, peperomias have a thick stem from which leaf stalks grow with a single leaf on the end of each. The stem stops at the point where the leaf stalks begin growing. In the spring and summer, peperomias grow a kind of flower that looks like a leaf stalk that turned white and fuzzy on the end and never opened into a leaf.

Peperomias do very well in shady light conditions, although they will grow in bright light too. Direct sunlight, particularly in the hot summer months, is not good for them, though they sometimes tolerate it.

One thing peperomias will not tolerate is over-watering. Particularly in winter, they should be allowed to dry out between waterings.

Peperomias are slow-growing plants and will very seldom outgrow their pots. Be careful not to break the brittle leaf stems whenever you do repot. If a stem or leaf gets dark or soggy, pluck it off. It has begun to rot from overwatering or high humidity. If this happens to your plant often, it is a warning that you are giving it too much water.

Whereas aspidistras and spathiphylla are propagated by dividing the crown into two plants, peperomias are propagated by cutting off one of the leaf stems and putting it in potting soil. The slow growth of peperomias applies here too, and it will be 4 to 8 weeks before the stem will develop roots. Small peperomia plants will grow up from the sides of the stem, at earth level. These should be cut off from the parent stem and repotted.

Peperomia caperata

3
Plants For Routine Care

Plants that need routine care are plants that at least should be looked at every day. They need good light, though not necessarily direct sunlight, and will thrive if you are attentive to their needs. If a plant needs unusual treatment, vigilance, or growing conditions, you will find it in the next chapter, beginning on page 66.

What does routine care consist of? Noticing the general appearance of the plant, for one thing. Do the leaves and stem appear healthy and fresh? Are there any yellowing leaves or spots? Is it growing straight? The time to catch trouble is early. If something appears wrong with your plant, analyze it and correct it.

The daily check should include touching the soil with your fingers. This is the best test as to whether the plant needs watering. You may think you can trust your eyes, but you can't. The composition of the soil and the changing light may fool you. Feel it, not just on the surface, but a bit under the surface as well. Consider your plant's requirements. Does it need moist soil almost all the time? Or should it dry out between waterings?

Some plants quickly turn their leaves and stems to the sun. If you want them to grow in a balanced even pattern, you should turn their pots a quarter turn every day or two.

The easiest method of insect pest control is to discover them when there are only a few on the plant. Pinch them with your fingers, rub them with alcohol, or remove the leaves that they are on.

For plants that tend to grow spindly, pinching their tips right from the start is a good way to get them to grow bushy. Daily inspection will let you see the new shoots that should be pinched right away.

Plants whose leaves are dusty and dirty should be washed. Many plants that do well in humid conditions like a good misting now and then.

Remember, the important thing about daily care is not that you have to do something every day, but that you have to notice what your plant is telling you.

You will find yourself less likely to put off a bit of routine care if you keep what you need in a household utility box, and carry it around with you.

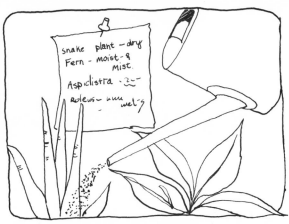

If you have bought a lot of new plants all at once, and can't remember how often each needs water, keep a list in your box or on the wall for a while until you have it memorized.

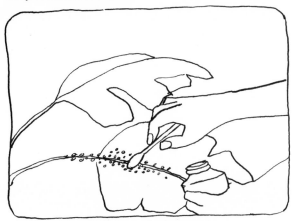

Both the sponge and the alcohol will come in handy as you find insects under leaves or on stems. You can kill them with your fingers, or sponge them off, or use alcohol on a cotton swab to kill them.

Just as you pinch a bit here and there as you see a plant needs it, get in the habit of looking for dead or dying leaves, rotting stems, and brown tips to snip off with your scissors.

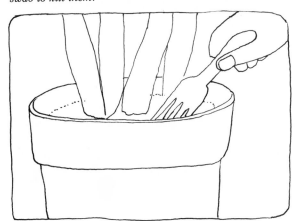

A fork is a good tool for breaking up the surface of the soil, and for digging in fertilizer for plants that are heavy feeders. It is easiest to do after you have watered.

Most days you will use the mister just to raise humidity and clean foliage, but occasionally the same bottle can be used to spray insecticide or fertilizer on your plants.

African Violets
Saintpaulia
(African violet)

If you have limited space, African violets ought to be one of your favorites. They never take up much room, and will greet you with stalks of colorful flowers all year round.

African violets grow outwards from a crown in a circular, or rosette, form. The leaves are fleshy and thick. Each leaf grows on the end of a leaf stem, or petiole, that is also fleshy and succulent. Because of the high water content of stems and leaves, African violets are prone to rot. Flowers grow on stalks that grow from the base of the petioles. There can be one or many flowers on a single stalk. African violet breeders have so increased the number of varieties that the flowers come in many shades of violet, pink, magenta, white, and combinations of these. Some plants have "single" flowers, meaning flowers that have five petals, and others have "doubles" which have so many petals that they appear almost ball-shaped. Avid fans of African violets also distinguish between different shapes of leaves, though all are deep green.

Overwatering is the easiest way to ruin an African violet. Some people advise watering from the bottom, by letting the plant sit in a tray of water for fifteen minutes, on the theory that it will only take as much as it needs. The trouble with this method is that the fertilizer salts that are necessary for getting African violets to flower will rise to the surface with bottom watering, forming a white deposit on the soil and pot. When leaf stalks touch this, they get burned and begin to rot.

We water only from the top, giving the plant enough water so that it runs out of the bottom

drainage hole. Then we check the moisture of the soil every day. The first day the soil is dry, we water again, and not before.

If your African violet is growing nice green leaves, but no flowers, there are three conditions to check. First, African violets need at least ordinary light to flower. In winter, they can be put even in direct sunlight, although the rest of the year direct sunlight will cause the leaves to burn. Give them as much light as you can, and then if you start to see brown spots or yellow rings on the leaves, you know it's too much light.

The second requirement for flowering is fertilizer. There are African violet fertilizers sold that are high in phosphoric acid and potash. Follow the directions on the label and don't over-fertilize. Treatment once a month is sufficient.

The third requirement for flowering is good humidity. Because homes are lowest in humidity in the wintertime, people simply assume their African violets won't flower during winter months. In fact, if you give them the humidity they need, all year round, they'll flower all year round. We recommend placing your African violet pots in trays of peat moss, and keep the peat moss damp all the time. Trays of wet pebbles will work as well. Don't keep the pots sitting in the water itself; the roots around the drainage holes will begin to rot.

Of the three flower requirements, humidity is the most important. Most homes have enough light for African violets, and the fertilizer only gives an added boost to the plant. But people who try it, find the humidity-raising trick makes a great difference in their success with this plant.

There are three ways of propagating African violets. In the simplest way, the plant does the job for you. Small plantlets, or "sucker" plants start growing at the base of the plant. People who want to keep the symmetrical rosette growing pattern of their plant simply pluck these off. If you want to use them for propagation, allow them to grow until the largest leaves are an inch wide. Then unpot the plant and use a sharp knife to cut off the suckers with their roots. Repot individually.

A second way of propagating is to cut a leaf petiole off. When cutting leaves from African violets for propagation or because they are diseased or rotting, always break the stem at the place where it grows from the center of the plant. This discourages stem, or crown rot.

Plant the leaf, with its stem trimmed to about an inch long, in a soil mix that drains well. Water the leaf as you would your plant. After some time, from a week to several months, small plantlets begin to form at the base of the leaf. When the leaves of these are ¾ inch wide, unpot the leaf and separate the plantlets with their root systems. Repot in small pots.

The third method of propagation is actually to pollinate the flowers. Each flower has a bright yellow pair of anthers in its center. Pinch these off, and crush them against your thumbnail to expose the pollen. Touch the pollen to the tip of the stamen, which is the long, needle-shaped part of the flower that sticks up in the air. The base of the pistil should begin to swell in a week or so. This part of the flower will stay green when the rest of the flower has fallen off. Leave it attached to the plant, cut down on watering, and in 3 to 6 months, the seeds will mature. When this happens, the base of the pistil, or seed pod, turns brown and dry. Break it off, and inside you will find thousands of dust-like African violet seeds. These can be sown on the top of a mixture of damp peat moss and vermiculite. When they sprout, thin the seedlings and transplant into their own pots.

Hedera helix

To build a climbing pole for ivies, hardware cloth or tightly-woven wire mesh can be rolled into a cylinder and tied to hold its shape. Put two thin pieces of wood through one end of the cylinder at right angles to each other. Each piece should be the length of the bottom of the pot in which you will place the cylinder. The sticks help hold the cylinder upright.

Fill the inside of the cylinder with peat or sphagnum moss. Plant the ivy in the pot and train it around the cylinder by pinning the strands with hairpins into the moss as they grow.

Ivies

There is a family of plants to which ferns belong; there is a family to which palms belong; even the orchids, with thousands of different colors and forms, all belong to the same family. But plants that are called "ivy" belong to many different families of plants. There is no botanical reason why they should be grouped together, except possibly that most of them have no erect stems. They creep along the ground, or hang from crevices, or climb up walls and trees. Except for one or two.

Hedera helix (English ivy)

The plant that most people think of when they hear the word "ivy" is English ivy, hedera helix. Even this plant has many different varieties, some with 5-lobed some with 3-lobed leaves. Some have heart-shaped leaves and some fan-shaped leaves. They come in white, yellow, green, and variegated colors. The most common has three triangular lobes on its dark green leaves. All the hederas can grow in cool temperatures, with ordinary light and regular watering. Don't keep them wet all the time, but an occasional misting is helpful.

Fatshedera lizei (tree ivy)

Early in the twentieth century, someone crossed a fatsia japonica with a hedera helix and produced a fatshedera. The japonica, or Japanese aralia, has large shiny green leaves, up to 16 inches long, and grows on leaf stalks that sprout in a clump. The fatshedera has the large leaves of the japonica, but its leaves are the 5-lobed shape of the English ivy. And fatshedera grows on an erect stem. Some people call it tree ivy. Both these plants need the same kind of watering as English ivy, but they do well if you can give them several hours of direct sunlight.

Cissus antarctica (kangaroo vine) *C. discolor* (begonia treebine) *C. rhombifolia* (grape ivy)

Another family of plants produced the cissus ivies: cissus antarctica, called kangaroo vine, cissus discolor, and cissus rhombifolia, or grape ivy. Antarctica has leathery green leaves with jagged edge ("toothed") leaves, 1 to 3 inches long. It can grow from 1 to 6 feet high, depending on how high you can provide a support for it. Grape ivy looks pretty much the same as antarctica, except that its leaves emerge from the stem in groups of three; on antarctica, they are single. Mature grape ivy has brown fuzz on the underside of its leaves. Both of these plants can be grown in ordinary light but not direct sun and should be allowed to dry between waterings. The cissus discolor, however, needs high humidity, and should be misted frequently or grown in a humid room like the bathroom. Leaves of the discolor are a pattern of purple, silver, white and green; the undersides are reddish-purple.

Plectranthus australis
(Swedish ivy)

So-called Swedish ivy, plectranthus australis, is actually a member of the mint family. It will take frequent heavy watering, and should be pinched back to develop new shoots along its stem. The silvery green leaves are heart-shaped and toothed, about one inch long. It can be grown in ordinary light. Cuttings are easily rooted in water.

Senecio mikanioides
(German ivy)

German ivy, senecio mikaniodes, has thin stems and single, bright green, 7-pointed leaves, 2 to 4 inches long. Pinch and prune it back often so it grows bushy. It roots from cuttings and needs ordinary light. Water when the soil becomes dry.

Hemigraphis colorata
(flame ivy)

Red ivy or flame ivy, hemigraphis colorata, has smooth, glossy olive-green leaves, with reddish-purple veins and underside. It will benefit from regular misting and a humid spot. Bright light will enhance the leaf color, although it will grow in ordinary light. Water when the soil has just dried out.

Cymbalaria muralis
(kenilworth ivy)

Kenilworth ivy, cymbalaria muralis, often grows wild in the eastern United States. It has ½-inch to 1-inch leaves with scalloped edges and bears tiny purple flowers. It stays a manageable size in a pot; it benefits from an occasional misting; and it will thrive in ordinary light. Water when the soil becomes dry.

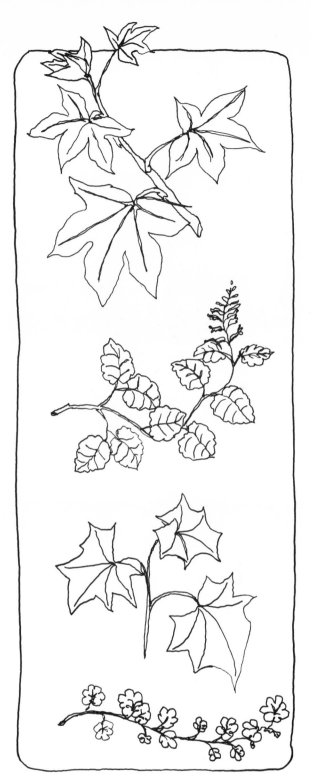

Ivies from top to bottom are: Fatshedera lizei, Plectranthus australis, Senecio mikanioides, and Cymbalaria muralis.

Begonias

Begonia is a whole family of plants, and there are many different types. Some are suitable for house plants, and others are not. There are indoor gardeners who grow nothing but begonias, and have a tremendous variety of plants. This is only a short run-down on the types that are commonly sold. We'd like to point out that some of the ones mentioned here definitely require more than routine care, while some are fairly easy.

Begonia semperflorens (wax begonia)

Easiest of all is the begonia semperflorens (the Latin name means "always flowering," which is a good description.) Its common name is wax begonia. If you have bright windows or sunny windows, semperflorens will do well for you. It can dry out between waterings, but it must have sun. Don't however, give it full sunlight in the hottest part of spring and summer days; its foliage will burn.

Semperflorens grows from a fibrous root. Its fleshy stems are covered with green, reddish-green, bronze, or deep red leaves about 1 inch long. The leaves are an oval that comes to a point. It is quite normal for the leaves at the bottoms of the stem to dry out and drop off. When a stem becomes too leggy, you can cut the whole stem off. Or you can try to force new growth at the bottom by pinching the tip of the stem. It's a good idea to keep the wax begonia trimmed back because it gets leggy after a while, although we have seen very large plants that people used as hanging plants and never trimmed. White, pink and red flowers take many different forms though they are seldom more than ½ inch wide. Some of the most common are globe-shaped and twin-winged. New flowers keep forming as long as the plant has good light.

You can propagate wax begonias by taking a stem cutting and putting it directly into a pot of moist soil.

Begonia rex (rex begonia)

The other large-selling type of begonia is the rex begonia. While almost no one fails to grow the wax begonia successfully, with the rex begonia almost no one succeeds. But who could fail to be impressed by the huge, gorgeous leaves, almost a foot long and vividly multicolored in a variety of patterns? And there they are, grow-

Begonia semperflorens

The semperflorens, or wax, begonia is almost impossible to repot without breaking some stems. We'd advise taking cuttings and starting new plants. For new plants, however, add a few handfuls of peat moss of vermiculite to your regular potting soil. Begonias don't like soil that packs tightly. The other begonias don't grow fast enough to need repotting often, but the same advice about soil mix goes for them too.

ing happily and healthily in the plant store. Why not take one home?

Why not? Because when you get home you find that in a few weeks, the plant's leaves have wilted and dropped off. As far as you can see, it's dead, so you throw it out and wish you had been a better gardener.

Actually, you did nothing wrong. In the first place, the plant is most likely not dead. Rex begonias go into dormant periods, which they signal by dropping their leaves, but they come back to life eventually and can be made beautiful again. The dormant period has most likely been brought on by the drastic shift in living conditions. In the greenhouse and in the flower shop or plant store where you bought it, it was heavily misted often and the humidity was kept much higher than it is in your home.

If you insist on keeping rex begonias around the house, the only way to do it is to get them through the dormant period. Put the plant, after its leaves have dropped, in a darker room. Water it only enough to keep the soil from getting powder dry. Don't try to fertilize it back to life. When the plant is ready, which may be in a month or three months, it will begin to put out new leaves again. When it does, move it into a bright room, but never into direct sunlight. Keep the air around the plant humid by using one of the methods described on page 17. Water when the soil is dry. Fertilize once a month with a fertilizer high in nitrogen.

Begonia rex-cultorum

Other Begonias

The Iron Cross begonia has emerald green leaves with a brown crossed pattern in the center. The pebbled look of its leaves also makes it distinctive. It should be handled the same as the rex begonia, although it dormancy period is not as extreme.

Stem begonias get their name from their long stalks, which resemble bamboo canes. They can grow several feet high and will flower if given direct sun. The shape of their leaves also gives them the name "angel-wing" begonias. Let them dry between waterings.

The begonias that have large, 3 and 4-inch blooms and are seen in flower beds outdoors are called tuberous begonias. Tubers, which resemble flat and irregular bulbs, are sold packed in peat moss. Usually pink shoots are growing out of the top side of the tuber. Plant these in a mix of half potting soil and half peat moss and keep moist till the shoots grow above the surface. We've never had luck with growing these in the house, but many gardeners claim it can be done.

Geraniums

There are many types of geraniums, or pelargoniums as botanists call them. Some are grown for their lovely flowers that appear in ball-shaped clusters; others have multicolored and patterned leaves that are the main attraction; still others have scented leaves and are grown for that quality.

Pelargonium hortorum (zonal geranium)

Most of the flowering types known as pelargonium hortorum, have roundish, scalloped leaves from 1 to 3 inches wide and a brownish ring around the center of the leaf. Some people call them zonal geraniums. They need a sunny window and should be allowed to dry out between waterings. After they flower, they should be propagated by rooting leaf cuttings. The parent plant can then be discarded because if allowed to grow, it will only become leggy and unattractive. Even during early growth, after a new cutting takes root, the plant should be pinched back frequently.

Some of the zonal geraniums have been bred to develop attractive leaves, with white, red, bronze, brown and gold colors as well as green. These varieties sometimes flower, too, but not as freely as the ordinary types. Their culture is the same as for the flowering zonal types. Don't mist any of these geraniums; they don't like humidity. Water when the soil has become dry.

Pelargonium domesticum (Martha Washington geranium)

The green-leafed Martha Washington varieties, which florists sell around Eastertime, produce beautiful flowers, but probably won't flower for you a second year. The reason is that these varieties need a three-month winter resting period at 60° temperatures. Without that condition, they won't set buds. If you want to try, cut the plant back sharply after its spring flowering, and let it grow in a sunny spot for the summer, with plenty of water. Let it rest during late fall and early winter in a cool room. Cut down on watering during the resting period too. Bring the plant back to warmth and more water in February or March.

Pelargonium tomentosum (scented-leaf geranium)

The scented-leaf geraniums, pelargonium tomentosum, are the easiest geraniums to grow. They don't need the direct sunlight that the

Pelargonium hortorum

Pelargonium domesticum

others require but may need constant pinching to avoid legginess. The many different leaf and flower types of these plants make them difficult to recognize. Most of them have plain green leaves, some with a textured surface, some roundish, some 5-lobed, and in all shades of green. The sure way is to pinch a leaf and smell. If you get a strong whiff of scent, — lemon-like, rose-like, or even mint-like — it's a geranium. Start new plants from stem cuttings and let plants dry between waterings.

Dracaenas

Dracaena fragrans massangeana
(corn plant)

Dracaenas come in a variety of forms; all are grown for their foliage. The dracaena fragrans massangeana, sometimes called corn plant, is the familiar house and office plant that has 6 to 12-inch long leaves, 3 inches wide, growing in a rosette, or cluster, from the top of a woody, thick stem. The leaves may be all green or colored with vertical stripes of yellow and cream. This plant really belongs with the "easy" plants, but we've put it here with the other dracaenas, which are fussier. The standard advice is to water the corn plant when the soil dries, but it takes an incredible amount of neglect and low light without obvious ill effects. Frequent watering and fertilizing don't seem to affect it either. This is an extremely slow-growing plant.

D. sanderiana
(corn plant)

Dracaena sanderiana has leaves similar in color and shape to massangeana, but they are always marked with vertical cream stripes and the plants are generally smaller. The leaves of sanderiana usually grow close together along the stem, instead of clustering at the top. Sanderiana should be allowed to dry out between waterings. It likes good light, if you can provide it, but tolerates low-light conditions.

D. marginata
(dragon plant)

Dracaena marginata has thinner, 12-inch or longer, pointed leaves with a thin red margin around the edges. It grows on a woody cane like massangeana, but it grows more quickly than its cousin. Let it dry out between waterings. The foot-high plants that most plant stores sell will grow to 3 to 4 feet high, although you may be successful in getting them to grow even larger.

When dracaena plants get too leggy, they can be propagated by air layering, a process that will take quite a long time because of the slow-growing habits of most dracaenas.

Dracaena fragrans massangeana

Nephrolepsis exaltata

Sometimes you will find a series of little bumps on the bottoms of fern leaflets. Don't be alarmed; this isn't a disease or some sort of leaf-burrowing insect. These are the reproductive spores of the plant. When they mature, they will fall off the leaf if you shake it. You can dry them on pieces of paper and plant them by sowing them on top of moist soil. When seedlings are about two inches long, pick them out of the soil with a fork and re-pot.

Ferns can also be propagated by division. In the case of ferns with rhizomes, cut the rhizome in two and prop it on top of new moist potting soil until it roots. Rhizomes shouldn't be buried.

Ferns

There is fossil evidence that ferns have been growing on earth for over 200,000,000 years. They now grow in the wild in all climates and areas of the world. There are thousands of varieties and many are suitable for indoor culture.

Nephrolepsis (Boston fern)

The Boston fern, nephrolepsis, is one of the most popular. It has long, 2 to 3-foot fronds with irregular shaped leaflets, 2 to 4 inches long, growing close together all along its length. There is a dwarf variety whose fronds are about half as long. Nephrolepsis needs good humidity and frequent ample watering. Otherwise its leaflets begin to turn brown and crispy. If you use it as a hanging plant, be careful not to let it get too dry. Mist often. It can stand any light except full sun. If it grows too large for its pot, it can be propagated by division.

Adiantum tenerum (maidenhair fern)

Adiantum has shiny black stems growing in a clump with branches of ¼ to ½-inch leaves shaped like little fans. The leaves have a pinkish tinge as they first appear, then turn light green. This plant will burn in a bright window: it needs a shady or dim environment. It also needs high humidity and should be misted daily or oftener. If you can put it on a humidifying tray, it will benefit. Keep the soil moist, but not wet.

Asparagus sprengeri (asparagus fern)

There are many kind of asparagus ferns, all having needle-like leaflets that are sometimes so fine and dense that they look like fur. They do not grow well in bright light, and require shade. Low humidity won't bother them as much as other ferns, but their soil should be kept from drying out completely.

Davallia fijiensis (rabbit's-foot fern)

Davallia, or rabbit's-foot fern, gets its popular name from its rhizome, or stem that grows along the ground like a root, which is supposed to resemble an animal foot. Davallia has feathery, dark green fronds of foliage growing from thin stems and branches, 12 to 18 inches high. Davallias do best in a shady window. They don't need deep pots because of the rhizome, which draws nutrients and moisture from the top of the soil. The soil should be kept fairly moist. Some davallias shed their leaves in winter; keep the soil from drying out, and they'll grow back.

Pteris cretica
(brake fern)

Pteris, or brake fern, has ragged, light-green leaflets, sometimes with cream-colored stripes, on fronds 6 to 12 inches long. They like to be kept moist and will benefit from an occasional misting. If you can grow them on a humidifying tray, do so. Don't put them in a bright window; they do best in ordinary light.

Polystichum setiferum
(English hedge fern)
P. tsus-simense
(Japanese hedge fern, holly fern)

Polystichum, or English hedge fern, has dark green, finely-divided foliage on 12 to 18-inch fronds. A Japanese cousin, polystichum tsus-simense, has a metallic green color and is often sold for use in terrariums because it doesn't grow large. Both will do well in ordinary or low light conditions. Let the soil get almost dry between waterings.

Cyrtomium falcatum
(holly fern)

Cyrtomium, or holly fern, has pointed leaf-lets, 1 inch wide and 3 inches long, that are shiny and leathery. The fronds grow 1 to 2 feet long. The leaflets should be misted or washed to keep the plant looking fresh. Keep the soil barely moist at all times. Cyrtomium likes ordinary or shady light conditions. It tolerates cool temperatures better than most other ferns.

Platycerium bifurcatum
(staghorn fern)

Platycerium bifurcatum, the staghorn fern, is not a plant we recommend for beginning indoor gardeners. It is an epiphyte, which merely means that it does not grow in soil. Most staghorn fern plants sold in stores are growing in wooden baskets filled with moss or attached to a tree bark or piece of cork. You water them by taking them off the wall once a week and soaking the base of the plant in a sinkful of tepid water. They need light that is bright without being sunny, although we have seen them growing in very dim conditions. The irregular, antler-shaped, skin-like fronds hang down from the center of the plant and should be sprayed or misted at least once a day.

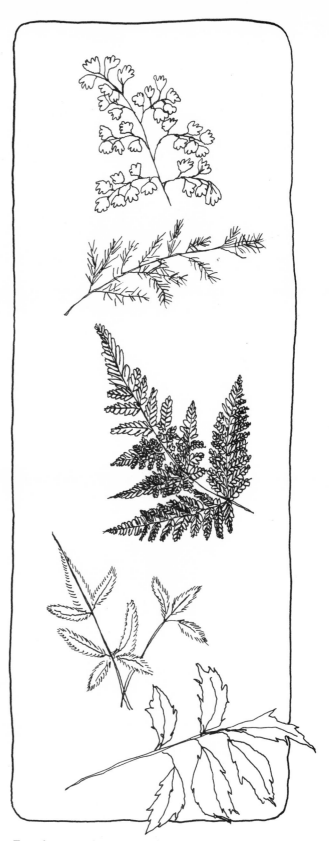

Ferns from top to bottom are: Adiantum tenerum, Asparagus sprengeri, Davallia fejeensis, Pteris cretica, and Cyrtomium falcatum.

Palms

The palm trees you see on the beach in Florida are coconut palms and need bright sunlight to flower and bear fruit. Don't make the mistake of thinking your indoor palm plants need the same treatment. They do well in bright or ordinary light, but don't like the burning rays of full sun. They should be kept moist and enjoy humidity as well. If the tips of your palm's leaves turn brown, it's probably because you're not giving it enough water. We let the soil of our palms dry out between waterings, but we mist them fairly often and keep them on a pebble tray in the dry winter months.

People look forward to having large palms of the type that decorate hotel lobbies in Humphrey Bogart movies. So they put their 6-inch palm in a large pot hoping to encourage growth. Unfortunately, this doesn't work. Most palms benefit from being pot bound, or planted in a pot that's just large enough for their roots to fit into. Potting in a pot that's too large can result in the soil packing tightly and, eventually, yellowing of the palm's leaves.

Beaucarnea recurvata (elephant's foot tree)

If you want a huge palm, you'll have to pay for one that will grow large — like the beaucarnea recurvata, or elephant-foot tree, which will certainly be a conversation piece in your living room. The trunk swells out at ground level, in the manner of an elephant's foot. At the top, leaves 3 to 4 feet long and about ¾ inch wide sprout out and hang down. This plant will thrive in a "small" container (2 or 3 feet wide), and can grow as high as 30 feet.

Dwarf Palms

At the other extreme, the smaller palms that you can buy at florists' or plant shops are called chamaedorea or howea palms. These are sometimes called "parlor palms," among other names, and rarely grow over a foot high. They are difficult even for experts to tell apart, and are identifiable only by their small size, and the growth of their leaves, which is pinnate.

We've received chamaedoreas, howeas, or neanthe elegans, which is another small palm, interchangeably from some dealers who didn't know what the correct botanical name was. No matter. The care for all is the same. Don't put them in direct sunlight. You'll be surprised how well they do in a dimly-lighted window or in a fluorescent-lighted office. The important thing is to keep the soil moist and, if you can, to mist them once a day. They appreciate some fertiliz-

In the case of all palms, if leaf tips brown or yellow, you can trim them off without damage to the plant. Trim them to a point to keep the plant looking natural.

Beaucarnera recurvata

If the bottom branches seem to yellow and die, it may be that you are giving too much light or not enough moisture. Analyze your situation.

ing, but not overmuch. Follow the directions on the fertilizer you buy. You will find that all of these dwarf palms grow slowly, but reliably. The stem of any of these small palms remains green, even as it thickens, to allow the growing stems to branch out.

Rhapis humilis (lady palm)

Many of the larger palms will develop brown, woody stems as they grow larger. One example is the rhapis, or lady palm, whose stems are covered with hairy fibers. The lady palm can also be distinguished by leathery leaves that grow in a palmate fashion. They can be reproduced from suckers that spring up from the base of the main stem. Cut these off and root them as you would cuttings.

Livistona chinensis (Chinese fan palm)

Livistona is another palm that grows large. On the young plants, 2 to 3 feet tall, the groups of leaves grow to one foot wide in palmate formation. As the plants mature, they grow larger. Fertilize these monthly except in winter, when they like a brief rest. Keep the soil moist throughout the year.

Phoenix roebelenii (Phoenix palm, miniature date palm)

Phoenix palms, or miniature date palms, are another small palm, seldom growing larger than 2 feet high, but they have longer (2 foot) fronds with longer (up to 9-inch) leaflets. They can be an attractive and compact addition to your indoor garden. Their soil should be kept moist at all times. Remember to water thoroughly till the excess runs out of the drainage hole, so the bottom roots get moisture too. Fertilize once a month. You will often find these palms in florists' arrangements of several plants. If they grow too large for the other plants in the arrangement, give them a pot of their own.

Caryota mitis (fishtail palm)

Caryota looks so different that many people don't think of it as a palm. Its leaves are pinnate, appearing in clusters along the many branches of the plant. Each leaf is a triangular, almost fishtail shape, accounting for the plant's common name, the fishtail palm. It takes the same moist and moderate light conditions of other palms. Keep caryota pot bound, and fertilize it once a month.

Chamaedorea elegans

The pinnate (like chamaedorea) have leaves growing out from either side of their branches from the bottom to the end of the branch, as evergreen needles grow out from a branch.

Livistona chinensis

The palmate (like livistonia) have all their leaves growing out from a central point at the end of their branches, in the same way that your fingers grow from your palm.

All palms fall into two main groups, the palmate and pinnate. These are easy to tell apart.

Gynura aurantiaca

Setcreasea purpurea

Both these plants are valued for their unusual purple color. The purple not only shows up best in good light, but is actually intensified by sun.

Gynura

Gynura aurantiaca
(purple passion plant)

Gynura aurantiaca, the purple passion plant, well deserves its popular name. It has furry purple leaves and stems. The leaves are sharp toothed, and hang down vine-like from the plant. Pinching the tips of the plant is the way to make it grow back bushy and give a colorful effect to a sunny window. As you can guess, the more sun this plant gets, the faster it grows, and the more intense will be the purple coloration of its leaves. Don't think because of its delicate purple hairs, that this plant is touchy or delicate. You can stroke its hairs all you like — the only thing that will kill it is lack of water. It loves a good watering, and you should keep it as moist as possible for good growth. Cuttings are easily made from its stems; they'll root easily in the same pot, if you want to create a whole bush of purple passion. If you let the plant grow without pinching it, some of those purple leaves will yellow and shrivel. Remove them, and pinch back more often. This plant won't require much feeding, but if you have it in the same pot for three or four years, it may slow its growth. Repotting or propagating from cuttings will rejuvenate it. If you give it a lot of light, it may develop little orange flowers. These can be left on the plant until they wilt.

Setcreasea

Setcreasea purpurea
(purple heart plant)

This is the other favorite purple friend of the home gardener. Some people call it the "purple heart plant." Its shade of purple is less brilliant than the gynura, and its leaves are long, slender and curving. They grow from divisions between the sections of the thick, succulent branches of the plant that arise in a clump from the soil.

Setcreasea needs plenty of water and good sunlight, although it does better in low-light conditions than the gynura. Keep its soil moist.

The lower leaves on this plant don't last long, and soon you have a very leggy plant. Pruning some of the branches down to the soil level encourages new branches to sprout. If you like, you can root the pruned branches in water or soil and start new plants.

Good light encourages setcreasea to sprout small short-lived flowers in the leaf axils.

Podocarpus

Podocarpus macrophylla maki (Chinese podocarpus)

These are slow-growing plants, and are sold at all stages of growth, from tiny plants in terrariums to large specimens in tubs. The woody stalk bears thin, green, pointed leaves all along its length, and will sprout branches with leaves, especially if pinched. The plant is really a coniferous evergreen tree, and can be trained as a bonsai, if you wish (see page 74). Most people raise it with occasional pinching back as a pot plant. It tolerates almost any kind of light, from strictly artificial to very bright. Direct summer sun can hurt it. It needs only the ordinary house humidity. You should water it when the soil becomes dry. Podocarpus is easily propagated by cutting off a branch that has sprouted to 2 to 3 inches, and planting it in moist soil or letting it root in water.

Podocarpus macrophylla maki

Dizygotheca

Dizygotheca elegantissima (false aralia)

Some people call this false aralia, because of its kinship to many of the ivy plants. You wouldn't call it ivy on seeing it. It has long thin leaves, leathery and deeply toothed. The different varieties of this plant have leaves that range in color from a reddish to a greenish-brown. The plant grows with a single, bark-covered trunk and leaf stalks which bear leaves in a palmate manner.

Moderate light is best for dizygotheca. It likes neither very sunny nor very dark conditions. Water it when the soil becomes barely dry. If you tend this plant well, it will eventually become 3 to 5 feet high, but it can be encouraged to a shrub-like appearance if you cut it back to 6 inches off the ground each year and let new sprouts arise from the base of the plant.

Cutting back the plant is also the remedy for the plant's losing its lower leaves. This occurs naturally through age, although dry air or very dim light conditions will also bring it on. A misting once or twice a week will help the plant to keep its lower leaves. Stem cuttings can be rooted in water or moist potting soil.

Dizygotheca elegantissima

Coleus

Coleus blumei
(coleus)

Coleus is the plant that is sold as little 2-inch specimens with brightly colored leaves at your local plant store in spring. By the end of the year, it can have grown to a 2-foot high shrub with hundreds of leaves, some of which are as large as the original plant you bought. This kind of result requires two essentials of care: good light and frequent watering.

The pink, yellow, orange, red and green patterned leaves come in all combinations. The more light these plants get, the more intense the colors are. This is one of the few plants that will even take direct summer sunlight, if you have a spot in your home to provide it. With all that sun and the rapid growth of the plant, it needs a lot of water. If you forget, it will remind you by drooping alarmingly. Fortunately, a good watering restores most coleus to their former vigor in an hour or so.

Coleus tends to be very leggy, and sheds lower leaves with reckless abandon. Don't worry about the loss of leaves, but do pinch back the growing tips of branches, to encourage bushy, bottom growth. Coleus is a very determined plant, you'll find, and will sprout twice for every pinch you make. Often it sprouts right out of the top of the plant again, and you have to be insistent: pinch the new sprouts and keep pinching until you get growth lower down the branches.

Coleus is one of the easiest house plants to propagate. If you buy a packet of mixed seeds at the beginning of the year, you'll soon have more plants than you know what to do with, and can pick and choose among them for colors and leaf shapes that you like.

Cuttings from coleus root more readily than anything else we know of. A 3-inch cutting will root in moist soil so easily that we don't see any point in rooting them in water.

Most people start coleus plants anew each year from cuttings. The plants get rather woody and leggy if kept more than a year, although it's certainly possible to grow the same plant, pruning it back each year to encourage fresh growth from the bottom of the plant.

Coleus blumei

Seed companies have been developing new types of coleus. Some of the new varieties have scalloped, lacy edges on the leaves, and others have long, thin leaves quite unlike the traditional heart-shaped coleus leaf. There is also an oak-leaf variety, whose leaves are shaped accordingly. Some of these new varieties are slower-growing than the traditional varieties, but if you have grown the old types and are tired of them, the new strains may renew your interest.

Maranta

Maranta leuconeura
(prayer plant)

Maranta is commonly called the prayer plant, because of its habit of folding its leaves upward at night. Turn on a lamp nearby, and the leaves gradually unfold again. In their native environments, this characteristic helps to funnel dew and moisture down to the roots of the plant.

Maranta leaves are 3 to 4 inches long, oval, and noticable for their red and brown markings. A typical variety has red veins with yellow or brown spots in each section of the leaf. The colors sometimes change as the plant grows older. The leaves grow on the ends of thick stems that arise in a clump from the base of the plant.

Maranta is tolerant of low-light conditions, and will not need a bright window to develop bright colors. Plants prefer to be kept moist and like an occasional misting.

Marantas take a winter rest; during which they need you to cut down on the watering, — but don't stop it altogether. Some people cut the stems back almost to the ground in the fall. In late winter or early spring, new growth will appear in the form of tightly-rolled leaves, which soon unfold. Begin watering more often at this time. Many indoor gardeners repot marantas at the end of the dormant period, to give the plants fresh soil and replenished nutrients. Maranta can also be propagated by division after new growth begins.

Maranta leuconeura massangeana

The calathea below is obviously a relative of the maranta above. Varieties of both can be mixed together for a striking foliage planting. Some calatheas have longer, more pointed leaves, and tend to grow taller.

Calathea

Calathea
(maranta)

Calathea, like maranta, is a member of the arrowroot family. In general calatheas are larger plants than marantas. Many calatheas have purple undersides to their leaves, although the tops of the leaves have markings similar to marantas. Some calatheas are distinguishable because they have red stems.

Calathea grows from a rhizome, which looks like a root growing above ground. It bears its leaves on the ends of stalks growing from the rhizome. Calatheas like a loose soil, with good drainage. It is a good idea to fertilize them once a month, except in winter when their growth slows, though not to the extent of marantas.

Calatheas like average light. Their real demands are for high humidity and warmth. Some stores sell them as terrarium plants, although the ones we've seen will soon outgrow most terrariums. Raise their humidity by keeping them on a pebble tray or a bed of peat moss, and mist often. Propagate in the spring by dividing the rhizome and repotting each half.

Calathea mackoyana

Fittonias

Fittonia verschaffeltia
(pink-veined fittonia)
F. argyroneura
(silver-veined fittonia)

These interesting plants have 2 to 4-inch oval leaves intricately veined with showy silver or pink markings. The veins stand out from the leaves and give them a ribbed texture.

Fittonias are commonly sold to amateur indoor gardeners with no warning about their difficulty; the result is a disappointing experience for people who are not prepared to provide the humidity that they need.

Both these fittonias will do best in a terrarium, but you can grow them in the open if you use pebble trays or beds of peat moss, and mist often. This is essential for healthy plants.

Light is not a problem with fittonia; they will tolerate dim light. Temperatures above 55° at all times are necessary, or the leaves will begin to drop. It is therefore not a good idea to place them on a cold windowsill or in an office where the temperature drops on weekends.

Keep the soil of your fittonias moist, but not soaking wet. Most growers propagate from cuttings each year, because even under the best of conditions, fittonias begin to get leggy after a time. Cuttings can be rooted in a plastic or glass container filled with moist sand, peat moss, or vermiculite. A cover of plastic wrap over the top of the container will ensure the humidity needed for the cutting to root.

Hypoestes

Hypoestes sanguinolenta
(freckle face)

Hypoestes has oval, dark green, 1 to 3-inch leaves spotted with pink spots that give it the name "Freckle-face." Good sunlight will increase the number and heighten the color of the freckles.

This too is a humidity-loving plant, suitable for terrarium use. Pebble trays or peat moss beds are useful in encouraging healthy growth outside a terrarium. Hypoestes don't need quite as much water as fittonia; the soil should be allowed to get barely dry between waterings.

Hypoestes needs continual pinching back, like coleus, to encourage bottom branches to sprout.

Fittonia argyroneura

Hypoestes sanguinolenta

Plants will produce small lavender flowers on spikes at the end of branches, but they must be pinched off as soon as they appear, because if allowed to flower, the whole plant will die back to the ground.
If this happens, don't regard it as a disaster and throw out the plant. Keep the soil barely moist and soon new growth will appear.

Pilea

Pilea cadieri
(aluminum plant)

This is a small attractive plant with 2 to 4-inch oval dark green leaves, quilted with streaks of aluminum-colored markings. Hence its popular name, the aluminum plant. The more light pilea gets, the shinier the aluminum streaks get, although it does well with only moderate lighting.

Humidity is helpful to the healthy growth of pilea, and this is another good terrarium plant, particularly if you buy the dwarf variety of it.

Some light pinching encourages bushy, full growth of pilea. If your plant starts dropping leaves, it's probably because of a dry or drafty environment. Plants that get leggy can be propagated by cuttings. Cuttings will root in moist sand, peat moss, or vermiculite. A closed container for rooting cuttings is preferred to supply the humidity this plant likes. It will root in open containers, however.

Let the soil of pileas dry out between waterings, and keep in a warm spot. These plants don't appreciate cold temperatures.

Pilea

Iresine

Iresine herbstii
(bloodleaf)

Bloodleaf is the common name for this plant because of the oval, pointed leaves which are partially or entirely colored a deep magenta. On the varieties which are entirely magenta, the dark patches in the coloration are chlorophyll that would be green except for the overlay of red. The leaves are ¾ inch to 2 inches long, and have a slightly quilted look.

Iresine dislikes cool temperatures, and will droop if placed near a cold window. It thrives on good light, although it can take full sun as well as shade. Keep the soil barely moist at all times. Like the coleus, drying out will cause iresine to droop, but a good thorough watering will snap it back to full vigor again.

Pinch iresines heavily, and they will reward you by branching out all along the length of their stems. You can create quite an attractive bush this way, and set in a warm window where sunlight filters through its leaves, iresine can be a spectacular plant.

Cuttings can be easily rooted in damp soil, sand, or vermiculite.

Iresine herbstii

Although it has a central stem, iresine soon grows too heavy for its stem to support, and thus is best grown as a hanging plant. Pilea is a good hanging plant too.

Tolmiea menziesii

Impatiens oliveri

Impatiens flowers are 1½ inches across, often in very brilliant colors of red, but some also white, or pink.

If you keep impatiens humid and give it good light, but not direct summer sun, it can flower all year round.

Tolmiea

Tolmiea menziesii
(piggy-back plant)

This plant has green stems, with leaves about 3 inches wide that are covered with fuzz. It is commonly called the piggy-back plant, because of its method of reproduction. Small plantlets form at the base of each leaf and ride on top of the flexible stems. These plantlets can be rooted by removing the leaf with its plantlet from the plant and putting it in moist soil, or by leaving the whole thing on the original plant and pinning it to the surface of the soil in the same pot or a smaller pot nearby.

The important thing to remember about tolmiea is that it needs moist soil at all times. If the soil is allowed to dry, the leaves shrivel quickly, and won't be revived by a fresh watering. The only thing to do in the case of leaves drying is to cut off the affected parts of the plant. If the whole plant has died down, keep watering it; eventually the plant will give you a second chance by sending up new growth.

Tolmiea thrives in almost any light conditions, although direct sunlight will dry out the soil quickly. It doesn't require a high humidity, but an occasional misting helps keep the leaves clean and fresh.

Impatiens

Impatiens
(Patient Lucy)

Impatiens gets its Latin name from a characteristic of its seed pods — when ripe, they open with a pop, spraying the seeds outwards as if they were impatient to grow. The English nickname, on the other hand, is Patient Lucy, which probably refers to the way it tolerates mistakes made by gardeners who want a flowering plant.

One mistake impatiens won't tolerate, however: dry air. This is an ideal plant if you have a large terrarium, or if you can supply enough humidity by growing on a pebble bed or tray of peat moss. Fertilize fairly often, once every two or three weeks, following directions on the package. You can use a fairly strong fertilizer, like a 15-30-15 formula.

There are many varieties of impatiens. Most grow on thick, fleshy stems colored pink or burgundy, about 1 to 2 feet high when mature. The leaves are oval and pointed, 2 to 3 inches long, some dark green, some reddish.

Pinch back hard, to keep the plant from getting leggy, especially in winter, when the dryer air will cause it to lose leaves. Keep the soil moist in summer, and let it dry out between waterings in winter.

Impatiens cuttings root easily and will produce another flowering plant in 6 months. Some people toss their plants out every winter and start new ones with cuttings from the old.

Cordyline

Cordyline terminalis
(flaming dragon)

This plant is often called a dracaena, and is familiarly known as flaming dragon tree or Hawaiian ti plant. Its manner of growth is similar to that of dracaenas, in that its 12 to 18 inch-long leaves grow outward from a fleshy stalk that becomes woody as the plant matures. Cordyline, however, has pink and cream leaves when they first sprout, gradually changing to a red-bordered deep green.

The humidity requirements of the cordyline are much greater than those of dracaenas. It should be grown on peat or pebble trays, and misted often.

Cordyline is not demanding in regard to its light requirements. Ordinary to bright light is sufficient, as long as you keep it out of bright summer sun. Water the plant when the soil is nearly dry.

Helxine

Helxine soleirolii
(baby's tears)

Baby's tears is one of the names given to this vigorous grower because of the tiny, tiny green leaves that grow from its thread-like vines in great profusion. It quickly covers any ground you plant it on, and sends curious shoots over the sides of the pot. Helxine is often used as a hanging plant because of this attractive quality. However, as a hanging plant, it sometimes gets neglected and will quickly let you know it wants more watering by dying back to the ground. As with tolmiea, the solution is to coax out new growth by keeping the soil moist.

Keep watering to keep the soil always moist for healthy baby's tears.

Helxine can be cut back at any time if it threatens to get out of hand. It can be propagated by dividing the clumps or by rooting cuttings in water.

Cordyline terminalis

Even with you best efforts to keep cordyline's humidity high the lower leaves may fall. If the resulting leggy plant is unattractive to you, it can be air-layered in the same way as dracaenas.

Helxine soleirolii

Baby's tears may be used as a ground cover in terrariums, where the constant moisture meets the requirements of the helxine.

Orchids

Cattleya
Paphiopedilum maudiae
(orchids)

Many people, hearing the word "orchid," think of expensive greenhouse plants that can only be grown with a great deal of expensive equipment and care. In fact, orchids grow wild in most areas of the world, including most areas of the United States. They can certainly be grown in your house if you pick the right varieties, and there are many spectacular plants available.

Greenhouse specialists on orchids divide them into three categories — "cool growing", "intermediate growing", and "warm growing". The "intermediate" kind fit the temperature levels of the average house.

It's safe to say that the paphiopedilum can be grown in all but the very darkest apartments and offices.

Paphiopedilum flowers resemble the lady's slipper variety of wild plants. The most common variety has a pale green and white flower. Some are speckled with brown and purple markings. The bloom is on a long, green, hairy stem that towers a foot or so above the relatively small leaves that stay near the surface of the soil. If given cool night-time conditions, fresh (but not cold) air during the day, and reasonable humidity from a pebble tray or bed of peat moss, this flower is capable of lasting for a couple of months before wilting. Paphiopedilum leaves are 4 to 8 inches long, oval and pointed. Some of them have dark green spots against a lighter green background. Other kinds have leaves that are all green. The kind you should get have the spotted leaves, because the all-green kind grow on plants that require cooler temperatures than you and your family would like.

Paphiopedilums do not require good light. If the leaves yellow, it is not because of underwatering — it's a sign that the plant has been getting too much light. Paphiopedilum only blooms in the winter. The rest of the year, you should continue to water it regularly, keeping it moist all the time.

Cattleya may be what most people think of when they talk of orchids. Its showy, fringed, purple, magenta and lilac flowers are of the senior-prom corsage type.

Paphiopedilum leeanum

Paphiopedilum and cattleyas are both epiphytes (doesn't grow in soil) which means they should be planted in sphagnum moss or osmunda, or pine bark.

Cattleyas come in two kinds: those that have two leaves on a stem, and those that have one leaf. The leaf or leaves are longish-oval, medium-green, and very thick and tough. You'll notice a swelling part-way down the stems that support the leaves. This swelling is the pseudo-bulb, which serves the same purpose on an orchid as the hump on a camel. It preserves a supply of water to feed the orchid during dry seasons. Because cattleyas have it, and paphiopedilums don't, the watering care of each is different.

Each year, cattleyas send up one stalk, which is slightly further across its pot than the stalk of the year before. Each stalk continues to live, but only the new one bears flowers. After some years, of course, the new stalk has advanced to the edge of the pot, and may even crawl over the side. When this happens, you'll have to repot. At repotting time, most people divide the plant, putting the first, or newest, two or three stalks in one pot and the "back buds," as they are called, in another. Both pots will have flowers the following year, because each string of stalks will send out a new stalk to begin another walk across the pot.

Cattleyas need very bright light, and if you have a window that gets four hours of direct sun a day, you can have the once-a-year gorgeous show of new cattleya blooms. The rule about high humidity applies to cattleyas too, but a pebble tray or bed of peat moss should handle their needs.

Cattleyas generally flower in the fall of the year. After they flower, and the last bloom dies down a month or so later, stop watering. Altogether. Keep the humidity trays moist, but give the plants a complete rest. The pseudobulbs will keep them alive. If you're going to repot and divide the plant, prepare for it during the dormant period by cutting the rhizome between the back bulbs and the new bulbs, or stems, at the front of the plant. After what will seem like an ungodly-long time since you stopped watering — 1 to 4 months — the front "bulb" will send out new growth at soil level. This is the rhizome from which the new stem will grow. It is also your signal to begin watering again. Repot at this time, if that's your plan. Put the plant off to the side of a new pot to give it plenty of room to grow.

Cattleya

We do not recommend that either of these orchids, the cattleyas or the paphiopedilums, be misted, because water nestling in the base of their fleshy leaves is likely to rot them.

4
Plants That Need Devotion

Up to now, the plants that have been discussed in this Part have been those that could be grown with little or only routine care. Some of them might require a change in your environment, such as additional light or humidity, but once that basic change is made, you can relax.

The plants in this chapter will be ones that we personally have found frustrating and difficult, or ones that require special kinds of care. The rewards for extra work are great, however, because among these are some of the most attractive plants sold for cultivation in the home. Many of these plants, in fact, are sold as gifts by florists who have no intention of revealing that the usual life span of this beautifully-grown $15 plant may be brief.

Armed with the information in this chapter, however, you can approach the cultivation of these plants with the reassurance that if you fail, at least you'll know why.

Some of these plants are just too tender for most people's homes. Their humidity requirements are too high, they're too sensitive to drafts, they dislike the change of temperatures that most houses experience, or they require periods of light and darkness that don't coincide with the ways most people live.

Other plants need a dormant period that can begin or end abruptly. Sometimes the dormancy is misread as death, and people toss out perfectly good plants that could bloom again (which may be good for you, for if you learn to recognize such plants, you can get them free from other people's trash barrels).

Don't let us discourage you from trying to grow any of these plants. Someday one of your friends may give you one as a present, and you'll want to fulfill their faith in your plant expertise. It's always fun to try something a little more difficult than we think we can handle.

Schlumbergera And Euphorbia

Christmas cactus
(Schlumbergera bridgesii)

Poinsettia
(Euphorbia pulcherrima)

Most people recognize these two holiday-blooming plants when they see them. Christmas cactus, has branches that resemble chains of flat, leathery green leaves, that bear brilliant red or orange flowers on their pendant tips.

These are jungle cacti, and are not adapted to direct sunlight. Keep them in bright light only. They like jungle humidity, so grow them on pebble trays and mist them often. Water when the soil is just dry.

To get the Christmas cactus to bloom again you must begin to cut back on its water in September. Keep it dry, waiting to water until the soil has been dry for three or four days. Gradually lengthen the time between waterings until buds form. At the same time, you must make sure that the plant gets 10 to 14 hours of uninterrupted and total darkness every night — like inside a closet. When the plant has set its buds, you can resume normal watering and replace the plant in its normal spot. Stem cuttings of schlumbergera or zygocactus will root and produce new plants. Put lots of peat and sphagnum moss in any new soil you pot schlumbergera in.

Poinsettia is even more familiar than Schlumbergera as a Christmas plant. The red leaves that form on top of the plant are bracts, adapted leaves, and merely surround the true flowers, which are quite small. If you give the plant good light and moist conditions, keeping the soil from drying out, the bracts may last for as long as three months. When they fall or fade, let the plant begin to dry out, giving it less and less water. In May, cut the plant back to 12 inches above the ground. Keep it out of hot afternoon sunlight all summer long. Keep pinching back new shoots as they appear. In the fall, put it on a schedule like the Christmas cactus, with 10 to 14 hours of total and uninterrupted darkness every night. Cool, but not below 50° temperatures, will help encourage flowering. The period of enforced night should last for at least 40 days. When (and if) the red bracts appear again, step up the watering so that the soil is always slightly moist, and give as much full light as winter conditions will allow.

Schlumbergera bridgesii

A relative of the Christmas cactus, called zygocactus, looks similar but bears its flowers earlier in the fall. Another similar relative bears flowers in the spring and is called "Easter cactus".

The formula for any of these cacti to bloom is to begin the low-watering, low-light regimen nine months after they stopped blooming the year before.

Euphorbia pulcherrima

Bromeliads

Ananas comosus
(pineapple)
Aechmea fasciata
(urn plant)
Billbergia
(bromeliad)
Nidularium
(flame-center bromeliad)

Ananas sativa

Aechmea fasciata

Did you ever buy a pineapple with the stem still attached? You can cut off that stem, bury it with the base an inch or so into moist potting soil, and it will often sprout roots. Then you'll have a bromeliad. All bromeliads grow like pineapple tops, with leathery, pointed leaves rising up from a central crown.

That sounds easy, and in fact it is. It's just as easy to raise a bromeliad you bring home from the florists, with its silvery-gray saw-tooth leaves and bright pink bract on a stem in the center. All you really have to do is keep water in the center of the plant, as you would in a vase, and that bloom will last for weeks or months. The difficulty comes in making the plant bloom again, for it is impossible except through propagation.

The aechmea, sometimes called the urn plant, is the bromeliad described above with the bright pink bract. There are other varieties of it, some with yellow bracts, some with dark blue bracts, and some with burgundy-colored leaves. If you find a white scaly or powdery substance on these plants, leave it alone. It's not a disease; it helps absorb water for the plant.

All aechmeas, and most bromeliads, have a "vase" of tightly wrapped leaves at the center of the plant. This vase should be kept full of water, from which the plant will draw most of its supply. Aechmeas enjoy bright light but not full sunlight. They will tolerate ordinary to dim light, particularly if you have purchased a plant that already has a bloom set. The soil around the plant should be watered whenever it starts to dry out.

Billbergia is a more upright-growing plant than aechmea. Billbergia's leaves are also thinner and narrower, and its scarlet or orange bracts are longer and thinner than those of aechmea. The same watering rules apply as for aechmea. Billbergia likes more sunlight, however. Give it direct sunlight if you can, except during the hottest parts of summer days.

Nidularium doesn't raise up its brightly colored bracts on a stalk the way aechmeas and billbergias do. Its pale green leaves with dark green spots grow outward from a tight center in typical bromeliad fashion, and it is from the center that fiery orange-red bracts grow.

Nidularium likes bright, but not direct, summer sun. In winter you can give it direct sun. Keep its soil mix moist and the cup formed by its leaves full of water.

There are many other bromeliads, but you should be able to recognize their pattern of growth from the three types described here. Most are actually easy to maintain during the period of their flowering. They aren't usually badly hurt if you go away and forget to water them, and there isn't a great need to fertilize them.

In the wild, bromeliads are usually epiphytes — they grow high up on trees, where their roots feed on the decaying vegetation of older bromeliads. For this reason, their roots are potted in mixtures of osmunda, sphagnum and peat mosses, sand, and fir bark. The roots penetrate the soil to a shallow depth, and you shouldn't put a bromeliad in a larger pot than the one it came in, even if you think its top growth makes it too big for its present pot. In fact, bromeliads should always be in clay, not plastic, pots with good drainage. If yours came in a decorative pot with no drainage hole, repot it.

Now flowering. Here's the awful truth: once your bromeliad flowers, it dies. Not right away, to be sure, but flowering means its life cycle is complete, and it starts withering and wilting and rotting, outer leaves first. If you keep its soil moist, it may produce small plantlets around the base of the plant. Leave these attached to the parent until the main plant has completely died down. By that time, the plantlets should have put out roots from the rhizome it grows on, and its leaves formed a cup to hold water. At this point these plantlets may, with great care, be grown to maturity and ultimately induced to flower.

When they become as large as the parent plant was, place them in sealed containers, like a terrarium or a plastic bag. Take care the plastic doesn't touch the leaves, or they will rot. In this sealed environment, you must add one other thing — a gas to stimulate bloom. Florists use preparations called Omnaflora or Brombloom. You can use an ordinary apple, and let it rot in the container.

Billbergia

To get bromeliad plantlets to mature and bloom, pot them individually in shallow pots filled with a mix of two parts wet sphagnum moss and one part sand. Then, you have several years to wait until the plants are mature.

After a couple of month's treatment with the gas, the plants should have set buds. Keep them in a bright location all this time, and don't open the container to water. When buds are set, you can remove the plant from the container and await flowering.

Codiaeum variegatum

Caladium humboltii

Caladiums and rex begonias look very similar, with 6 to 12-inch leaves colored in vivid reds, pinks, greens, yellows, and purples. The caladiums have leaves that are very thin, almost like tissue paper, and their leaves are shaped like arrowheads. Begonia leaves are not symmetrical, as caladiums' are.

Codiaeum

Codiaeum variegatum pictum (croton)

The brightly-colored leaves of the croton, or codiaeum, are all but irresistible. Coming in shades of red, yellow, green, and purple, with all four colors splashed in different patterns on the leaves of a single plant, the codiaeum just begs to be taken home and displayed proudly. Our advice is: pass it by.

More than almost any other plant we know about, the codiaeum reacts with shock to the conditions in the average home — and you'll react with shock, too, when the lovely leaves all drop off the plant.

Codiaeum needs very, very high humidity. In addition, it will not tolerate cold drafts, sudden dropping of temperatures, or direct sunlight. We have grown a codiaeum of a certain type in an apartment with some success. If you are determined, try putting the plant, pot and all, inside a much larger pot and packing wet peat moss inside the space between the smaller and larger pots. By keeping the peat moss and the soil constantly moist and spraying the leaves daily, you will (hopefully) have generated enough humidity to keep the leaves attached to the plant. If the plant gets leggy, air-layer it. And if you get branches, they can be cut off and rooted in peat moss or vermiculite.

Caladium

Caladium hybrids (calamity plant)

We call this the calamity plant because of what happens to it. Ever have a florist tell you "All these large, beautifully colored leaves are gonna die in six months."? Well, they are. But don't toss out the plant when they do. The plant is only dormant and can be brought back to life. When the leaves start to die down, give less and less water until all the leaves are dead. Then dig up the tuber from the soil, dry it out, and store it in a plastic bag in a warm place (above 55°) for 3 to 4 months. Then repot in fresh soil, and keep moist. To get the tuber started again, you may have to put the pot in a very warm window or in a pebble tray on a radiator. During the growing season, keep caladiums' soil moist and mist them often. They're not fussy about light.

Aphelandra

Aphelandra squarrosa
(Zebra plant)

The cream-white veins of aphelandra are set against a dark green shiny leaf and would make it a plant worth growing for its beauty, even without the brilliant yellow bloom (sometimes orange) that rises from the center of the 2 to 3-foot stalk. The plant does best in bright light, but not direct sunlight. Keep the soil moist during the life of the bloom — which is not a flower, but a cluster of bracts.

Always put aphelandras on a pebble tray or bed of moist peat moss. They have to have high humidity or the leaves will quickly drop. It should also receive frequent fertilizing while it is in flower — as often as every 2 weeks.

Problems with aphelandras arise when the yellow bracts begin to die down. The lower leaves of the plant fall off. It begins to get leggy and top heavy. Pinch the growing tips off the plant to get new growth from the roots or branches from the side. We recommend cutting these new shoots and repotting them in a mix of half peat moss and half potting soil. When they start to grow, give them as much humidity as you can. They may flower the following year. Or, you can cut the original plant back to the ground and wait for new growth from the roots. Water very sparingly until the new growth is well established, but keep misting and growing on a pebble tray or bed of peat moss.

Cyclamen

Cyclamen persicum
(cyclamen)

Another plant sold by florists when in full, gorgeous bloom, cyclamen has pink, white, or red flowers rising on pink stalks amidst dark green or silvery green leaves. Keep the plant moist and in a bright location. Temperatures under 65° will make the blooms longer lasting.

The bulb-like ball from which the flower and leaf stems grow is called a corm. When the flowers die down, you can let the corm dry out. Wait for the leaves to yellow and their stalks to dry out and shrivel down to the corm. Rest the plant for a summer, watering it occasionally to prevent a total drying out. Then in the fall, repot it and begin watering often to revive the plant.

Aphelandra squarrosa

Cyclamen

Although cyclamen are notorious for refusing to bloom a second time, we do know people who continued to water as usual after the flowers died down, never letting the soil dry. New leaves continue to spring up from the corm, but no flowers. Our friends are content with an unusual-looking foliage plant that stays green the year round.

Gesneriads

Sinningia speciosa
(gloxinia)
S. speciosa pusilla
S. concinna
S. x-varieties
(miniature sinningias)

There is a whole family of different kinds of gesneriads. The most famous are the African violets, but since they can flower all year long with moderate care, we have given them a separate section in this book. (See page 44.)

The next most popular gesneriad is the gloxinia. There are two areas of difficulty with gloxinias. One, they have a dormant period, during which all growth dies down to the tuber (which resembles a bulb). Two, they need extremely high humidity if they are to flower.

The most successful and least expensive way to buy gloxinias is to buy a tuber from a reputable grower or seed catalog. Put it in a 4″ wide pot, buried just beneath the surface of the soil. Give it a good watering, and put it in a warm spot, even a pebble tray on a radiator. Keep watering to keep the soil moist. When the sprouts start up, move the plant off the radiator, and give it plenty of bright light, but not direct sunlight. If you mist the plants once a day and keep them on a bed of wet peat or a pebble tray, you should get buds. Even then the buds may blast (shrivel before opening) if the humidity isn't high enough. Fertilize often. If you dilute your fertilizer solution to 1/10 its recommended strength, you can fertilize with each watering.

Unfortunately, most beginning gardeners don't grow gloxinias from tubers. They buy them after seeing them in full bloom in the local super market or plant store. These plants are spectacular, and well they should be. They've been grown in very humid greenhouses, with heavy fertilizing under conditions designed to force growth. The trumpet-shaped gloxinia flowers are 3 to 5 inches long, brilliant reds and purples, and the leaves are fresh and green and fuzzy, some of them 8 to 9 inches long. The unwary buyer thinks these must be good plants because look at all the buds on them.

But what usually happens when you take the plant home is that the flowers collapse almost overnight, the leaves turn to brown mush, and the buds never open.

If this happened to you, you may have thrown away what was left of the plant. We did, the first time it happened to us. Here's what we should have done: Cut away rotting leaves at the base or tuber. Gradually reduced watering. Put the plant in a cool place — under 65°. Water only once a week, to keep the tuber from drying out.

Sinningia speciosa

There are miniature sinningias that are as tiny as ¼ to 1-inch leaves, on plants 2 to 8-inches across. Sometimes they bear fairly large flowers, and in any case are wonderful for terrariums. In some apartments, a terrarium may be the only way you can provide high enough humidity for sinningias, and the miniatures are certainly easier to handle than the full-size gloxinias. They like good light but not full sun. Also, they don't go completely dormant the way the full-size plants do. You can grow them all year round. When they get a bit leggy, pinch them back to the ground, and new growth should spring up. Fertilize once a month or oftener when they are in flower.

Given this care, eventually the tuber will send up new growth. Then you can cultivate it according to the directions above for planting a fresh tuber.

Columneas

Columnea
(goldfish plant)

Columneas are gesneriads usually used as hanging plants. In the wild, they are epiphytes. They can thus be grown in baskets of sphagnum moss or fir bark. You can also use a mix of 1/3 soil, 1/3 sand, and 1/3 peat moss. The important thing is that they get frequent watering with good drainage.

Most columneas produce their red, pink, or yellow tubular flowers all year round. The flowers remind some people of goldfish. Fertilize with half-strength fertilizer every two weeks. Flowers usually grow all along the length of the stems. They like bright light and can take direct sunlight in winter and early spring. Cool temperatures (below 60°) are best for columneas.

Pinching back columneas often is a help to bushy, fuller growth. If you let the stems go unpinched, they can grow several feet long. Many people make it a practice to prune back severely all the branches once a year, encouraging overall new growth. This is always a good idea, if the plant loses lower leaves and looks straggly. You can easily root the stem cuttings that result from such a pruning.

Like all gesneriads, columneas love humidity. It's hard to give hanging plants good humidity unless you hang them up with a dish of moist peat. So mist them often, trying for twice a day if you can.

Columnea microphylla

Achimenes

Achimenes hybrids
(nut orchid)

If you've mastered gloxinia culture, you can easily grow these handsome hanging gesneriads. They bear loads of 1 inch-wide trumpet-shaped flowers in white, pink, red, and purple. Water heavily, keeping the soil moist. Keep them in good humidity and fertilize often during their growing season, from spring to fall. Pinch often and propagate from the cuttings. Achimenes need good light, but protection from full sun. They start to die back in September, when you should slow down the watering. After all growth has died down dig up the tubers and save in a plastic bag till March. You can plant several tubers in one pot for a bushy plant.

Bonsai

Let's get it straight: Bonsai is a method of growing plants. If you see an ad for a $2 bonsai, what you'll receive is a baby tree seedling that, trained properly, can become a bonsai plant — but it is you who will be doing the training. Proper training is a years-long process. In Japan and China, where the process developed, true bonsai growers pass the plants on for generations. Those magnificently gnarled and shaped bonsai trees you've seen in pictures can be over a century old. And you do not buy them for two dollars.

Still, knowing the principles of bonsai can give you a start that will enable you to experiment with bonsai and, if you enjoy the patient and painstaking care, you might take it up as a full-time hobby. There are many books on the subject presenting the philosophy and detailed, sophisticated techniques of bonsai gardening.

We suggest you try bonsai techniques with a fast-growing herb — rosemary would be a good candidate, and so would germander or sage — to practice techniques in a compressed amount of time. This is definitely not the classic process of bonsai, which uses real trees. If you insist on a real tree, plant citrus seed in ordinary potting soil and begin from there, or buy a dwarf or seedling tree. (See Chapter 31.)

Bonsai Pots

The Japanese word bon-sai means tray gardening. Your first step is to find a suitable tray, or pot. This is not as easy as buying a clay pot for your house plants, which are more tolerant of drainage problems than bonsai. Bonsai are stunted trees, and a great deal of the stunting is done by cramping the roots. If your tray has improper drainage, it will result in rotting of the roots as they begin to fill the pot. Bonsai growers make extra drainage holes in the bottom of the pot, and shape the bottom with paraffin or cement to slope toward the drainage holes. In addition, they line the bottom of the pot with a layer of pebbles or broken crockery.

Pots should be shallow — usually no more than 3 inches deep for a young plant, and often shallower. The soil should be kept moist until the seed germinates.

First Pruning

Root pruning is all that is done to the seedling tree in its first year. But for an herb, you can begin to prune shoots after 2 months growth. A convenient, but inelegant method of beginning root pruning is to plant the seed in a peat pot

This is only one of the many basic forms traditional to the art of bonsai. Other famous ones are small forests, an ancient weather-beaten look, or a windblown effect.

and snip off the roots as they penetrate the sides of the pot.

After the first year in other plants shoot pruning starts. Shoot pruning can begin in a manner similar to pinching house plants. You pinch the growing tips of the plant to encourage growth lower on the stem or trunk. Be persistent in pinching and repinching if growth starts again in the same place. Your tree is strong. Pinching won't kill it.

Dwarfing

Dwarfing is accomplished by pruning branches. This is where the real art of bonsai comes in, for which branches you remove or shorten helps to determine the shape of the tree.

The shape of the tree is also affected by bending and training the branches. This can be done with insulated copper wire wrapped around the branches and trunk. Tying the ends of the wire to a support, and gradually increasing the angle at which the branch or trunk bends is the primary method of training. Before you begin to prune and train, plan on paper the shape you want your tree to be. If you try to figure it out as you go along, you will end up with a misshapen freak, not a bonsai. After your plan is clear to you, prune and train the tree accordingly.

Routine Care

Your bonsai-trained tree is still a tree, and for proper growth, it must have a seasonal change in temperatures. If it is deciduous, it must be allowed to lose its leaves and go into dormancy in fall and winter. You should place it in a protected spot, like a screened porch, for these seasons. Most trees dwarfed this severely will not withstand freezing temperatures. On very cold nights it may be necessary to move the tree to a cold basement or hall.

As the tree ages, you will have to fertilize it artifically. Oriental growers use organic fertilizers of their own devising. If you have no place to get these, and most of us do not, you will have to use chemical fertilizers.

Always keep the soil of the tree from drying out. This does not mean flooding it every day; during the dormant period, you will have to water very seldom.

After three years, the bonsai should be given a soil mix that is 2/3 potting soil and 1/3 sand. At this time, it can be moved to a permanent container. The root ball should be cut back by one-third periodically — every three years. This process will shock the plant, and it should be done in the spring and the tree protected from direct sunlight for two to four weeks after root pruning.

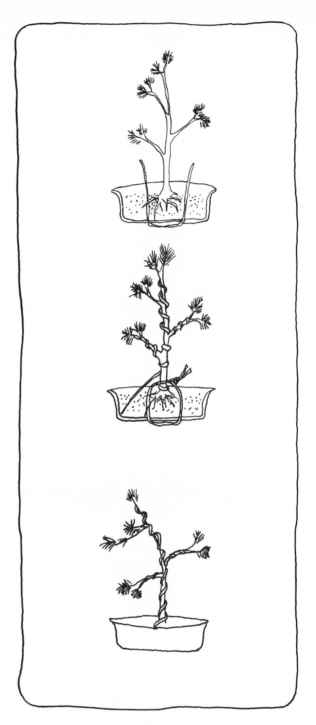

These illustrations suggest one method widely used to train a bonsai tree.

A wire is inserted through the bottom of the pot and twisted around the trunk to support the tree. Then heavy wire is braced against the side of the pot and twisted around the length of the stem. Thinner wire is twisted around the branches. Finally the first bending of the tree can be done. Over the next few months, the supporting wire is removed and the tree is gradually bent more and more to get a windblown look.

5
Special Plants

In this chapter, we've listed some plants that can be useful, for special purposes. We have some that you can use if you want a big, dense jungle in your living room or studio apartment. We have two plants that are virtually indestructible as hanging plants, and some suggestions about hanging gardens generally.

We have included indoor vegetable plants for those who like fresh tomatoes and salads even in the middle of the city, and plants to grow from the remains of your dinner . . . the avocado of course, but many others as well.

Finally, there is a section that may get you started on herbs — how to pot them indoors and grow them on a kitchen windowsill for all sorts of uses (even medicinal).

All of these sections are only introductions to special types of planting. The field of horticulture is vast and endlessly fascinating, and if this book has awakened your interest in it, then we will feel successful.

Curiosities

We're including these three plants just because people find them fun to grow. They're unusual, some people find them repulsive and they may not be easy to find, but we guarantee that your kids will love them.

Mimosa pudica

Mimosa can be grown from seed. Started in the spring, seeds can produce full-size plants by fall. This is another plant that needs good humidity, and should be grown on a pebble tray or bed of peat. Spraying with lukewarm water is a good way to keep it healthy. Don't put mimosa in direct sunlight, and keep the soil from drying out completely.

Mimosa pudica
(sensitive plant)

The sensitive plant is so called because of its fern-like foliage which folds close to the stem when touched — yes, it really moves, and quickly too. After a while it unfolds again. It also has tiny pink flowers. It will grow a foot tall by maturity, but tends to die down after it has flowered. This is a good plant to start anew from seed each year.

Dionaea muscipula
(venus fly trap)

Here is the exotic venus fly trap, model for dozens of far-fetched science fiction movies where giant versions of this devour men alive. Want to know the only places in the world where this plant is found in nature? North and South Carolina. So much for its exotic quality.

Venus fly trap doesn't have to have insects to eat. You can "feed" it (though it does not need to eat) flecks of ground meat, and watch it close on its prey. The flowers of the plant are white and appear in a little cluster on a stalk. They only grow if the plant is given good light. Dionaea prefers cool (below 60°) temperatures.

Hydrosme rivieri
(voodoo plant)

Here's a plant that flowers before it produces leaves. Up comes a stalk, 3 to 4 feet high, colored a dark purple with red spots. It looks like a big calla lily. Not really a flower, this stalk is a carrier for tiny little flowers that grow in clusters on a fleshy spike at the top. Afterwards, more stalks grow out of the ground, with large, 3 to 4 foot wide leaves on the ends. Terrific, huh? Why doesn't everybody grow one?

Apparently because of the smell, which is described as repulsive, carrion-scented, and just plain bad. You can't say we didn't warn you.

Dionaea muscipula

We've seen florist shops selling a dry pack of soil and seeds for this plant lately. If you get the seeds by themselves, you can grow them easily in wet sphagnum moss. A mix of peat moss and sand, watered with acid fertilizer once a month, will also do as a growing medium. Whatever you use, keep the soil mix well-watered, and don't let it dry out.

Hydrosme needs plenty of water while it is growing. After the leaves start to die down, the watering should be reduced and the plant placed in a temperature of around 50°. Repot it and resume heavy watering in about 6 months. The dormant period is usually from fall to spring.

Hydrosme rivieri

Plants For Groves and Jungles

Did you ever visit a plant store that sells a great many large plants? It's an impressive, beautiful sight. All those plants, many of them really trees, give an atmosphere that many people want to create in their homes and apartments. But remember: that plant store with the large plants is extremely humid. It has to be, to keep those plants healthy.

With a small plant, like the African violet, it's possible to raise the humidity in the vicinity of the plant with a pebble tray or bed of peat moss. When you fill your home, or a corner of it, with a 6-foot plant, however, you have to raise the humidity of the entire room to get it to where the plant wants it. And then the room isn't comfortable for people.

There are two solutions. One is to have large plants that are so hardy that they take a long time to die, even years. That's why ficus and schefflera are so widely sold as giant house plants.

The other solution, a more sensible one, is to buy these plants when they are small. As they grow in your home, they become used to the dry conditions and can tolerate them better even when they grow large. Unfortunately, this solution means you can't have a jungle in your house tomorrow just by going out and buying one.

Ficus elastica
(rubber tree)
F. benjamina
(Benjamin fig)
F. lyrata
(fiddle-leaf fig)

The ficus, or fig, family is a large one with many varied types of plants. The most familiar is Ficus elastica, the rubber tree. The large, thick, green leaves and gray-green stems and branches have a springy consistency.

Some people believe the rubber tree is indestructible, because it grows in so many conditions and takes so much abuse. It can take low light, low humidity, and overwatering without actually dying. But what it likes to have is high humidity, good light without direct summer sun, and watering only after the soil dries out.

Ficus benjamina is more shrub-like than the rubber tree, but it will grow to your ceiling and beyond, and can be trained as a single-trunked tree by simply removing all stems other than

Ficus elastica decora

Ficus benjamina

the strongest one. It's a quick grower, sometimes increasing in size by 10 inches a year if it's treated right. It has many smaller-size 3 to 4-inch leaves and thin branches. Pinch the tips of the branches to encourage bushy growth. We give this plant as much light as possible, including direct sun unless the leaves seem to be burning or wilting from the heat. The larger the plant is when you get it, the more light it will require. Mist often, at least when you first bring the plant home, and let the soil dry out before re-watering. Always water ficus plants thoroughly, so the water runs out the drainage hole.

Ficus lyrata, or fiddle-leaf fig, gets its name from the narrow waist of its wavy-edged leaves. It likes warm temperatures, and will respond to cold drafts by dropping some leaves. Keep it above 65° if you can. Its leaves are similar in size to the rubber tree's, but they are thinner and sometimes show the veins in a cream pattern. Water it when the soil dries out, and mist often. Give bright light, but not direct sunlight.

Schefflera actinophylla

Schefflera actinophylla (umbrella tree)

On the end of each branch of the schefflera grow four or five thin oval green leaves. Perhaps someone thought these resembled umbrellas, and gave the plant the name umbrella tree. Cut back the tip of the stem often to encourage branching. Schefflera appreciates bright light, and though it will tolerate lower-light conditions, it will grow less quickly. Let the soil dry out between waterings, then water thoroughly. Like all these large plants, it needs misting. In plant stores, where they have drains in the floor, they hose them down with a spray nozzle daily. Too bad for your living room.

Araucaria excelsa (Norfolk Island pine)

The Norfolk Island referred to is not off Virginia; it's off Australia. Will the Norfolk Island pine grow in your apartment? Theoretically, yes. But remember the smaller it is when you get it, the better chance it has of surviving. And then you can have a live Christmas tree all year round. Give it bright light and high humidity. Water when the soil dries out. Fertilize every month with an acid fertilizer. If the plant is fairly large, it may prefer cool temperatures of 50° to 55°, but smaller ones can adapt to house temperatures.

Araucaria excelsa

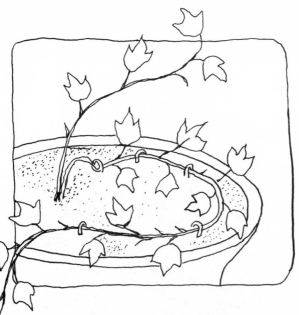

Pinning and tying is one way of getting bushy growth from your hanging plants. Most ivy-type and vining plants, including the climbing types of philodendrons as well as tradescantia and zebrina can be grown by pinning and tying. Pinning and tying consists of taking advantage of the ability of these plants to send out roots all along the length of their stems.

Bruise or break the stem of the plant slightly with your thumbnail, then pin the bruised spot against the surface of the soil with any homemade device, such as a hair pin or paper clip. Do this along the length of the stem, winding it around the surface of the soil inside the pot. A circular pattern may be easiest. Each place that you have bruised and pinned to the soil will send roots down and new shoots up. The result will be not only a far bushier plant, but one that is far stronger because of the more extensive root system supporting the plant.

Plants For Hanging Gardens

One of the most attractive ways of displaying plants is from hanging pots in your windows. The best kinds of plants for this purpose, of course, are plants that will hang, although if you want to train vines upwards along the support that the pot hangs from, that can be effective too.

We'll tell you the two biggest problems with hanging plants right now. They drip, and they need watering more often than pots that sit on your windowsill. The drip problem can be taken care of to some extent by getting a hanging planter that has a built-in tray to catch the water. Even then, you can easily over-water to the point that the overflow tray overflows. The best solution, it seems to us, is to hang the plant over a windowsill on which you grow plants that will enjoy the bath. Growing African violets underneath a hanging plant is our idea of living dangerously.

The need of hanging plants for more frequent waterings is real. It may be that the better air circulation dries them out faster. It may be that because we can't see the surface of the soil we don't realize when it's time to water. Reach up there every day and feel the soil to see if it has dried out.

One authority that we trust on almost every other bit of advice says the easiest way to water hanging plants is to put a few ice cubes in the pot. When they melt, the plant is watered. Frankly, this makes us nervous because we have always found that plants do better with lukewarm waterings. If it works for you, however, fine. We just get a watering can with a nice long stem.

Any of your hanging plants, by the way, will give you a pleasant surprise if you climb up and reverse the pot so that the "sunny" side faces the room. The heavier foliage will now be on display until it gradually turns toward the window again.

Some older apartments have aging plaster that can be difficult to securely fasten hooks into. A fairly large hanging plant when well watered can weigh up to ten pounds or even more, and you won't believe the mess it creates when it comes crashing to the floor. If you're worried that you won't be able to hang your plants securely, try this suggestion. Go to a sporting goods store and get a chinning bar that will expand to press against the sides of a doorway. Hang the chinning bar near the top of your window frame, and suspend the plants from that.

A warning that we gave in the earlier chapter on pot selection bears repeating here: Never buy hanging plants that have picturesque fiber ropes as hangers, particularly if they loop through the inside of the pot. After you water the plant enough times, the rope will rot and down will come the plant, pot, earth, and mess.

The heart-leaved philodendron does very well in hanging pots, as do scindapsus, most ivies, vines, and several other plants we've pointed out in the sections on specific plants.

Tradescantia fluminensis variegata
Zebrina pendula
(wandering jew)

Two plants we've saved for now that seem particularly suited to hanging-plant use are tradescantia and zebrina. These two are practically the same plant and are universally called wandering jew. Tradescantia has green, silver and white striped leaves, and zebrina purple, silver and white stripes. Both bear inch-long oval pointed leaves growing along trailing stems. They grow until they are pinched, then shoot out somewhere else. Cuttings root in the same pot or other pots as fast as you can cut them.

Wandering jew should be watered when the soil gets dry, but will stand a considerable amount of neglect. If you forget all about your plant for a month or so, the stems start to dry out from the ground up. When you discover this, you can snip off the part of the stem that is still fleshy and replant it. It will forgive you and root again. Tradescantia and zebrina will grow in fairly dim light as well as sunny, and they respond to misting or high humidity. We don't know a better plant, except heart-leafed philodendron, to hang in a shaded bathroom window.

Zebrina pendula

Herbs

If you have a bright kitchen window, nothing will give it more cheer than a row of pots, each growing a different herb with which to flavor your family's meals. There are herb garden kits sold in almost any place that has plant supplies. In our opinion, these are overpriced. The peat pots that most of them include are fine for starting seeds, but what will you do when the plant quickly starts poking its roots through the sides of the pot? That's right: go back to the plant supplier and buy real pots.

Better to start with individual seed packets of the herbs you want to grow, and plastic pots that have a top diameter of 3 to 4 inches. Make sure the pots have drainage holes, and that you have a tray to catch the excess water. Any good potting soil will do. Plant the seeds according to the directions on the seed packets. Usually pushing them just beneath the surface will do. Keep the soil well watered, but not soggy, until the seed germinates.

Chives

Taking the easiest first, we start with chives. It looks like thick grass and tastes like mild onions. Can't be beat in vichyssoise, omelets, and Bloody Marys. Plant a lot of seeds, and let them all sprout. They will, and quickly. The more you thin, or prune, for cooking, the better it grows. Let the bunch grow without using it for too long a time and the ends start to dry out. Snip them off and encourage new growth. They say this plant will send up purple flowers. Outside it will, but not in your kitchen. Not enough light. Keep the soil of chives moist.

Basil

Another quick-growing plant, you can start harvesting basil in about a month. Take a little, leave a little to grow on. Most Italian cooks wouldn't start spaghetti sauces without fresh basil. Basil is an annual plant, which means if you let it flower, it will have completed its growing cycle and die. Therefore, cut off any buds that form. Keep snipping from the top, and it will send out new shoots on the bottom. The more light you can give it, the better, and don't let it dry out.

Parsley

If you plant some parsley seeds in the soil and start to water, you'll want to give it up as a lost cause before it germinates. Here's a tip: soak the seeds in a moist paper napkin for 2 to 3 days, and then plant. Even then, let the plant mature

Basil, and all the other herbs except chives and parsley, can be used fresh or dried. Dry herbs by harvesting them at their prime, and hanging the stems in small bunches upside-down in a well-ventilated area out of the sun. When dry, discard the stems, crumble the leaves and store in tightly-closed jars. Chives and parsley have a better flavor frozen than dried. Wash and dry, cut to convenient size, and freeze quickly in sealed plastic bags.

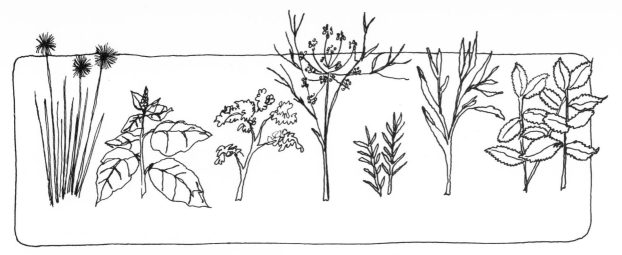

From left to right: chives, basil, parsley, dill, rosemary, tarragon and mint.

before harvesting. When the initial shoots start to get branches, you can begin a cautious harvest. Keep checking to make sure the soil isn't drying out. Parsley is a biennial, but we advise re-seeding it every year for your indoor garden.

Dill

Dill seeds germinate fairly quickly, but the plant doesn't respond to pruning as readily as some other herbs. If it doesn't grow as quickly or as thickly as you'd like, plant a second pot of it. Don't let the soil dry out.

If you're intending to use the dill seeds, you'll have to grow it to the end of its cycle, which will be 6 to 8 months. The seeds appear on the flowering ends of the branches. There may not be enough on an individual plant to make a spoonful. We advise using the plant for its greenery, and buying your dill seeds in a jar.

Rosemary

Another plant that's a slow starter. Sometimes you can buy plants; if not, soak the seeds before planting and be patient. When the plant comes up, it likes humidity, so use your misting techniques on it. Let the soil barely dry out before watering again. Pinch back tips to harvest; the plant itself can live a long time.

Tarragon

Good for window sills that don't get much sun, tarragon should be grown from plants. The French tarragon has the best flavor. Let its soil get dry before you water again.

Mint

Mint should also be grown from a cutting or young plant. It's in the same family as the coleus, so you know it's an easy plant to grow. Give it light, and keep it well watered, and you'll have more than you know what to do with.

Growing Vegetables At Home

Midget vegetables are now available that put vegetable gardening within the reach of anyone who has a patio-terrace, balcony, or even a really sunny window sill.

You can start some of the longer-season varieties indoors in small pots while the weather outside is still frost and snow. We think peat pots are best for starting seeds that will be transplanted, because you don't have to disturb the roots later. Just plant pot and all. Fill the peat pot with a light and airy soil mix, with plenty of vermiculite, perlite, and peat moss. Make sure the seedlings don't dry out, but don't keep them soggy either. A little water will go a long way with them.

Tomatoes

This is just about the easiest vegetable to grow on your porch, in a pot, that we know of. If you're starting from seedlings, start them as early as you can get the seeds, because in the dim sunlight of the average house in winter, they'll grow slowly. If you're only planning on one or two plants, it's a good bet to buy a plant that's already potted up and grown a foot or two. These generally cost around a dollar, and they'll repay that investment many times over the summer in juicy, fresh, vine-ripened tomatoes.

For the miniature tomato varieties, such as Tiny Tim, you won't need a pot much bigger than 8 inches across. We advise plastic pots because tomatoes use a lot of water, and the plastic pots won't allow evaporation through the sides of the pot as clay pots will.

Transplant from the small container you buy a young plant in, to a large 12 to 16-inch diameter plastic pot. If the plant is out in the sun where it should be, you'll have to give a full-size plant two or three quarts of water a day. Tomatoes wilt quickly when left unwatered, but rewatering helps them come back again. Green tomatoes on a bush when it goes very dry and is then rewatered will crack, so it pays to keep up with your chores.

Tomato plants will benefit from a strong fertilizer, such as 6-18-6, every two weeks during their growing season.

Eggplant

Eggplant is a little harder to grow than tomatoes but the care and watering of both is

Tomato "Atom"

about the same. There are good varieties of midget eggplant that take up much less room than the full-size varieties. When starting seeds indoors, which is almost a must because of the long growing season, you can put the pots in a pebble tray on top of a radiator. The germinating seeds like an average temperature near 85°. They like long hot summers outdoors, too. Fertilize at least as heavily as for tomatoes, once every two weeks with 6-18-6 fertilizer. And water well every day.

The midget eggplants can be grown, when full-sized plants, in a 10 to 12-inch diameter pot. The standard midget variety is Morden Midget. There are also some small regular varieties, such as Early Beauty Hybrid (Burpee) and Imperial Black Beauty (Stokes) that will give you plants under two feet tall that can be grown in 14 to 18-inch pots.

Cucumbers

Midget cucumbers can easily be grown in an 8 to 12-inch diameter pot, with a trellis two feet high to train it on. Start this plant right in the pot as soon as the weather is warm outside. Plant two or three seeds to a pot, for proper fertilization.

Tiny Dill (Farmer and Park) is the variety we've tried, and the ½-inch yellow flowers that last only a day are almost worth starting this as an indoor plant. Keep the vines from falling over after they germinate. If your trellis is too high for them to reach, use a popsicle stick as a support until they grow a little taller.

Don't let the cucumber soil dry out. Since the fruit are almost all water, this will mean a daily watering when the plants are full grown. Pick the cucumbers when green, even if there are too many for you to use right away. If the cucumbers mature on the plant, it stops bearing fruit.

Corn

Oh, yes, you can have your own just-picked ears of corn for dinner this summer and fall. And if you've never tasted how good fresh-picked corn is, you'll be glad you set aside the space. We grow corn in window boxes, one stalk of Faribo Golden Midget variety to each foot of box. Corn doesn't seem to have very deep roots, so if you fertilize once every two weeks with 10-10-10 fertilizer, you won't have trouble. We've found that if it gets windy, it's a good idea to stake your young midget corn plants. We use

Patio Pik cucumber

a pencil and twist-ties. The mature plant will only be about 2 feet tall, and will bear one or two 4-inch ears to a plant. When you've harvested, tear up the plants and start a new crop. Corn likes sun all the time and watering when it gets dry. We had a problem, on our city terrace with pigeons eating the corn seeds that were planted, but tying strips of cloth to the terrace railing created a scare-pigeon of sorts and allowed the corn to germinate.

Cantaloupe And Watermelon

Cantaloupes the size of softballs and watermelons the size of ordinary cantaloupes are in the selection of midget edibles you can grow in pots. An 8 to 10-inch pot will do for the cantaloupes, and a 12 to 16-inch pot for the watermelons. These should be planted two or three to a pot, like the cucumbers, so there will be enough flowers to pollinate each other. Provide a trellis or support for the cantaloupe and watermelon vines to grow on.

Minnesota Midget cantaloupes will mature in two months of good weather, on vines that are about 3 feet high. They can be started indoors and moved outside a couple of weeks after the frost season is over. Fertilize every two weeks with 5-10-5 fertilizer. Keep well watered, particularly as the fruits mature. They are ripe when the stems come off the vine with a slight tug.

Golden Midget is the widely-grown midget watermelon variety. When it's ripe, it lets you know by turning its skin yellow (from green). Cultivation is the same as for cantaloupe.

Garbage Garden

It's ecologically sound to use waste products, rather than turning them into a trash disposal problem, right? So here's how you can get some beautiful plants by saving them from your garbage can.

This shows how easy it is to start your very own mango tree after you have finished dessert.

Citrus Trees

Oranges, lemons, grapefruits, limes — all have seeds that are thrown away. Take one of those seeds, put it in a pot of moist soil, and keep it moist. Within a year, you'll have a foot-high citrus tree, with shiny, dark green leaves. Pick off one of the leaves and rub it between your fingers. Smell the oil that comes off, and you'll be able to tell which of the citrus fruits your plant was grown from.

Secrets of citrus plant growing are: keep the seedling in moist soil, because they dry up easily. When the plant gets well established, you can let the soil dry out between waterings. Always give the citrus plant the best light you can, although we've seen them sprout and eke out an existence in a fluorescent-lighted office.

Here's the question that every child in your family will ask: will it bear fruit. The answer is, yes, after three or four years (but they aren't good to eat — too sour).

Sweet Potato Vines

A lot of people know the trick of planting a sprouting sweet potato in water and watching it sprout. But a sprouting sweet potato is getting rare these days because they are now sprayed with a chemical growth inhibitor. In case one does sprout for you, keep it in water till the best sprout is almost a foot high. Use this as the main stem of your plant, snip off the others, and bury the entire potato in a pot, with only the stem above the surface of the soil. Given good watering and light, you can have a lengthy vine. Pinch the tip to produce more shoots.

Cucurbit Plants

"What are cucurbits? I'll bet our kids won't eat them." You'd lose your bet, because cucurbits include watermelon, cantaloupe, cucumbers, and squash. Looking at the seeds, you can see the similarities. All will produce fast-growing climbing vines for you. Dry out the hard seeds from mature fruits on a paper towel

A sweet potato vine after it has grown for awhile.

after washing off any leftover bits of fruit. Plant them in at least a 6-inch pot, because they will start fast and furious. You'll need a trellis to train them on. If you feed them regularly and provide a large dose of sunlight every day, you'll certainly get flowers and possibly fruit, although by that time the original pot will long since have been outgrown. Try cucurbits anyway, to see how far you get.

Apple Trees

If you can get an apple that was ripened on a tree, its seeds will certainly sprout. Plant them in a 10-inch diameter pot or larger, and water well, because, you know, you're growing a tree. It's a deciduous tree, at that, so it's mandatory to give it cool weather in the fall and winter so it can lose its leaves and go into dormancy. If you dread the thought of an apple tree in the living room, you can start practicing your bonsai techniques on the seedling.

Avocado Trees

Avocado growing has become an obsession with some people. The search for the perfect method of sprouting, planting, and pruning

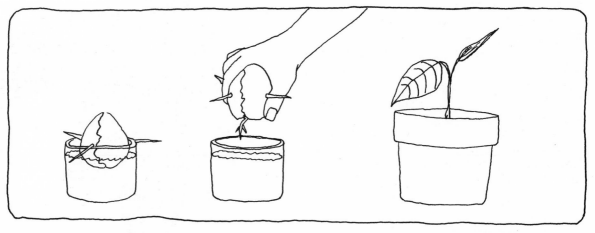

The avocado pit that has already started to grow a root is the best candidate for getting a tree started. But if yours has no root, start it in water until a root grows. Transplant it before the stem sprouts. Then be patient, because the stem takes a while to come up.

goes on. Here's the truth. The seed inside an avocado will sprout eight times out of ten. Some, however, sprout more readily than others. If yours has visibly sprouted inside the fruit, and already has a root growing out of a crack in the bottom, plant it in ordinary potting soil in a 10-inch pot with the tip of the pit above the soil. Keep moist, and put in your brightest window.

It shouldn't have direct summer sun until the stem turns green and sprouts a few leaves. But good light always, right from the start.

If your avocado has not sprouted inside the fruit, you can put three toothpicks an equal distance from each other around the side of the seed, and put it into a glass of water. The flat end of the seed is the bottom. The toothpicks rest on the side of the glass and prevent the seed from sinking to the bottom. Rinse the seed off and dry with paper towels before you stick the toothpicks in, and you'll be able to grip it better. The skin can be taken off to expose the shriveled, pale surface below, but it's not necessary. It will eventually fall off.

When the seed in the glass of water sprouts white roots — which may be in a week or six months — plant the seed in soil. Don't wait for the stem to appear. The stem will sprout sooner or later, and meanwhile the roots can get a better start if they grow in soil.

The indoor avocado specialists say to prune off the top of the growing stem every so often to make it sprout branches. The people who raise avocado plants for a living say it sprouts branches without pruning, and can be damaged by main-stem pruning.

We've got two 5-foot avocado trees with numerous branches in our apartment. Neither has ever been pruned. We have another, 4-foot avocado plant that has scars on its stem to show the many times it's been pruned. It has no branches. We'll take the professionals' advice every time.

Fertilize an avocado plant once a month, except when it stops growing to rest, and mist the leaves often. Keep it in bright light, and you'll have a beautiful plant.

Persea Americana

Part II
Cacti &
Succulents

NORTH & SOUTH, INDOORS & OUT

BY WILLIAM C. MULLIGAN

Some barrel cacti (Echinocactus wislizeni) shown in their natural setting. Garden plantings should suggest elements of a plant's native habitat for best effect.

6
The Most Unusual Family of the Plant Kingdom

Cacti and the other succulents represent an incredible diversity of plants—from miniatures to giants, leafless to leafy, cuddly soft to impossibly thorny. Often the subject of erroneous myths, these unusual plants are viewed with apprehension by many growers, but they're actually easy to care for and make strikingly beautiful plantings both indoors and out.

Cacti and succulent grower/hobbyists are sometimes considered a strange breed, not only because the objects of their affection are so bizarre and mysterious but because these people are so enthusiastic in their praise of the water-retaining desert and tropical dwellers and cultivate them lovingly, often to the exclusion of all other plant forms.

Cacti and succulent growers certainly are not strange, but they are definitely attuned to the universal in plants. Shrewdly, they are aware of the challenge and enjoyment of being a part of nature's mysterious ways.

As the plant craze sweeps the country and gains momentum, more and more people are discovering that they favor certain plants or plant families and are concentrating their efforts on those; ferns, bromeliads, begonias, African violets—each has its own fans and fan club. But no group offers as much plant versatility and variety or deserves a larger host of fans than the cacti and succulents.

What Are Cacti and Succulents?

Succulents are plants that are capable of storing large amounts of water over a long period of time. As the earth evolved and atmospheric changes took place, scarcity of water in many areas caused these plants to adapt themselves cleverly; leaves evaporate water easily, so they became smaller or disappeared altogether—as in the case of cacti—and the stems either became the whole plant or took over from the leaves, to a great degree, the job of water retention and photosynthesis.

All cacti are succulents but not all succulents are cacti. Succulents comprise selected plants from many different families—the amaryllis, daisy, milkweed, and lily, among others. The *Cactaceae* family, of which all cacti are members, is, by the water-retaining nature of its plants, included in the group categorized as succulents. In other words, all plants called cacti are members of one botanical family, but the group of plants referred to as succulents is comprised of water-retaining plants from various families. Some non-cactus succulents such as the columnar euphorbias may look like cacti, but the true cactus has specific characteristics that distinguish it from look-alikes. On close examination one of the most evident is the formation of areoles. Cactus plants are dotted with these little soft protuberances from which sprout the spines, flowers, and new growth. Some of the euphorbias are covered with similar spines, but you'll see that they are not cacti if you look closely—the spines are not borne from areoles.

The conception of many that all cacti are spunky desert dwellers that bravely endure scorching sun and heat is not entirely correct. Some are epiphytes (air plants) that live in trees in the world's tropical jungles. Not as hard-pressed to retain moisture as their desert relatives, these cacti are less fleshy and have more leaf-like growth.

By far the greatest variety in form is found among the desert cacti. From large columns or candelabra shapes to the tiniest of spheres, these plants have devised all kinds of ingenious ways to overcome their environment. The ball shape of some cacti is one of nature's cleverest designs; it combines the greatest volume for water retention with the least amount of plant surface for evaporation. And the ribs of many cacti enable them to expand and contract accordion-fashion, as they swell when water is available and shrink when it isn't. The spines (some stiff and sharp, others as long and soft as hair) of cacti are a means of protection, not only from predators but also from the scorching desert heat, much the same as an animal's skin is kept at an even temperature with the help of its fur coat.

Climate and Locale

Just as you might ask a new acquaintance, "Where do you come from?" it's important to know the native habitats of the cacti or succulents you wish to add to your household. If you duplicate or at least closely approximate the conditions of their home environments, your plants will be comfortable and healthy.

All cacti are indigenous to the Western Hemisphere, but many have escaped to other parts of the world. Surprisingly, some grow in the cold climates of Canada and southern Chile. Most, however, are found in the desert regions of the United States and Mexico and in the warm areas of the West Indies and Central and South America.

The other succulents can be found just

Giant Saguaro cacti (Carnegiea gigantea) *rise as high as 30 feet—huge sentinels in the bleakness of their desert surroundings near Tucson, Arizona.*

about anywhere in the world. Their great diversity includes plants suited to every known climate and locale. They grow in the rain forests, deserts, plains, and mountains of the Americas (*Agave, Echeveria, Euphorbia*), Asia (*Sansevieria, Sempervivum*), and Africa (*Aloe, Cotyledon, Crassula*).

Something for Everyone

Transform an outdoor garden into a desert or tropical landscape, or create miniature succulent and cactus landscapes indoors with dish gardens and container plants. Whatever, you'll soon discover the rewards of growing these

The great diversity of cactus and succulent plant forms are displayed in this western garden exhibit at a fair.

Mammillaria pseudocrucigera. *Some of the most beautiful of all blooming plants, even among those cultivated, are the desert cacti.*

fascinating plants. Though many look as though they're about to say, "Take me to your leader," they never cease to be interesting in the way they grow, and in their striking shapes, foliage and coloring. And when you least expect it, a prickly little cactus may give birth to a spectacular bloom. Cactus flowers are especially vivid in color, and one bloom will often outsize the plant from which it bursts forth.

Our most popular Christmas plant, the poinsettia (*Euphorbia pulcherrima*), is a succulent that will grow well indoors or outdoors

A cereus cactus specimen plant—living sculpture that commands admiration.

Aloe arborescens *(candelabra aloe) in flower in its tropical habitat.*

Agave americana *'Marginata' is a sizable native of Mexico and the southwestern United States. Both aloe and agave are available in smaller varieties suitable for home containers.*

in temperate areas. Although precise amounts of light and dark are required for it to bloom again (the brilliant red "flowers" are actually leaf bracts—the yellow centers are the real blooms), a potted poinsettia gift plant makes a handsome and welcome year-round foliage plant. (See page 67.)

Another plant of the Euphorbia family that's a splendid container candidate is the crown-of-thorns (*Euphorbia splendens*). It has brown thorny stems and bright red or coral-colored flowers.

Other succulents among the many that make attractive houseplants are the stylish agaves (of the Amaryllis family) and aloes (of the Lily family), both with long, tapering leaves that radiate from the plants' centers. Especially interesting is the partridge-breast aloe (*Aloe variegata*) that bears red and yellow bell-shaped flowers.

The Crassula family offers an endless variety of unusual yet attractive succulents. Among these are: *Sempervivum tectorum* var. *calcareum*, artichoke-shaped rosettes that are suited for container growing indoors or as rock-garden or border plants outdoors. The burro's tail (*Sedum morganianum*), with clusters of red flowers and trailing growth that can reach lengths of up to five feet, makes an ideal hanging-basket plant. The pen-wiper plant (*Kalanchoe marmorata*) has beautiful bluish-gray leaves flecked with maroon. White flowers bloom at the end of a long stem that rises up from the plant's cluster of thick leaves. The true jade plant (*Crassula argentea*) is an especially pleasing yet easily cultivated container choice. It survives too much or too little sun or water, grows very fast, and bears racemes of pale pink flowers.

Of the Lily family, the oxtongue (*Gasteria maculata*), as its name implies, has thick, tongue-shaped leaves that are dark green with white flecks. Long, narrow stems produce little hanging red flowers. Another member of the Lily family, the fairy washboard (*Haworthia limifolia*), has leaves similar in shape to the oxtongue but crossed with a series of ridges, hence the plant's name. Hanging, bell-shaped flowers are green outside and white inside.

Among the interesting succulents of the

*The branching growth of a jade plant (*Crassula argentae*) (above) and* Echeveria glauca *rosettes (below) complement each other in this strawberry jar planter.*

The velvet leaf Kalanchoe beharensis *is one of many attractive plants of the many kalanchoe species.*

Milkweed family are string of hearts (*Ceropegia woodii*) and hairy starfish flower (*Stapelia hirsuta*). String of hearts makes a fine hanging plant, with its long, trailing stems that bear heart-shaped, mottled leaves and unusual black flowers. The hairy starfish flower grows clumps of cactus-like stems, but its most distinctive feature is described by its name; its large, star-shaped blooms are hairy on the inside and maroon in color.

The thick, tongue-shaped leaves of Haworthia limifolia *resemble those of gasteria, aloe, and other unusual members of the Lily family.*

Stapelia flowers look so like starfish that they have been given that name. Their slight odor of carrion attracts blowflies for pollination in the wild.

A seashore planting of succulents.

Lithops bella, *a split rock in bloom.*

The Mesembryanthemum (*Aizoaceae*) family contains probably the most unusual of succulents. Many sit on the soil surface and appear to be nothing more than smooth, egg-shaped rocks. Species of the genus *Lithops* look like rocks that have been split; each has a cleft separating what are actually two very thick, somewhat globe-shaped leaves. Bright yellow flowers grow out of the cleft. Tiger jaws (*Faucaria tigrina*) has white-speckled, tooth-edged leaves and large yellow flowers. The faucarias include almost forty species, all fitting this general description.

Other families, some of whose members are unusual and attractive succulents, are Geranium, Portulaca, Grape and wandering Jew.

Yuccas (foreground) and sedum ground cover, both hardy, thrive in full sun in a northern garden.

Knobby tiger jaws (Faucaria tuberculosa) *is one of the many faucarias that grow in this interesting pattern.*

Ideally Suited to Today's Oft-Absent or Vacationing Gardeners

Living with greenery is an increasingly popular trend; more and more people are recognizing the warmth and decorative beauty of plants and the enjoyment of tending them. And while many of us are filling and surrounding our houses with growing things, we don't always have as much time as we would like to devote to their care. Cacti and succulents are the answer to this dilemma; they make handsome and unusual additions to any environment, yet require relatively little upkeep.

An unusual outdoor container planting of hardy echeveria and sedum that can be brought indoors when weather turns too cold or wet in winter.

Yuccas withstand frost and in summer shoot up stalks with showy blooms every other year. Only the yucca moth can pollinate this plant.

Give most cacti and succulents plenty of sun outdoors, in a greenhouse, or on a window sill indoors and you don't have to worry about much else. They can adapt to low levels of humidity and need only minimal amounts of water. Pests are seldom a problem because the skin of these plants is just too tough to be inviting.

Cacti and succulents are ideal plants for a weekend house at the seashore or in the country. At relatively low temperatures, they can be left in a sunny window and will require watering only about once a month. And the faster growing succulents will so change their

A dramatic effect is achieved with an arrangement of stone slabs planted with various succulents.

A raised bed is attractive and provides needed drainage for cacti and succulents.

Containers of tender succulents may be brought indoors easily with the onset of cold weather to provide an inside garden in a sunny window or glassed-in area.

shapes that your being absent part of the time will add to the enjoyment of growing them.

The versatility of cacti and succulents is excellently suited to today's trends in outdoor gardens. In areas of the country that are subject to frost, containers of cacti and succulents can be placed in the ground in imaginative arrangements, and brought inside in winter, which is the normal dormancy period for these plants.

Cobweb hen-and-chicks (Sempervivum arachnoideum) make a handsome winter hardy ground cover.

Some cactus genera—Opuntia, Pediocactus, and some species of Echinocereus—can withstand frost and may be left outdoors all winter. In spring and early summer these will reward you with large, breathtaking blooms.

If you're fortunate enough to enjoy the frost-free environments of Florida and the southwestern United States, then there is an almost infinite variety of cacti and succulents from which to choose to ornament your outdoor garden. Plant a lawn of blooming ice plants (of the Aizoaceae family) for a blanket of color, or such flowering plants as Echeveria, Sedum, or Sempervivum. For a desert garden of dramatic shapes, combine pin-cushion plants (Mammillaria) with columnar (Cleistocactus hyalacanthus) and golden-barrel (Echinocactus grusonii) cacti.

Ocotillo (Fouquieria splendens) (left) and opuntia provide two starkly contrasting shapes among the great variety of succulent plants.

Ice plant (Lampranthus emarginatus) is covered with purplish-red blooms but makes a handsome ground cover of gray leaves in frost-free climes, even when not in bloom.

This furry-looking columnar cactus (Cleistocactus) will enhance a southern garden, either in this striking arrangement or grouped with barrel and other columnar cacti.

Sedums and sempervivums in a dry wall planting. Provided with plenty of sun, these are hardy in northern areas and provide accents for flagstone steps and around trees.

Winter-hardy Sedum spectabile *makes an unusual, imposing flowering border set off against a carpet of trailing sedum.*

Flowers in Abundance

Cactus flowers are unequaled in the plant world for sheer size and brilliant color. The whites, yellows, purples, and reds that provide relief from the browns and greens of the desert can also be vivid accents in your garden. Many cacti will not bloom until reaching an advanced age and need lots of sun and heat to do so.

Coryphantha borwigii *and its related species such as lobivia, and those of rebutia, gymnocalycium, and notocactus bear spectacular blooms on small plants.*

Some will flower when young and even in containers indoors. Rebutias, for example, will often bear 2- to 3-inch blooms, sometimes on as small as a 1-inch plant, completely covering it with a mass of bright color.

No discussion of cactus blooms is complete without mention of the Christmas cactus (*Schlumbergera bridgesii* and hybrids). These are branch-type cacti that grow link fashion,

Orchid cacti (Epiphyllum x hybridus) *display showy blooms, some fragrant, in colors ranging from red and pink to yellow and white.*

with showy white or red flowers at the ends of the "branches." The flowers bloom around Christmastime in a profusion of color.

For the ultimate in exotic blooms, try one of the night-blooming cacti (species of *Cereus, Hylocereus, Epiphyllum, Monvillea,* and *Selenicereus*). These are similar in growth habit to the Christmas cactus, but the blooms are larger and truly spectacular. Opening only after dark and closing before dawn, they're heavily scented and often reach as much as 12 inches in diameter.

The orchid cactus (species of *Epiphyllum*), as its name suggests, represents another group of attractive bloomers. These are of the tree-dwelling, epiphytic variety which require more water than the desert types but have adapted themselves to survive drought conditions, and won't suffer if the drought happens to be your vacation trip. Some orchid cactus are night bloomers and others are day bloomers, depending on the species, and colors range from white, cream, and amber to lavender, purple, and red.

Among succulents other than cacti, colorful blooms are offered by the agaves, aloes, hoyas, and ice plants.

The abundance of choice is obvious, and success with all of these—whether flowering or not—is easier than you think if you take time to consider each plant's native habitat and the degrees of sun and moisture and the kind of soil it enjoys there. Your selection is limited only by the conditions you can provide in and around your own home. Don't expect the impossible, be attentive to any signs of distress or deterioration among your plants and you will become a successful cactus and succulent grower.

7
Caring for Desert and Jungle Dwellers

Beyond a few basic cultural requirements, cacti and succulents need minimal attention. Even if you forget to water them for a period, their moisture-retaining ability will keep them hale and hearty. And while most other plants need high humidity, cacti and succulents prefer the lower levels (10 to 20 percent) of the average home. However, considerations of soil and light described below are of the utmost importance. And we must be aware of and allow for the once-a-year period of dormancy characteristic of many of these plants.

Tender Care for Newcomers

When moved to a new environment, plants of any kind need time to adjust; they may require anywhere from ten days to two weeks to adapt to the conditions of your home and will demand greater care during this period than any time thereafter.

Whether your newly purchased plants arrive boxed from a mail-order house or in mint condition from a local nursery, try not to do anything that will add to the shock they have already suffered in transit, with one exception. A soft, sometimes mushy rot may appear on a newly arrived plant, a sign of overwatering. Don't throw it out. Cut out the rot with a clean razor blade, let the wound dry for several days. All will be well. Keep new plants in partial shade for a few days and water moderately. Then place them in a sunny window or, if you prefer, under lights (see page 118). But don't put them among plants you already have unless you are sure the newcomers are free of pests and disease. Even plants from the most reliable of nurseries may be pest-ridden, so before you contaminate your entire plant collection take the precaution of immersing your new plants in water for a few hours almost to the rim of their containers. If there are any pests in the soil, they'll come to the surface in short order.

If you receive a new plant unpotted (bare root), root it in the ground outdoors or indoors in a container of soil as soon as possible. Don't water for a few days unless the plant appears especially dry or shriveled, in which case you might moisten the ground or potting soil sparingly.

Container Culture

Soil: Contrary to popular belief, cacti and succulents will not grow in pure sand. They need the nutrients and moisture-retaining capability provided by a mix of ingredients. A good, basic mixture for cacti and succulents consists of equal parts garden loam, sand, and leaf mold, but keep in mind that the most effective mix for healthy growth depends on the climate conditions of your locale. In warm weather areas a light, well-drained mixture is best, and in cooler areas where less watering is required, a heavier soil is more suitable.

To make desert cacti feel more at home, add extra sand and some gravel to the basic mix; for jungle dwellers such as rhipsalis and epiphyllum, the preferred mix is one part osmunda or fir bark to one part garden loam. For the health of your plants a potting mix should provide good drainage combined with moisture retention, so be sure to mix all ingredients thoroughly to insure a loose, friable texture.

Commercial mixes available at your local nursery or garden center are thoroughly blended and sterilized against pests and bacteria. Unless these prepared soils are combined specifically for cacti and succulents (such packaged mixes are available), a little doctoring may be necessary. Many experienced growers have had great success with commercial mixes to which they add a small amount of vermiculite and sand for drainage, and a few tablespoons (to a 6-inch pot) of manure and bone meal for added nutrients. The bagged soil-less mixes perform well and are becoming increasingly popular for houseplants, but they contain no nutrients. Use them only if you are prepared to follow a steady and time-consuming feeding program.

Light: Most cacti and succulents require direct sun during some part of the day for successful flowering and optimum growth. If this isn't possible, don't give up the ship. These plants are remarkably adaptable, and although they may not grow quickly or bloom often, if at all, they will survive in indirect light or partial shade. Rebutia and lobivia cacti respond better than most to these less-than-ideal conditions.

Potted plants should be turned periodically to provide even light on all sides of the foliage, but not if the plant is about to bloom. Any change in light at that time may cause the flower buds to drop.

Of the succulents other than cactus, almost all do best in direct sunlight. Members of the Mesembryanthemum family, especially, thrive in the desert conditions of full sun and little water. Exceptions among the succulents are *Kalanchoe blossfeldiana* and *K. pumila*, which grow best in partial shade.

As an indication of the amount of light your plants are getting, it's helpful to know that foliage cacti and succulents respond to sufficient light with deeply colored foliage, while the absence of optimum light causes the foliage to grow pale or less vibrantly colored.

Moisture: This area of plant culture is the one that inspires the greatest lack of assurance among growers, especially novices. It's the kind of thing for which there are no hard, fast rules, but with experience and genuine attentiveness to your plants, you'll develop almost a second sense regarding their watering needs.

In general, the desert-dwelling cacti require less moisture than the other succulents. Another rule that can be applied generally is never water either type on cold or overcast days, because these conditions coupled with excess moisture promote the growth of fungi. Also, plants in large pots do not need as frequent watering as those in smaller pots; a 4-inch pot will use up all of its moisture in a day, while a 10-inch pot will take a week to dry out. Another general rule: When plants are sprouting new growth, give them plenty of water, but hold back during their period of dormancy.

With each watering, water thoroughly until drainage seeps from the bottom of the container. Don't water again until the soil has dried out.

Fertilizers: Unlike most other houseplants, cacti and succulents, under ordinary conditions, do not require frequent feeding. They will achieve acceptable growth without fertilizer, one exception being older, specimen plants in large containers. Because these grow more slowly, they don't need frequent repotting; they must be fed regularly, preferably during spring and summer, however.

For any plant to survive, it must have: potassium for good stem growth and flowering and seed production; nitrogen for healthy leaves and new growth; and phosphorus for proper development toward maturity. Although cacti and succulents extract most of what they need of these from their potting mixes, I would recommend a moderate feeding program as an insurance factor, especially if you have the time or if you are not likely to repot your plants frequently.

Add a little bone meal once a year (1 teaspoon to a 6-inch pot), or apply a weak solution once a month of 10-5-5 fertilizer (numbers refer to the ratios, successively, of nitrogen, potassium, and phosphorus present in the formula). Feed these to your plants only during the spring and summer months, which is their active growing period.

Potting and Repotting: Cacti and succulents will grow well in almost any kind of container as long as it's of the proper size and has holes in the bottom for the drainage of excess water. The standard terra-cotta pot is the old standby of experienced growers because it provides good drainage, comes in an assortment of sizes, and is relatively inexpensive. But if you have a penchant for decorative containers without drainage holes, simply plant in a terra-cotta pot and drop it inside whatever decorative container you've chosen. After watering, be sure to empty the outer container of any water that has drained from the clay pot.

Container size is a very important consideration. If too small, there will not be enough soil to provide the plant with adequate nutrients, and if too large, the soil will hold more moisture than the plant can absorb, increasing the likelihood of rot. Follow these rules of thumb: A ball-shaped cactus should be planted in a pot with a rim that is 2 inches wider than the diameter of the plant; a columnar cactus should be provided with a pot that has a rim diameter measuring half the height of the plant. In both cases, the pot should be deeper than it is wide.

Before planting, always scrub old or new pots with hot, soapy water to remove dirt and possible insect eggs. Rinse well and then submerge them in water overnight so they'll be completely waterlogged and will not absorb moisture from the soil.

For the actual planting, first place shards of clay (break an old pot into small pieces) at the

For safe removal of cactus and soil-root mass from pot, tap the pot on table edge while holding cactus with several thicknesses of newspaper.

bottom of the container to insure drainage. Cover these with a thin layer of sphagnum or peat moss. This will keep the soil from filtering down into the pieces of clay. Add about 2 inches of potting mix, and then set the plant in it. Add or remove soil, as needed, until the plant is at the proper height. Then pour the remaining soil around the plant. To keep your fingers free of sharp spines, shape a piece of paper like a chute, place some soil in it, and then tilt the "chute" so the soil slides into the container. For those cacti and succulents that are especially sensitive to moisture, substitute a thin layer of attractive gravel for the very top layer of soil. This will keep the plant from coming into contact with excessive moisture and adds an exotic touch.

Wait at least several days before watering a newly potted plant, so that any damaged roots will not rot and will have time to heal.

A welcome dividend of cacti and succulents is that they grow relatively slowly, necessitating much less frequent repotting than other plants. Those in 4- to 7-inch containers will require repotting no more than every two years, and those in larger containers can go three years before needing to be repotted. Spring and fall are the best times to repot, but if this isn't possible or if your plants are in desperate need of repotting, you will do no harm giving a plant a new container during summer or winter.

Remove a plant from its old container by inverting it and tapping the pot rim edge sharply against the edge of a counter or table-top. During this operation, you can hold a prickly plant with a double thickness of newspaper. When the plant and soil mass are free of the container, pour in the last of the soil with a paper chute and tamp it down with a narrow stick. For easy and safe handling of a spiny cactus while removing soil from its roots and placing it in the new container, roll up a piece of newspaper and flatten it into a long, narrow strip; wrap this around the cactus and join the ends to form a handle. For smaller cacti, substitute scissor-type kitchen tongs for the newspaper. Like porcupine quills, cactus spines will detach themselves and remain in your fingers. They also will penetrate gloves;

the tongs and newspaper are the only ways to handle cacti safely.

Rest and Recuperation: Like hibernating bears, most cacti and succulents need a once-a-year period of rest (varying from a few weeks to several months), when growth ceases and both moisture and nutrient needs lessen. This occurs during the winter months for most cacti and some succulents, and at other periods of the year and for varying lengths of

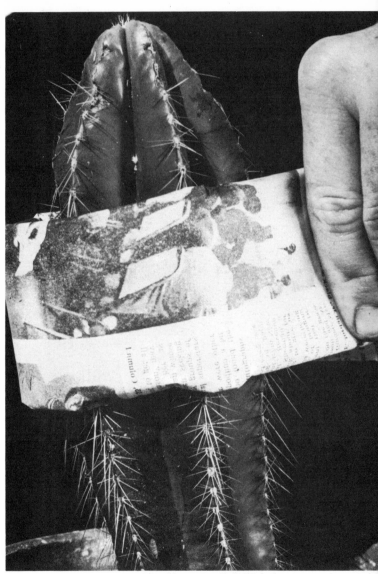

To plant in new pot, position cactus and hold it in place with a "handle" fashioned from rolled-up newspaper.

time for the remaining succulents. Exceptions are kalanchoes, aloes, and agaves, which have no readily discernible periods of dormancy.

During their resting time, your plants will need cooler temperatures at night (around 55°F.) and only enough water to keep them from shriveling. A sort of perked-up look and fresh new growth is the signal that your plants have awakened. When this occurs, they'll need more heat and normal watering.

New Research: The science of plant cultivation is not always as exact as researchers and growers would like it to be. Plants are living organisms, and like people, their well-being is subject to an almost infinite number of variables. Medical researchers are constantly discovering more effective ways to care for the human organism, and horticultural researchers, although on a smaller scale, are finding new and better ways to cultivate plants.

You're probably familiar with the study being done in the area of extrasensory perception as it applies to plants. The essence of the theory is that plants react to human brain waves or thought processes. This may be great news for those people who are tired of talking to their plants; they need do no more than encourage them with good, positive thoughts. A book called *The Secret Life of Plants* by Peter Tompkins and Christopher Bird is a provocative and comprehensive report of the experiments being done in this field.

Cacti and succulents are not exempt from experimentation, and growers are making some startling discoveries that refute the traditional and generally accepted rules. One of these growers, Michael Tifford, has had success treating cacti and succulents much the same as other plants. The following is from an article by Elvin McDonald that appeared in the August 1974 issue of *House Beautiful*.

Tifford, a wholesale grower of bedding and house plants on Long Island, began to grow cacti from seeds. Originally, he followed the established rules, but both sprouting and growth were disappointing. Reasoning that almost anything would be an improvement, Tifford began to experiment. He first tried treating the cactus seeds and seedlings as if they were ordinary bedding plants or vegetables—say petunias and tomatoes—or the ferns like the holly-leaf or the Boston.

His greenhouses have an atmosphere of fresh, moist air, no steam bath, mind you, but

To keep fingers away from spines, form a single sheet of paper into a chute to add soil around a newly potted cactus.

no sauna either. In the fall and winter seasons, all the glass and plastic coverings are cleaned to admit maximum light, but some shading is added from early spring until the late summer.

Probably most important, however, is moisture in the soil. Tifford uses a growing medium that is both humusy and gritty and he keeps it uniformly moist. There is, of course, a distinct difference in the meaning of the words "moist" and "wet." Tifford's rule is that a cactus or other succulent watered in the morning should be only moist or approaching dryness by night-

fall. It should not be allowed to remain wet overnight. In other words, right compares to a moist sponge from which you cannot squeeze any water; wrong is a wet sponge that yields a trickle of water. Tifford has found that when any cactus is too hot and too dry, it goes dormant, the same as in the desert.

Tifford's revolutionary treatment of cacti has produced phenomenal results. Year-old seedlings are four times the usual size and healthier than plants grown in the traditional manner. Older plants flower much more freely.

8
Cacti/Succulents in the House

Deciding which cacti and other succulents to begin a collection with is no easy matter; in fact, it can be downright mind-boggling when you consider the thousands of possibilities. After you have read this Part and studied the pictures, you will have some idea of the selection available. It's also a good idea to visit one of the major public displays of cacti and other succulents, (for addresses, see Appendixes). You can also send away for the catalogs and listings of specialists who ship by mail (also see Appendixes).

Just in case all of this research leaves you even more bewildered and undecided as to which cacti and other succulents are most likely to perform well as houseplants, I have prepared a listing of the kinds that do well for me in a New York City apartment, or that have been recommended by other authors and friends whose judgment I respect.

The small dimestore plants are varied and some grow quite slowly. Six or eight of them of different heights and colors in a single glass or ceramic bowl will last for several years. Changing in shape constantly, they produce young knobs and projections that fall off and take root when inserted between the stones or into the colored sand that covers the soil. If there is no drainage, water sparsely or the roots will rot. With drainage, it isn't necessary to dampen more often than every week or two.

Planters or groups of larger pots arranged on cork (to protect the floor) in the corner of a glass-walled room create a desertlike garden to offset a cold winter. Or a sunny windowsill completely covered by a shallow pan and covered with sedums and sempervivums brought in in the fall absorbs the winter sun.

Cacti should be planted or grouped together for best effect and the same with succulents, but there are exceptions for those with an artistic eye. And in these days of large interior plants, nothing is more striking than a single columnar specimen of almost ceiling height, or a special table with large striking cacti or succulents of suitable kind or shape.

Recently, many apartment dwellers have added gro-light fluorescent units to their indoor gardens. As winters progress, a sunny window may lose hours of bright light, and many a loved plant has hung sadly or grown spindly, or dropped leaves like snowflakes. Many fluorescent light manufacturers are still experimenting with growth, blooming, and distance of light from plant. Among the most successful plants under light are the cacti/succulents which need the long hours of light but also flourish in the dry air of central heating. You can have your desert or jungle and apartment, too.

Astrophytum asterias (sand dollar) can grow to an attention-getting size.

Best Houseplant Cacti/Succulents

Latin Name	*Popular Name*
Adromischus cooperi	plover eggs
A. maculatus	calico hearts
Aeonium canariense	giant velvet rose
A. tabulaeforme	green platters
Agave victoriae-reginae	queen agave
Aloe striata	coral aloe
A. variegata	partridge breast; tiger aloe
Aporocactus flagelliformis	rat-tail cactus
Ariocarpus fissuratus	Mexican living rock
Astrophytum asterias	sand dollar
A. myriostigma	bishop's cap
Beaucarnea	
Cephalocereus senilis	old man
Cereus peruvianus monstrosus	curiosity plant
Ceropegia woodii	string of hearts
Cleistocactus straussi	silver torch
Coryphantha elephantidens	elephant tooth cactus
Cotyledon barbeyi	hoary navelwort
Crassula argentea	jade plant
C. cultrata	propeller plant
C. deltoidea	silver beads
C. perforata	necklace vine
C. perfossa	string o' buttons
C. pseudolycopodiodes	princess pine

A Collection of Container Cacti.
1. Echinocactus grusonii *(golden barrel)*.
2. Haagocereus bicolor.
3. Cephalocereus nobilis.
4. Cleistocactus straussii.
5. Cephalocereus chrysacanthus.
6. Echinocactus grusonii *(golden barrel)*.
7. Nyctocereus serpentinus cristatus *(snake cactus)*.
8. Mammillaria geminispina.
9. Coryphantha.
10. Machaerocereus eruca *(creeping devil)*.
11. Melocactus.
12. Mammillaria prolifera.
13. Mammillaria geminispina.
14. Coryphantha.
15. Notocactus haselbergii.

Best Houseplant Cacti/Succulents

Latin Name	Popular Name
C. rupestris	rosary vine
C. teres	rattlesnake tail
C. tetragona	miniature pine tree
C. tricolor jade	tricolored jade
Echeveria derenbergii	painted lady
E. elegans	Mexican snowball
E. pulvinata	chenille plant
Echinocactus grusonii	golden barrel
E. horizonthalonius	eagle claws
Echinocereus sasayacanthus	rainbow cactus
Echinocereus	hedgehog cactus
Echinopsis multiplex	Easter-lily cactus
Espostoa lanata	Peruvian old man

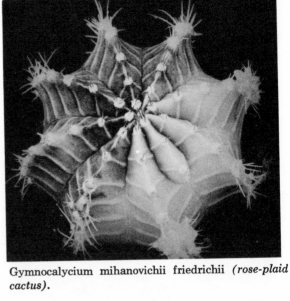

Gymnocalycium mihanovichii friedrichii *(rose-plaid cactus)*.

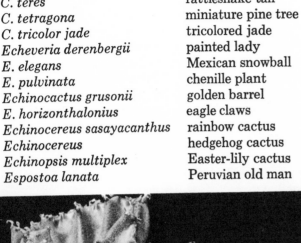

Euphorbia lactea cristata *(elkhorn or brain plant) is one of the most statuesque and variable succulents for the house and summer garden.*

Hoya carnosa variegata *(wax plant) is one of the many trailing hoya hybrids that form clusters of star-shaped fragrant flowers.*

Huernia kennedyana.

Best Houseplant Cacti/Succulents

Latin Name	Popular Name
Euphorbia caput-medusae	Medusa's head
E. fulgens	scarlet plume
E. heterophylla	mole plant
E. lactea cristata	elkhorn; brain plant
E. mammillaris	corncob cactus
E. mammillaris 'variegata'	Indian corncob
E. pulcherrima	poinsettia
E. splendens	crown of thorns
E. tirucalli	pencil tree; milk bush
Faucaria tigrina	tiger jaws
Furcraea gigantea	giant false agave
F. selloa marginata	variegated false agave
x Gasterhaworthia *	royal highness

* x indicates hybrid.

The tiny brilliant scarlet blossoms, like drops of blood, of the crown of thorns (Euphorbia splendens) are probably the reason for the popular name.

Best Houseplant Cacti/Succulents

Latin Name	Popular Name
Gasteria verrucosa	oxtongue; pencil leaf
x Gastrolea beguinii *	pearl aloe; lizard tail
Gymnocalycium leeanum	yellow chin-cactus
G. mihanovichii	plain chin-cactus
G. mihanovichii friedrichii	rose-plaid cactus; red cap
Haworthia	
Hoya carnosa	wax plant
Huernia	
Kalanchoe beharensis	velvet leaf; elephant ear
K. pinnata	air plant; miracle leaf
K. tomentosa	panda plant
Lemaireocereus marginatus	organ pipe
Leuchtenbergia principis	prism cactus; agave cactus
Lobivia	cob cacti
Mammillaria bocasana	powder puff
M. camptotricha	birdsnest
M. candida	snowball pincushion
M. elongata	golden stars
M. fragilis	thimble cactus
M. hahniana	old lady cactus
M. lasiacantha	lace-spine cactus
M. plumosa	feather cactus
Myrtillocactus	branching candelabra cacti
Nopalea	tall, almost treelike plants
Notocactus submammulosus	lemon ball
N. rutilans	pink ball cactus
N. scopa	silver ball
Nyctocereus serpentinus	(cristate) snake cactus
Opuntia basilaris	beaver tail
O. bigelovii	cholla cactus; teddy bear
O. clavarioides	black fingers
O. cylindrica	emerald idol
O. dillenii	tuna
O. erectoclada	dominoes
O. erinacea	grizzly bear
O. fulgida mamillata monstrosa	boxing glove
O. microdasys	bunny ears
O. microdasys albata	angora bunny ears
O. microdasys albispina	polka dots
O. microdasys 'Lutea'	honey Mike
O. oricola	prickly pear
O. rufida	cinnamon cactus
O. schickendantzii	lion's tongue
O. streptacantha	tuna cardona
O. strobiliformis	spruce cones

* x indicates hybrid.

Notocactus submammulosus.

Sedum autumn joy is a glorified form of **Sedum** spectabile *with 6-inch pinkish flowers spreading 30 inches wide and 30 inches tall. It is hardy.*

Best Houseplant Cacti/Succulents

Latin Name	Popular Name
O. turpinii (glomerata)	paperspine cactus
O. vulgaris (moncantha)	Irish mittens
O. vulgaris variegata	Joseph's coat
Oreocereus celsianus	old man of the Andes
O. fossulatus	mountain cereus
Pachypodium	can be dwarf or treelike
x Pachyveria haagei *	jewel plant
x P. scheideckericristata *	jeweled crown
Parodia maassii	Tom Thumb cactus
Portulacaria afra variegata	elephant bush
P. afra variegata tricolor	rainbow bush
Rebutia	tiny specimen called crown cactus
Rhipsalis cassutha	mistletoe cactus
R. warmingiana	popcorn cactus
Sansevieria guineensis	bowstring hemp
S. trifasciata	snake plant
S. trifasciata 'hahnii'	birdsnest
Schlumbergera bridgesii	Christmas cactus
S. gaertneri	Easter cactus
S. gaertneri makoyana	cat's whiskers
Sedum morganianum	burro tail
S. pachyphyllum	jelly beans
S. rubrotinctum	Christmas cheer
S. sieboldii	October plant
S. spectabile	autumn joy
S. treleasei	silver sedum
Stapelia hirsuta	starfish flower
S. variegata	star flower
Trichocereus	relatively large plant; a genus of organ pipe cacti
Zygocactus truncatus	Thanksgiving cactus

* x indicates hybrid.

Specimens as Sculpture

In recent years the general trend in houseplants has been away from small tabletop or window-sill specimens to ceiling-reaching trees and great cascading hanging baskets, often with medium-sized shrubs in between. The same is true of cacti and other succulents in particular. In fact, some of these are absolutely stunning as pieces of living sculpture. Uplight, downlight, or crosslight one of them and you will be amazed—and delighted—with the different effects possible.

Some of the best kinds from which to select a large, important specimen include:

Latin Name	Popular Name
Agave	
Aloe	
Astrophytum	sand dollar
Cephalocereus senilis	old man cactus
Cereus peruvianus monstrosus	curiosity plant
Cleistocactus	
Echinocactus grusonii	golden barrel
E. horizonthalonius	eagle claws
Euphorbia caput-medusae	Medusa's head
E. grandicornis	cowhorn
E. tirucalli	pencil tree; milk bush
Kalanchoe beharensis	velvet leaf
Lemaireocereus marginatus (Pachycereus)	organ pipe
Myrtillocactus	
Trichocereus	

Perhaps it is unnecessary to say, but nevertheless a word of caution: Be very careful in placing spiny or sharp-needled plants where you or any other person might walk into them. One shudders at what might happen from the careless placement of a large agave, for example, with its dagger-sharp leaf tips.

What about light for these large plants? And care? They are usually costly investments, and besides, one develops an attachment for these rather quickly; a casualty is not to be taken lightly. For one thing, be *sure* the plant you purchase is established in a container of

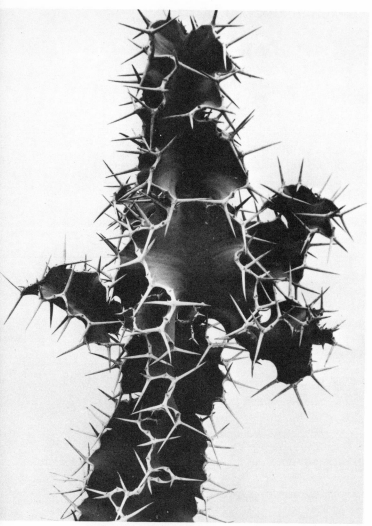

The interesting growth habit of Euphorbia grandicornis *(cowhorn euphorbia) makes a dramatic statement in any room setting.*

other approach to containerizing large cacti and other succulents is to grow them in a utilitarian container which has a drainage hole. Slip this inside a slightly larger decorative jardiniere, but be sure that water does not collect and stand in the base. If you place a waterproof saucer inside, woven baskets make great containers for specimen cacti and other succulents. Those with Indian design motifs seem especially appropriate.

For convenience it is a good idea to place the containers for large specimens on some kind of dolly. This provides instant portability so that you can wheel them around the house for a change in decorative effect, or to receive greater light. A dolly also facilitates an easy indoor-outdoor existence if that fits your scheme; in other words, you can wheel the specimen outdoors for real recuperation and growth in ideal light during warm dry weather, but well before frost is expected they can be rolled back inside.

The amount of sunlight received indoors in most houses and apartments is hardly sufficient even under the best of circumstances for long-range health of most cacti and other succulents. The use of supplementary artificial light is not only beneficial to the plants' health but the cosmetic effects are obviously desirable. Incandescent floodlights (General Electric's Cool Beam or Sylvania's Cool-Lux, for example) are the answer. These may be mounted in ceiling track systems, in uplight or downlight units, or in any stand-mounted socket. These floodlights should be used only in ceramic sockets. Spotlights are not suitable; they concentrate the light too much and may cause burned spots on cacti/succulents.

Floodlights of the type suggested are available in sizes ranging from 75 to 300 watts. These should be placed approximately 2 to 4 feet away from the plants. As the sole light source for a large specimen, it may be necessary to use two or three floodlights, perhaps of 150-watt size, burned 12 to 16 hours out of every 24. Plugging them into an automatic timer is more satisfactory than remembering to do the on-off work yourself—besides, who will provide days and nights if you go away for several days?

soil, that is to say, well rooted. It follows that the best investment will be a specimen that has been nursery-grown, not one recently ripped up and robbed from the desert.

A large clay pot with a drainage hole and a matching saucer makes the best container for a large specimen. Remember, however, that unglazed clay saucers seep some moisture through the bottom, enough to eventually spoil a fine wood floor or carpeting. You can avoid this problem by cutting a circle of cork to fit underneath the saucer; that little extra moisture will evaporate through the cork. The

If floodlights are used merely to supplement natural light, they may need to be burned for only six to eight hours in the evening when, incidentally, you will most enjoy the effects of dramatic lighting.

What to Grow If You Have No Sun

Best known for their tolerance of less than abundant sunlight are the succulents *Beaucarnea, Ceropegia, Hoya,* and *Sansevieria.* One grower friend of mine, Francesca Morris, who lives in a Westchester suburb north of New York City, has excellent success in north-facing windows with ceropegia, hoya, and sansevieria; she also keeps an epiphyllum in this same exposure in the wintertime. In his new book, soon to be published, *The Encyclopedia of House Plants,* Elvin McDonald also suggests the following cacti/succulents tolerant of less than perfect natural light indoors:

Rattlesnake tail (Crassula teres) *will grow with no direct sun, indoors or in a semi-shady spot in a southern garden.*

Latin Name	Popular Name
Acanthocereus pentagonus	big-needle vine
Acanthorhipsalis monacantha	spiny rhipsalis
Aeonium canariense	giant velvet rose
A. haworthii	pin-wheel
Aichryson	
Bowiea volubilis	climbing onion
Chiastophyllum	
Cissus quadrangularis	veld grape
C. rotundifolia	Arabian wax cissus
Clusia	
Crassula argentea	jade plant
C. cultrata	propeller plant
C. deltoidea	silver beads
C. perforata	necklace vine
C. perfossa	string o' buttons
C. pseudolycopodiodes	princess pine
C. rupestris	rosary vine
C. teres	rattlesnake (tail)
C. tetragona	miniature pine tree
Cryptocereus	
Deamia testudo	tortoise cactus
Disophyllum	
Epiphyllanthus	
Epiphyllopsis	
Epiphyllum x hybridus *	orchid cactus
Erythrorhipsalis	
Euphorbia tirucalli	pencil tree; milk bush
Gasteria caespitosa	pencil leaf
Hatiora salicornioides	drunkard's dream
Haworthia	
Heliocereus speciosus	sun cactus
Huernia	
Kalanchoe tomentosa	panda plant
Lepismium	
Leuchtenbergia principis	prism cactus
Monvillea	
Nopalxochia	
Opuntia vulgaris variegata	Joseph's coat
x Pachyveria clavata cristata *	
Pedilanthus tithymaloides	redbird cactus
Pereskia aculeata	lemon vine
P. grandifolia	rose cactus
Pfeiffera	
Portulacaria afra variegata	variegated elephant bush
Pseudorhipsalis	

* *x indicates hybrid.*

Latin Name	Popular Name
Rhipsalidopsis	
Rhipsalis cassutha	mistletoe cactus
R. warmingiana	popcorn cactus
Schlumbergera bridgesii	Christmas cactus
S. gaertneri	Easter cactus
S. gaertneri makoyana	cat's whiskers
Sedum morganianum	burro tail
Selenicereus grandiflorus	queen of the night
S. pteranthus	king of the night
S. urbanianus	nightblooming cereus
Senecio rowleyanus	
Weberocereus	
Zygocactus truncatus	Thanksgiving cactus; crab cactus

Christmas cactus (Schlumbergera bridgesii) *offers a continuous profusion of showy rose-red to orange-red flowers, in season.*

Burro tail (Sedum morganianum), *a handsome trailer in a well-chosen planter, will do well without a great deal of sun.*

The Fluorescent Way

If you have no natural light indoors sufficient to sustain healthy growth of cacti and other succulents, fluorescent light provides a ready substitute. It is, at this time, limited to the culture of seedlings, young plants, and kinds that remain fairly small at maturity—say no more than 8 to 10 inches tall.

Fluorescent-light culture of cacti/succulents is at present a fairly new idea. The most up-to-date experience of a successful home gardener was reported by Henry F. Lee in the September 1974 issue of *Green Scene*, a magazine published by the Pennsylvania Horticultural Society. Dr. Lee recommends the use of Gro-Lux Wide-Spectrum tubes placed in standard reflector units and burned 16 hours out of every 24. For a growing area approximately 18 by 24 inches you will need a standard industrial fixture with either two or three 20-watt tubes; for an area 24 by 48 inches you will need a fixture with two or three 40-watt tubes. Replace the tubes at least once a year, preferably every six months, otherwise the light is

The beautiful flowerlike shape of the Dudleya candida *is emphasized by the light of the sun. When the plant is brought indoors in winter, an incandescent grow light can do the same for it.*

too dim for the best growth of your plants.

For recommended varieties to grow under fluorescent lights, study Dr. Lee's listings in the accompanying chart.

Cacti and succulents all grow and bloom faster under fluorescent lights because of the longer duration of light. Here a collection includes an old man cactus, a little partridge, aloe, and others.

Cephalocereus senilis, *the old man cactus, is a fuzzy white curiosity and a relatively friendly one; its long spines are somewhat stiff but safe to the touch.*

Selected List of Choice Plants Grown from Seed Under Lights

Cacti

Latin Name	Popular Name
Astrophytum asterias *	sand dollar
Astrophytum myriostigma	bishop's cap
Cephalocereus senilis	old man cactus
Cereus peruvianus monstrosus	curiosity plant
Cleistocactus straussi	silver torch
Dolichothele longimamma	finger-mound
Echinocereus * (many species; beautiful long-lasting flowers)	rainbow cactus
Ferocactus acanthodes	fire barrel
F. covillei	Coville's barrel
F. nobilis	
Gymnocalycium mihanovichii friedrichii *	rose-plaid cactus (one of the best bloomers)
Gymnocalycium * (several others)	chin-cactus spider cactus plain cactus
Leuchtenbergia principis	prism cactus
Lobivia * (several)	
Mammillaria bocasana *	powder puff
M. bombycina *	silken pincushion
M. elongata *	golden stars
M. geminispina (bicolor)	whitey
M. gulzowiana	
M. insularis *	
M. klissingiana	
M. longiflora *	
M. nivosa *	
M. pseudocrucigera	
M. pyrrhocephala *	
M. zuccariniana *	
Notocactus crassigibbus * (long-lasting flowers)	
N. haselbergii *	white-web ball
N. magnificus	
Parodia aureispina *	Tom Thumb
Setiechinopsis mirabilis *	

* *Successful flowering under lights.*

Other Succulents

Latin Name	Popular Name
Aloe (many species; mixed seed starts well in sphagnum)	
A. haworthia	
Argyroderma (several)	
Cheiridopsis (several)	victory plant
Dinteranthus puberulus * (germinate seeds in the dark)	
Faucaria * (many species)	tiger jaws
Hoodia gordoni	
Huernia * (many species)	
Lapidaria margaretae	karroo rose
Lithops * (many species)	stoneface cleft stone
Odontophorus *	
Schwantesia *	
Stapelia * (many species)	
Tavaresia grandiflora *	thimble flower
Titanopsis calcarea	limestone mimicry

Successful flowering under lights.

Aloe haworthioides, *perhaps the handsomest of the small aloes, with white spurs on dark green spiky leaves, can be grown from seed under lights.*

For the display of cacti and succulents in your home, there are no hard and fast rules concerning arranging and grouping. Try to achieve a distinctive effect by relying on your own sense and knowledge about the plants' natural habitats. Cacti often stand alone in the desert, and for that reason a single potted cactus lends an austere and dramatic focal point to any room setting.

Cacti and nonleafy succulents grouped in bowl or dish plantings or in individual containers will inevitably evoke the image of the desert. And if you like, you can further this effect with the addition of small rocks or pieces of sun-bleached wood or bone. Standard terra cotta containers or planters of rough-

Lapidaria margaretae, *a miniature (pot is 2 inches across) of the same family as ice plant, will form 2-inch yellow flowers.*

White-web ball (Notocactus haselbergii) *has brilliant red flowers that last a week and keep on budding for four to eight weeks.*

Miniature Lithops *(stonefaces) are no larger than 1 inch in diameter. Real stones are combined with succulents in this clever tray planting.*

hewn material will complement this likeness.

To recall the lushness of the tropical jungle, group epiphytes, cacti and leafy succulents together or along with appropriate nonsucculent plants such as orchids, dracaenas, bromeliads, and tall Kentia or Areca palms. Terra cotta containers that are molded in various shapes or woven baskets of all kinds work best in achieving the tropical look.

Above all, don't be afraid to be original or adventuresome. Experiment with the contrasts and similarities of totally unrelated plants. If you want to set ferns alongside cacti, no one could be displeased by the beautiful counterpoint of these two opposite ends of the plant spectrum.

This free-form pebble-finish concrete planter is filled with small, ground-hugging crassulas with the bold Crassula falcata *planted for accent.*

9
By Choice
Not Chance-Collecting

The variety of cacti and succulents available is truly fascinating, but it can also be bewildering. One way to comprehend this vast grouping is to consider basic types according to size, predominant color of the foliage, body or spines, and the flowering or growth habits. The photographs in this chapter have been selected with these basic types in mind. For every plant shown you will likely find several others that are similar. As a beginning collector you might, for example, choose one plant from each category, presuming of course that you can provide the space and suitable growing conditions. On the other hand, you may wish to collect plants within a single category, for even the look-alikes have distinct differences which provide endless fascination to the true collector. Spine formations, for example, may appear at a glance to be the same, but look again—perhaps using a magnifying glass—and you will discern infinite variety.

A few decades ago, our grandmothers covered every available sill and table with African violets, behind a sun-softening curtain to protect the foliage from burning. Today, many of us have our own plant craze, and none is more satisfying than cacti and succulents. Some genera—aloe, agave, opuntia and many others listed in this book—are so broad that a compulsive collector can easily turn to any one of them. Often, after a few years of seeking variety, one settles down to the expertise of collecting one genus, joining its society (see Appendixes) and visiting its shows, even taking tours with a master horticulturist to see for oneself the great collections.

This country provides a tropical and subtropical environment in Texas and Florida, where the variety can easily overwhelm the first-time visitor. To see the native Caribbean trees there, especially in bloom, or catch sight of a fifty-foot century plant standing alone in the scrub with its twenty-foot bloom is not to be forgotten. Nor is it perhaps so different from the obsession of setting aside a sunporch encased in glass with euphorbias in all their dozens of forms.

With more than two thousand species of the cactus family to choose from (all originating in the Americas) and several tens of thousands of succulent (water-storing) plants from thirty families of plants all over the world . . . well, why not specialize in collecting? Nobody ever collected them all.

Euphorbia lactea cristata.

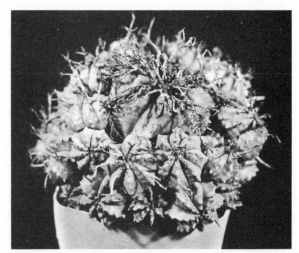

Euphorbia valida.

Euphorbia obesa.

Euphorbia hermentiana.

Astrophytum asterias.

Aeonium arboreum variegatum.

Coryphantha poselgeri.

Echinocereus knippelianus.

Frailea asterioides.

Gymnocalycium denudatum.

Mammillaria abbescens.

Horrida minor.

Lithops helmutii.

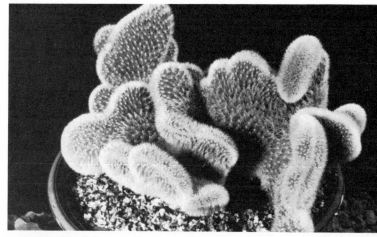

Hildewintera acriespina *crest*.

Mammillaria bombycina.

Kalanchoe pumila.

Neoporteria mammilloides.

Neobuxbaumia polylopha.

Notocactus rutilans.

Pachyphytum *'Blue Haze.'*

Rebutia heliosa.

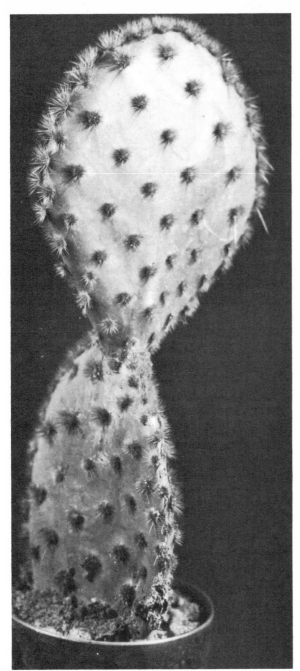

Opuntia acicularis.

Sedum furfuraceum.

Senecio scaposus.

Oreocereus trollii.

Stenocactus multicostatus.

Euphorbia species.

Turbinicarpus schmiedickeanus.

10
Unusual Ways of Display

Part of the pleasure to be derived from growing a collection of cacti and other succulents lies in displaying them so as best to emphasize their natural beauty. Lighting effects are discussed in Chapter 8.

The trailers and creepers suggested for hanging baskets in the text which follows may also be cultivated in pots and displayed on a shelf or pedestal where the stems can cascade freely.

Cacti and Succulents for Hanging Baskets

Cacti and succulents are among the best of all plants for growing in hanging baskets. Indoors the main problem lies in providing them with sufficient direct sunlight, especially during the short and often dark days of late fall and winter. Otherwise they are uniquely suited to growing up in the air. One problem with most leafy basket plants is that when they are hung in the upper parts of a room—where they are most often desired for decorative effect—the temperatures up there are too hot in winter. And basket plants outdoors often suffer from drying out too frequently. The cacti and succulents included in the following list won't thrive if you are totally negligent about watering them, but, on the other hand, most of them won't suffer any great setback if the growing medium dries out occasionally for a few days.

Hanging basket containers you might use for cactus and succulents include:

- redwood boxes and cradles. Line these with polyethylene plastic (with drainage holes punched in the bottom) so that the growing medium does not all wash away between the slats; or you can line them with pieces of unmilled sphagnum moss or florists' sheet moss.
- wire or plastic hanging baskets (with open mesh construction). First line these with a thickness of unmilled sphagnum moss or florists' sheet moss; then add a liner of polyethylene plastic with holes punched in it for drainage.
- clay or plastic hanging pots. These are excellent, providing they have drainage holes. Cacti and succulents have a natural affinity for pottery, but not unless the container has provision for drainage. This is a rule you

might get by with breaking indoors where you control the amount of moisture, but not outdoors where rainfall reaches the containers.

After you have selected a hanging basket and lined it appropriately, fill with your favorite growing medium for cacti and succulents and proceed with planting. Some growers report success with the new soil-less mixes in hanging baskets, partly because these mixes are very lightweight and thus provide a more easily managed and mobile planting. With any soil-less mix—Jiffy Mix, Redi-Earth, or Supersoil, for example—it is necessary to feed a little with every watering while the plants are in active growth. A "little" means feeding at one-fourth to one-fifth the strength recommended for normal feeding. For example, if the directions say "one teaspoon fertilizer to one quart water," you would reduce the amount to one-fourth teaspoon fertilizer to one quart water.

Aloe ciliaris: Climbing aloe. Firecracker aloe. Hanging basket. May be used as a ground cover in frost-free climates. Spikes of red flowers in season.

Aporocactus: species and varieties. Rat-tail or whip cactus. Sprawlers and spreaders, excellent for hanging baskets. Flowers may be crimson, pink, or old rose. Likes sun and warmth. Occasionally seen trained upward on a wire or wooden trellis, espalier-fashion.

Bowiea volubilis: Climbing or sea onion. Twining, graceful, even bizarre stems grow upward from a green bulb that sits partially out of the soil. In time these stems develop a cascade effect. Will survive in a bright north window but prefers at least morning or afternoon sun indoors. May be cultivated as a curious—if not beautiful—hanging-basket specimen, or trained upward on a light trellis.

Ceropegia: species. Rosary vine. Hearts entangled. Long, dangling, wiry stems set with heart-shaped or small, slender leaves. Some are plain green, others marked in a silver mosaic. The strange, intricately formed flowers are truly fascinating if you examine them closely. Great hanging-basket plants indoors or outdoors. As houseplants the ceropegias have an amazing tolerance for varying light levels, from that of a north window to a sunny southern exposure.

Echeveria: Belonging to the Crassula family, the range of these many-colored plants runs to the hundreds of species. Rosette shapes dominate, and the waxy white rosettes are surely the most appealing.

Epiphyllum: species and varieties. Orchid cactus (see illustration, page 102). Many recent hybrids have been bred specifically for growing in hanging baskets. Essentially they need shade from hot summer sun but plenty of direct sun the rest of the year. Plant in sandy but humus-rich potting soil. Feed and water freely in the summer; give no fertilizer in winter and water only enough to keep the stems from shriveling. The spring and summer flowers are spectacular, but well-grown plants are attractive in any season. Closely allied *Aporophyllum, Chiapsia nelsoni, Disapora,* and *Disophyllum* require similar care and make excellent basket specimens.

Harrisia: Night-blooming cereus (one of many so-called). May be grown as a large hanging-basket plant in a spacious sunny window in warmth.

Hoya: species and varieties. Wax plant (see illustration, page 112). Sometimes classified as succulents and often seen in the company of cacti and other succulents. These make beautiful hanging-basket plants. The foliage—which may be plain green; green-flecked with silver; or a combination of green, creamy white, and rosy pink or burgundy—is always attractive. In season the clusters of star-shaped flowers are exquisite—and fragrant.

Kalanchoe: Two species, *K. scandens* and the better-known *K. uniflora* (kitchingia), may be used as basket plants. *K. uniflora,* from Madagascar, makes a fine houseplant in a sunny window. Dangling lantern flowers of dark rose appear in the spring.

Kleinia: species. Several of these are satisfying to grow in hanging baskets. They include *K. heereianus* (gooseberry kleinia), *K. pendula* (inchworm plant), *K. radicans,* and *K. tomentosa.* In the house they need as much sun as you can give them.

Mesembryanthemum: Ice plant (see illustration, page 101). Both of these names are applied to a variety of creeper, trailers, and sprawlers that make attractive hanging baskets. As houseplants, all need a generous measure of sun. Specific names include: *Aptenia cordifolia variegata, Carpobrotus edulis* (Hottentot fig), *C. chilensis* (sea fig), *C. acinaciformis, Cephalophyllum alstoni, C. spongiosum, C. tricolor, Cryophytum crystallinum, Delosperma echinatum, Dorotheanthus bellidiformis* (Livingstone daisy), *Hymenocyclus croceus, H. herrei, H. purpureocroceus, Lampranthus multiradiatus* (sun rose), *L. emarginatus* and *Oscularia deltoides.* All are characterized by fairly small succulent leaves and an abundance of brilliantly colored daisy-like flowers.

Othonna crassifolia: Pickle plant. Drooping stems set with succulent leaves like miniature cucumber pickles. The flowers are half-inch yellow daisies. Provide an abundance of sun all year, plenty of water in summer but on the dry side in winter. An excellent and fairly easily obtained hanging-basket plant.

Peperomia: species. This popular houseplant is succulent-like, and certain kinds make splendid hanging baskets. Peperomias are touchy about water—too much or too little and they have a habit of turning up their toes, collapsing of rot at the base of the stems, and dying. Yet they are mostly carefree, easily cultivated plants in the light of an east, south, or west window. Best for hanging baskets are these species: *P. cubensis, P. fosteri, P. glabella, P. obtusifolia, P. prostrata, P. quadrangularis, P. scandens,* and *P. trinervis.* Houseplant baskets of these will summer well outdoors in partial shade, hanging from the branches of a tree, for example.

In a heavy ceramic pot, with pockets in the sides like a strawberry barrel, a single genus— Echeveria (see page 58)—has been planted. Most echeverias are of the rosette form. In fair weather, this one is hung from the bough of a tree in the garden.

The hybrid Disophyllum *on delicate white stems sends out its fragile white blossoms.*

Peperomia scandens 'variegata' *is an ideal hanging plant. When the young upright stalks begin to hang down naturally, the pot can be suspended in a basket.*

The mistletoe cactus—Rhipsalis cassutha—*has several look-alikes which are not pendant enough for a hanging basket such as the pencil tree.*

Portulaca grandiflora: hybrids. Rose moss. This old-fashioned annual, most often seen carpeting dry, sun-baked areas in the garden, makes a superb hanging-basket plant outdoors in the summer. Plant seeds or set out started plants in baskets as soon as danger of frost has passed in the spring. You may expect flowers eight or nine weeks later—and then until fall frost. The best of today's hybrids have double flowers nearly three inches across. They are available in mixtures or in separate colors—all of which are spectacular.

Rhipsalis: Mistletoe cactus. These are mostly spineless with strange, slender, cylindrical branches, many of them with the unusual habit of shooting off new branches at acute angles. Grow in a mixture of fir-bark, sand, peat moss, and garden loam; water freely except not so much in the winter. Protect from hot, midday sun. Excellent houseplant hanging baskets, especially if you can provide a little better than average humidity in the winter. These look especially attractive in the company of stark, contemporary furnishings. The related and similar *Hatiora salicornioides* (drunkard's dream) and *Pseudorhipsalis macrantha* are equally fine basket plants.

Sansevieria parva: This succulent member of the Lily family has the fascinating habit of sending down long runners to two feet with baby plants on the tip of each. Like the common snake plant, in whose family it belongs, *S. parva* has a truly cast-iron disposition; hot or cool, moist or dry, sun or shade, it makes a striking basket plant when well grown and groomed.

Sedum: Live forever. This genus is rich in creepers and danglers suited to all kinds of airborne plantings. Mostly they are popular and widely distributed. Consider: *S. acre, S. dasyphyllum, S. lineare variegatum* (especially fine as a houseplant), *S. mexicanum, S. morganianum* (the choice burro or donkey tail sedum), *S. palmeri, S. sieboldi,* and *S. stahli* (coral beads or Boston bean). Of all, *S. morganianum* is surely the choicest; it is, in fact, a favorite among *all* hanging-basket plants. When you want to purchase the burro's tail sedum, growers inevitably will show you a fine old specimen with which they will not part, but then you'll have the pleasure of seeing your young (and relatively inexpensive) rooted cutting grow into an equally fine specimen. Outdoors, *S. morganianum* is best given protection from strong winds and stormy rains; otherwise many of the leaves will be broken off the stems.

Senecio rowleyanus: This strange succulent, with many African relatives, has creeping branches and berry-shaped leaves that distinguish it from the others.

Stapelia: Starfish flower. Carrion flower. These succulents with leafless, knobby stems have only one fault—and that lasts for a fairly brief time: The flowers smell of carrion. There are many different kinds; favored as a houseplant hanging basket is *S. variegata* whose fantastically marked flowers give off less of the offensive odor than some of the larger ones. Indoors it needs direct sun in an east, south, or west window. Easily cultivated.

Zygocactus: Thanksgiving, Christmas (see illustration, page 118) and Easter cacti. This grouping also includes *Rhipsalidopsis rosea*, *Schlumbergera bridgesii*, *S. gaertneri* (sometimes called a rhipsalidopsis), and *S. russelliana*. Besides these species there are dozens of new hybrids available today, many of which flower more freely. All bloom when days are naturally short; you'll upset their timetable if you allow artificial light to reach them at any time between sundown and sunup in the fall months. During these short days it is important to keep them on the cool side (preferably not over 65°F.), to water less and not to feed at all. All of these prefer a humus-rich potting soil, the same as you might use for begonias or African violets. They make excellent hanging-basket plants, preferably in a window that receives some direct sun in the winter months. While these jungle cacti do well in the dappled shade of a tree outdoors in summer, as houseplants they really do require some direct sun in order to grow well.

Green jade (Echeveria agavoides) *produces the larger leaves and trailing sedum produces the smaller ones in this wire basket.*

A remarkable sight, a round jug with round openings festooned with Senecio rowleyanus, *or a string of pearls.*

Bursera fagaroides, *in a Japanese bonsai planter, captures the illusion of an actual ancient miniature tree.*

Cacti/Succulents as Bonsai

Many fine specimens of hundreds of different cacti and other succulents take on the appearance of aged bonsai—miniaturized trees—when they are planted in traditional bonsai containers. Larger, older specimens may require the root room of a fairly deep, bowl-shaped bonsai dish. Smaller and young plants may be established in more shallow bonsai trays.

Some of the best plants for giving the instant effect of bonsai are:

Latin Name	Popular Name
Agave victoriae-reginae	queen agave
Anacampseros rhodesica	
Bursera fagaroides	
B. hindsiana	
B. odorata	
Euphorbia nivulia	
Fouquieria fasciculata	
Jatropha berlandieri	
Opuntia ramosissima	
Pachycormus discolor	
Plumeria acutifolia	West Indian jasmine; temple tree
Trichodiadema densum	miniature desert rose

Euphorbia nivulia, *one of the forms of this genus with normal-looking leaves, also in a Japanese bonsai planter.*

The crown of the Trichodiadema densum, *known as the miniature desert rose, must be heavily pruned over a long period to achieve this effect of foliage and centuries-old trunk.*

While the plants in the preceding list are fairly rare, there are two more suited to bonsai training which are popular and widely distributed: *Crassula argentea* (jade plant) and *Portulacaria afra* and *P. afra variegata* (elephant bush). After a few years of cultivating these with the roots cramped in small quarters, they begin to develop aged, enlarged, gnarled stems and smaller leaves in keeping with a bonsai.

Bowl and Dish Gardens

One of the most pleasurable ways to enjoy a collection of small cacti and other succulents is to combine them in a miniature desertscape which can be planted in any container that seems appropriate to the size, texture, and color of the plants. You can use pottery, plastic, clay pot saucers, bonsai dishes and trays, even clear Plexiglas. Since these containers have no provision for drainage, it will be necessary to first add a layer of gravel, followed by a layer of charcoal chips, then the final layer of your favorite planting medium for cacti and other succulents.

Before you actually begin planting, it is a good idea to sketch the dimensions of your container on a sheet of newspaper. Then arrange the plants within this area while they are still individually potted. You can try all kinds of spacing and different combinations until the effect is exactly what you have in mind. Use this as your planting scheme, removing one plant at a time, unpotting and repositioning it in the desertscape container. To assist in handling spiny plants, take a sheet of newspaper and fold it over and over into an inch-wide strip; wrap this around the spiny body and clasp together with your fingers. This makes a fine holder that will not damage the plant, and the spines will not wind up in your fingers.

Water bowl and dish gardens of cacti and other succulents very carefully. In the beginning the medium should be moist, but not too. If you can imagine potting soil as being wet, nicely moist, barely moist, or nearly dry, then try to keep your desertscape within the range between barely moist and nearly dry.

As the finishing touch for a desertscape,

A great fashion is the garden under a glass dining table. The Trumans introduced this at the White House.

Little Joshua trees is the name given to this collection of Sedum multiceps *dwarfed by a specimen stone.*

Easiest Cacti/Succulents for Bowl and Dish Gardens

Latin Name	Popular Name
Adromischus	plover eggs
A. maculatus	calico hearts
Aloe variegata	partridge breast; tiger aloe
Astrophytum asterias	sand dollar
A. myriostigma	bishop's cap
Cotyledon	
Crassula argentea	jade plant
C. cultrata	propeller plant
C. deltoidea	silver beads
C. perforata	necklace vine
C. perfossa	string o' buttons
C. pseudolycopodiodes	princess pine
C. rupestris	rosary vine
C. teres	rattlesnake tail
C. tetragona	miniature pine tree
Echeveria derenbergii	painted lady
E. elegans	Mexican snowball
E. pulvinata	chenille plant
Echinocereus	hedgehog cactus
Echinopsis multiplex	Easter-lily cactus
Euphorbia caput-medusae	Medusa's head
E. fulgens	scarlet plume
E. heterophylla	mole plant
E. lactea cristata	elkhorn
E. mammillaris	corncob cactus
E. mammillaris 'variegata'	Indian corncob
E. pulcherrima	poinsettia
E. tirucalli	pencil tree; milk bush
Faucaria tigrina	tiger jaws
Gasteria caespitosa	pencil leaf
Gymnocalycium mihanovichii	plain cactus
G. mihanovichii friedrichii	rose-plaid cactus; red cap; Oriental moon
Hatiora salicornioides	drunkard's dream
Haworthia	
Hoya carnosa	wax plant
Kalanchoe daigremontiana	devil's backbone
K. pinnata (Bryophyllum)	air plant; miracle leaf
K. tomentosa	panda plant
Lithops	stoneface; cleft stone
Lobivia	
Mammillaria bocasana	powder puff
M. camptotricha	birdsnest
M. candida	snowball pincushion

sand is the obvious choice as a ground cover. Gravel chips and small sandstone pebbles are sometimes effective also. In addition, small pieces of driftwood may be used. Children in particular like to include figurines and other Lilliputian objects in a desertscape which may also tell a story of fact or fantasy.

If the walls of your container are transparent and fairly deep, consider adding more than the usual three layers of gravel, charcoal chips, and potting soil. You might work with different colored sands, for example, creating a painted-desert effect with different colors undulating and contrasting like a geological cross section of the earth.

With the possible exception of hoya and *Scilla violacea*, the cacti and other succulents listed on these pages are not suited to planting in moist, woodsy terrariums and bottle gardens.

The tall devil's backbone (Kalanchoe daigremontiana) *appears like graceful palms above a desert oasis, in this dish garden.*

Latin Name	Popular Name
M. elongata	golden stars
	lace cactus
M. fragilis	thimble cactus
M. hahniana	old lady cactus
M. lasiacantha	lace-spine cactus
M. plumosa	feather cactus
Monanthes	
Notocactus mammulosus	lemon ball
N. rutilans	pink ball cactus
N. scopa	silver ball
Opuntia basilaris	beaver tail
O. bigelovii	cholla cactus; teddy bear
O. clavarioides	black fingers
O. cylindrica	emerald idol
O. engelmannii	tuna
O. erectoclada	dominoes
O. erinacea ursina	grizzly bear
O. microdasys	bunny ears
O. microdasys albata	angora bunny ears
O. miscrodasys albispina	polka dots
O. microdasys 'Lutea'	honey Mike
O. oricola	prickly pear
O. rufida	cinnamon cactus
O. schickendantzii	lion's tongue
O. streptacantha	tuna cardona
O. strobiliformis	spruce cones
O. turpinii (glomerata)	paperspine cactus
O. vulgaris (monacantha)	Irish mittens
O. vulgaris variegata	Joseph's coat
x Pachyveria *	
Pelecyphora	jewel plant
	jeweled crown
Portulacaria afra	elephant bush
P. afra variegata	rainbow bush
Rebutia	
Rhipsalidopsis	
Rhipsalis cassutha	mistletoe cactus
R. warmingiana	popcorn cactus
Scilla violacea	silver squill
Sedum morganianum	burro tail
S. pachyphyllum	jelly beans
S. rubrotinctum	Christmas cheer
S. sieboldii	October plant
S. stahlii	coral beads
S. treleasei	silver sedum

* x indicates hybrid.

Snowy echeveria in a wok can be the table center-piece one moment and a terrace decoration the next.

A fantasy of cacti and succulents beside a permanent clump of cactus.

11
How to Multiply Cacti/Succulents

Plant propagation is a means of increasing not only your plants but also your enjoyment and involvement with them. The pleasure of nurturing a plant from seed, or the excitement of a successful graft, must be experienced to be appreciated. In addition to the satisfaction involved, making more plants from one offers the advantages of saving the cost of nursery-grown stock, or of obtaining a new plant from a rare one that may be difficult to acquire. And you can be sure that the plant you raise is the variety you want—ready-conditioned to your own particular climate.

Like other plants, cacti and succulents can be grown from seed, propagated by cuttings, or grafted one to another. Special techniques are involved with each, but cacti and succulents are more-than-willing parents, and with a little help a handful of plants can become an indoor or outdoor garden.

Seeds

If you don't mind the time involved, growing from seed is the best way to acquire a large number of plants at little expense. Seeds can be obtained from a nursery or harvested from your plants' seed pods. The best time for sowing seeds is spring or early summer, especially in temperate areas, so the seeds will have time to sprout before winter.

You will need a shallow container, and since drainage isn't crucial, almost anything handy will do. For large numbers of seeds, though, a nursery flat, a commercially available plastic seed flat, or a large, shallow box are recommended. You can divide these into compartments and sow different seeds at the same time. Be sure you label each or you'll lose track of what seeds are sown where.

Use vermiculite or a basic mix of equal parts peat moss and coarse sand. Don't pack the mix down, but allow it to fill the container rather loosely. Moisten the mix thoroughly and tip the container to empty it of any excess water. Place large seeds just below the soil surface by hand or with a pair of tweezers, and sprinkle tiny seeds, such as those of crassula, over the surface of the mix. Cover with a sheet of clear glass or plastic. Or you can use a piece of plastic food wrap.

Put the seed flat in a warm (78°F.), bright place, such as a window sill, but not in direct sunlight. Indoor plant lights, burning 14 to 16 hours out of every 24, are very good for germinating seeds. Keep testing the soil to be sure it is evenly moist. The enclosed container will hold moisture for long periods of time, and the seeds will probably not need watering more than once every two or three weeks. Always water with a fine mist or an eye dropper, so as not to disturb the delicate seeds. The germination period (the length of time required before the first sprouts appear) can vary from a few days (Stapeliads) to a year (some cactus species).

It will take a sharp eye to see the tiny seedlings, but when these are several months old and of manageable size, they need to be given plenty of light and air. Transplant them, several to a pot, and place, uncovered, in a sunny, well-ventilated location. When the containers become crowded, transplant individual plants into pots no larger than 2 inches. Larger pots hold moisture too long.

Cuttings, Divisions, and Offsets

The natural growth habit of cacti and succulents makes them well suited for propagation by cuttings, divisions, or offsets. Offsets are the little "baby" offshoots of new growth that form on the flower stalks of agaves, aloes, crassulas, and haworthias and at the bases of various other succulents. When a few inches in size, these may be pulled or cut off and rooted in their own containers.

Plants that form a dense mat of individual crowns, such as sempervivum, can be propagated by division. This means that the crowns can be pulled apart and replanted individually. Each crown, after separation from the others, retains its own root system, making it well on the way to being a self-sufficient plant.

Cuttings can be taken from either leaves or sections of stem that have leaf nodes. Good candidates for propagation by leaf cuttings are crassulas, kalanchoes, gasterias, and haworthias. Cut off either a whole leaf or a leaf section and mark it to remind you which end is up. Then set it aside for a few days to dry.

Plant one or many sections of leaf, bottom ends down, in light, sandy soil (three parts sand to one part loam). Don't push the leaves too deeply into the mix; they need only break the soil surface, and there will be enough contact for roots to form. Place in a warm, shaded location and keep the soil evenly moist. When the cuttings begin to look healthy or richer in color, you'll know that roots have formed. You can then dig up each leaf or leaf section and plant it in its own pot.

Whichever of these methods of propagation you choose, remember that the offspring will need warmth, even moisture and protection from direct sunlight until they have formed roots. Also, the best time of year for propagating is spring. At that time your plants are completely rested and ready for new growth.

Grafting

This technique is more a curiosity and a source of enjoyment for the adventuresome grower than it is a practical means of propagation, although it is sometimes the only way to get a stubborn plant to respond. Basically, grafting involves joining one plant to another

Flat graft (left) is best for rounded or globular scions; cleft (center) and side (right) grafts help make more slender scions succeed.

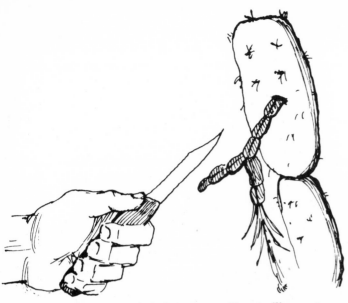

The stab graft is best for grafting trailing cactus species to fleshy stem cactus stock (opuntia, in this case). Make upward stab in stock and insert scion.

Until the graft takes, hold scion in place with rubber bands (as shown), toothpicks or long cactus spines.

with the hope that the host plant (understock) will support healthy growth in the guest plant (scion). And it is often the case that two grafted plants grow as one better than either would by itself. But in actuality, grafting of cacti is most often done to create even more bizarre and unusual shapes than already exist in this fascinating family of plants.

Only members of the cactus, euphorbia, and milkweed families can be grafted. These have in common what is called a cambium layer. This is the layer of growth that surrounds the plant, and the two plants to be joined must be matched at this point for the graft to succeed.

The four methods of grafting commonly used for succulents are: the flat graft, in which both the understock and the scion are cut straight across and joined; the cleft graft, in which a wedge-cut scion is fitted into a cleft-cut stock; the side graft, in which both stock and scion are cut at the same angle and joined; and the stab graft, in which a deep upward cut is made in the stock and the scion is wedged into it. Each method has its own advantages and works best with certain plant combinations. The flat graft is least difficult and is used especially for ball-shaped scions; the cleft and side grafts for tall, narrow stocks and scions; and the stab graft for flat, trailing plants.

The best time to graft is during the summer months when both stock and scion are in full, vigorous growth. It's especially important that you select healthy stock. Cut with a clean, sharp knife and join the pieces as quickly as possible. Be sure the cambium layers of both meet, and secure the scion in place with spines, rubber bands, or toothpicks. Once the graft takes, the spines will dissolve naturally, but toothpicks (which will leave slight scars) or rubber bands must be removed.

Before being joined, the stock and scion should be trimmed so that both parts fit as closely as possible. If too much sap runs from the cut surfaces, soak the pieces in water for a few minutes. This will dissolve the sap and make joining the pieces easier. Keep your newly grafted plants in shade for a few days and check rubber bands occasionally to be sure they are not too tight.

12
Positive Answers to the Negatives

If you buy only healthy, well-cultivated plants or seedlings from a reputable nursery, and care for them properly, they will be provided with a built-in resistance to disease and bothersome garden pests. Only neglected and poorly grown cacti and succulents suffer any real damage from the various ills and predators that threaten them. Preventive medicine is the best kind; it is far easier to build immunity with good soil, sun, and moisture than it is to eliminate infestation once it has taken over a plant. But there are safe and effective steps you can take if any of your plants falls prey to infection.

Pests

There are various bugs and almost microscopic animals that, given the chance, will enjoy chewing at or sucking the juices from cacti and succulents. Plants are especially susceptible indoors where these parasites have no natural enemies, and are therefore free to multiply and ravage as they please. Outdoors, ants are the principal problem because they act as temporary hosts to the insects that actually do the damage. Ants carry aphids and mealybugs from plant to plant, in return for which they eat these pests' secretions. Control ants in your garden and greenhouse with a good ant poison and you'll control dangerous pests. But never sprinkle ant powder or any of the other ant killers directly on your plants.

Aphids: These are tiny, greenish-colored insects that pierce the skin of cacti and succulents and suck out the juicy sap. They will cause twisted leaves and areas of discoloration on foliage. Flower buds and fruit will also be affected. To eliminate these pests, use malathion or spray with a nicotine sulfate–soap solution. You can make this yourself by adding one teaspoon mild soap flakes and one-half teaspoon Black Leaf 40 to one quart warm water. Water plants thoroughly the day before you intend to spray and wash off the residue a few hours after spraying.

Mealybugs: More difficult than aphids to kill, these sucking parasites are fuzzy white or gray insects about the size of a grain of wheat. They attack spines, stems, and roots of succulents, especially if the plant is overly dry. If you discover only a few, they can be picked off individually with tweezers. Or you can touch them with an alcohol-soaked cotton swab to kill them instantly. For heavier infestations, spray with malathion or the nicotine-soap solution. Mealybugs on large plants outdoors can often be knocked off with a strong jet of water from a hose.

Scale: The most stubborn of all pests to eradicate because of their hard outer shells, scale will look like pinhead-sized brown or whitish protuberances on stems and around the areoles on cacti. For minor infestations, dip a toothbrush in the nicotine-soap solution and scrub the infected areas. For more serious cases, use malathion according to the directions on the container.

Root-knot Nematodes: These are microscopic, wormlike animals that attack the roots of succulents, such as echeverias and euphorbias. They are evidenced by swellings along the roots and plants that turn pale in color and stop growing. Affected plants should be dug up, their roots pruned drastically and allowed to dry out for a few days. Plant in fresh soil, preferably sterilized. If you have any doubts about the soil, sterilize it by heating it in a 180-degree oven for an hour.

Thrips and Red Spiders: These tend to appear when plants are kept too dry and warm, especially indoors where ventilation is apt to be inadequate. The first signs are small yellow or white spots on stems or leaves. Fortunately, these mites are easily eradicated with malathion or the nicotine-soap solution.

Snails and Slugs: These chewing villains are the chief predators of cacti and succulents outdoors. Help keep your garden free of them by clearing weeds and thick brush, where they tend to breed. To kill them, scatter metaldehyde, a poisonous bait, on the soil around your plants. Beetles, grubs, and sow bugs are additional garden pests that can pose a threat to cacti and succulents, and these chewers also can be eradicated with metaldehyde.

Diseases

Fungus infection is the chief disease a cactus or succulent plant is likely to develop. But again, like pests, it will attack only those plants that have been neglected or mistreated in some way. If a plant has been overwatered, underwatered, or has been bruised or cut and not cared for, it will be susceptible to the growth of fungus and the decay it causes.

When a fungus infection takes hold of it, a plant will droop and become discolored. To restore it to good health, it's necessary to find the point of infestation and cut out all of the decay until only healthy tissue remains. Then dust the open wound with sulfur or captan and allow it to dry out.

Another disease cacti and succulents sometimes develop is black rot, an infection that enters a plant through a break in its skin. Healthy tissue will turn into a soft, black mass, which eventually will spread throughout the plant. If caught in time, this disease can be dealt with in the same way as fungus infections.

Other Problems

In addition to pests and diseases, cacti and succulents that are poorly cared for are subject to various physiological disorders. Some of the symptoms appear to be the same as those caused by insects or fungus, but if you can find no evidence of these and your plant still shows signs of ill health, take stock of its growing conditions to be sure it's getting the air, light, heat, and moisture it needs.

For example, too much sun will cause foliage to develop yellow spots that will eventually turn brown and crusty. Frost-bitten plant tissues will turn soft to the touch, and if only small areas are affected, these should be cut away as soon as possible. Allow the rest of the plant to dry out and then resume normal culture. Succulents receiving too little air and light will develop abnormal growth that is long, rangy, and twisted. This phenomenon is called etiolation, and it can be corrected simply by supplying needed sun and ventilation.

If you keep in mind the fact that all of the afflictions described in this chapter are the result of negligence, and cultivate your plants with preventative care, then you'll never really have anything to worry about. Above all, don't become one of those gardening zealots who is constantly spraying and fertilizing unnecessarily. Chemical sprays are ultimately harmful to plants and should not be used unless you are certain your plants are infected. And stimulants, hormones, etc.—often used indiscriminately to compensate for otherwise inattentive cultivation or to satisfy impatience—are unnecessary. Don't succumb to the temptation of using them, but give your plants only what nature provides; it has done pretty well the past billion or so years and is difficult to improve upon. Finding out what nature wants for such varied groups of plants is up to you.

13
Nature's Curiosities

If you like to read science fiction, you will almost certainly want to grow some of the strange cacti and succulents illustrated in this chapter. Some are mere mimics—living stones and purple baby toes, for example. Others, like the elkhorn, mimic many strange and sculptured forms. The windowed succulents offer a study in the remarkable ability of plants to adapt to natural growing conditions. In the desert these curiosities have small, translucent areas at the ends of their stems that continue to admit needed sunlight even though the rest of the plant may become covered with sand.

If far-out plants appeal to you, consider one of the globes that sends out strange tentaclelike growths, or an old man cactus covered with silky, long white hairs. There are some cacti and succulents that have irregularly flattened or fasciated growth that you may find appealing—or a monstrosity. In fact, the Latin word *monstrosus* appears frequently in listings of cacti and succulents.

A monstrose plant forms multiple shoots of irregular growth from its growing tip. A fasciated or cristate plant is one that has developed twisted, snakelike growth, that can take different forms among botanically identical plants. Scientists still argue about the causes of these oddities; they've been attributed to damage or disease, excessive or inadequate feeding, or environmental conditions. Whatever, they're sought after by many growers to the extent that they become avid collectors of nothing else. It is, of course, a matter of personal taste, but a few of these tend to go a long way in a plant collection. Each is like a piece of living sculpture. Select with care, then give each a container uniquely suited to showing it off. Although you may cultivate the plants wherever you can give them the best care, from time to time bring each one to a living area where it can be lighted dramatically and properly appreciated by you and your friends.

All the bizarre plants illustrated in this chapter are available commercially in this country, either from local specialists or by mail from one of the growers listed in the Appendix. But some are rare indeed, so rare that importers and growers will exchange single specimens like rare coins. True aficionados will only lend their best-loved plants just as museums or galleries lend their most-desired paintings.

Senecio fulgens—*scarlet kleinia.*

Euphorbia ornithopus—*elkhorn euphorbia.*

Lobivia densispina *crest—lily cactus.*

Dorstenia hildebrantii.

Gerrardanthus macrorhizus.

Bowiea volubilis—*climbing onion.*

Cotyledon reticulata.

Senecio pendulus—*green marble vine.*

Othonna herrei.

Frithia pulchra—*purple baby toes.*

Melocactus violaceus—*Turk's cap.*

Gibbaeum album—*flowering quartz.*

Thrixanthocereus blossfeldiorum.

Sarcocaulon herrei.

Part III
Miniature
Gardens

BY ELVIN McDONALD

ABOVE: *Bubble bowl terrarium has a clear glass cover to keep plants inside in a moist atmosphere. A covered terrarium like this one needs bright reflected light, but if hot sun shines directly on it, temperatures inside will be too high for good growth. This kind of terrarium will grow to perfection in a bright north window or in a fluorescent-light garden. Keep outside of glass polished clean.*

LEFT: *To plant a terrarium, collect suitably small plants that require similar conditions for healthy growth. Here the choices for a terrarium that will be constantly humid and moist include small-leaved English ivy, a young Fluffy Ruffles fern, Dracaena sanderiana, dwarf palm, and rooted cuttings of mistletoe fig. The growing medium has been mounded into an interesting, naturalistic terrain.*

14
The Miracle
of the Terrarium

Almost two hundred years ago English gardeners began to bring ferns and flowering potted plants indoors from their conservatories and glasshouses and enclose them individually in bell jars and other glass containers. The benefits were obvious. Delicate leaves and pampered flowers enjoyed a relatively warm and moist atmosphere in these enclosures. However, it was not until around 1829 when Nathaniel Ward, an Englishman variously described as botanist, surgeon, and scientist — all of which he may well have been — discovered that a little soil and some plants sealed in a glass container could exist, indeed thrive, indefinitely, forming a perfect microcosm of nature. Actually, the discovery happened by accident. Dr. Ward enclosed a chrysalis with some garden soil in a jar. Since any healthy garden soil contains seeds and possibly other living plant matter, in time green growth appeared. What happened to the chrysalis we do not know, but Dr. Ward had the good sense to appreciate what was happening with the plants inside the jar and to document his findings in a scientific journal.

So it is that we honor Dr. Ward as the father of the Victorian Wardian case, which has, in the form of terrariums and bottle gardens, truly come of age. Those earlier gardeners had the idea, but they didn't write it down in the proper fashion. If we trace the development and early practical application of Dr. Ward's discovery, it is easily understood why the idea works so well for us today. Following that first sealed jar, he built large glass cases, which were used by early explorers to keep newly discovered plants alive during long sea voyages. It was not long before these practical cases were made up into the ornate glass enclosures for exotic plants which we associate with the Victorian drawing room. Keeping tropicals in those drafty, chill rooms was hopeless until the Wardian case came along.

Wardian cases soon became popular in drawing rooms in the more genteel American homes. Presumably this practice continued until central heating arrived. Just how those elegant under glass gardens evolved into the terrarium of today is not so easily traced. Conjecture has it that teachers, wishing to re-create Dr. Ward's discovery for students, began to refer to the glass jars and other containers as terrariums — *terra* meaning "earth" and *arium* meaning "home." It was probably one of those students who decided once again that

ABOVE: Peperomias and dwarf palm provide a woodland home for a pair of fine feathered figures in a carriage lantern hanging terrarium.

BELOW: Covered bubble bowl is planted with grape-ivy, hoya or wax plant, and a rooted tip cutting of crassula.

the time was right to try some small exotic plants in a glass enclosure and the old idea found a new life.

In the 1940s I remember as a small school child reading in gardening books about converting fish tanks into terrariums and removing the bottoms of five-gallon water jugs to make bell-jar coverings for temperamental plants. I had a lot of fun digging up seedlings from our Western Oklahoma ranch pasture land and watching them grow in the various terrariums I rigged up. In those days the prescribed method for removing the bottom from a glass jug was to score a line with a glass cutter where the break was desired, then tie a kerosene-soaked string in the scored line, set fire to the string, and immediately plunge the bottle in cold water. I never succeeded with this method, but today my own children seem to have mostly successes with the simple bottle-cutting kits which are sold everywhere.

By the late 1950s, when I first moved to New York, terrariums were being widely used as propagating boxes for rooting cuttings of such plants as African violets, gloxinias, and rex begonias. New or old, discarded fish tanks were the most popular choices, although I remember making one excellent propagating box simply by taping four pieces of glass together, setting them inside a slightly larger wooden seed flat and covering the top with a fifth piece of glass. In a north-facing window, as well as under fluorescent lights, this made a great place to grow miniature plants. I also remember tramping through the Connecticut woods property owned by a friend and scooping up a little of this and that and placing it in a five-gallon aquarium. This rather haphazard planting yielded a phenomenal array of mosses, ferns, violets, and a clump of bluets that bloomed for weeks in a north window of my New York City apartment.

By the early 1960s terrariums were beginning to be more decorative. One perfect,

OPPOSITE: Plexiglas acrylic sheeting is an excellent raw material for making your own terrarium. This decorative display includes a closed terrarium planting of ferns, podocarpus, Norfolk Island pine, and Trileaf Wonder (Syngonium) atop another cube enclosing a piece of sculpture. Pots of African violets on marble chips complete the setting.

A brandy snifter planting that was cultivated under fluorescent lights (a bright north window would also be fine).

Plants include miniature caladium, miniature gloxinia, and three kinds of selaginella.

flower-covered African violet was often seen planted in a large brandy snifter. The miniature gloxinia, *Sinningia pusilla*, was new on the scene and right away we realized that it needed constant warmth and high humidity. Some kind of terrarium was the answer. This era also brought bags and rolls of thin polyethylene plastic. Gardeners more intent on success with plants than esthetics found it a simple matter to enclose almost any container of plants in this wonderful new material. This was also the decade of awakening to the meaning of such words as environment, ecology, and pollution.

However awed, overwhelmed, or even angry those words made us feel, they brought into the 1970s an interest in gardening that is unprecedented in history. Ecological problems of this planet concern us all, yet few of us actually deal with them. It may sound foolish, but it is true that each time another person begins to grow plants at home, the world gets a little better. But growing plants at home is not always a successful venture. For some it is a real disappointment. Lack of experience and forgetting to water are only part of the problem. Modern houses and apartments, however well heated in winter and cooled in summer, tend to be as dry as the desert. We have hot, dry drafts more lethal to delicate plants than the chill of a Victorian parlor. And we travel frequently, for business or pleasure, leaving potted plants to certain neglect. A well-conceived, healthy terrarium is the best way to have thriving plants within the circumstances of today's lifestyle.

The farther we get from a farming society, and the higher up we live in sky-reaching apartments, the more we become strangers to nature. And there lies the most important benefit to be derived from growing miniature gardens in glass — or clear plastic — containers. It goes much farther than plunking a few little plants in a jug or plastic bubble. It is plants and people together, or more vitally, plants and you, the individual, living healthfully and relating to each other. The growing pleasure of a terrarium lies in creating a living, changing, interrelating microcosm of nature. Only certain kinds of plants go well together. It may remind you of the desert, of a woodland dell where you had a secret hid-

Instant terrarium: A rooting leaf of 'Cleopatra' begonia is given the moist environment it likes by simply covering it with a drinking glass.

ing place as a child, or of a Japanese landscape you may never have visited but whose peacefulness you felt. Within the confines of a glass or plastic container you hold in your hands all of these miracles. The range of possibilities and realizing them are what this book is about. Whether you talk to your plants or play music for them is of less importance than the time you spend nurturing growth, appreciating the curve of a leaf, the furl of a flower petal, and the smell of good moist earth.

The Miracle of the Terrarium **157**

Watermelon-begonia (Peperomia), *pothos, strawberry-geranium* (Saxifraga), *dwarf palm, aluminum plant, and* Dracaena godseffiana *get along well together in a Plexiglas bubble bowl.*

15
Terrariums – Types, Planting, Maintaining

All you need to know to plant and to maintain a single but immensely satisfying terrarium could be written on a single page, yet the full scope of the subject easily merits an entire book. If you learn the basics, then you will be able to apply them to almost any situation, regardless of the container or plants available.

In the most general terms all terrariums may be classed as either open or closed. These two words are very important for they relate to the amount of natural light a terrarium planting can tolerate.

Open terrariums can tolerate some direct sunlight shining on them. However, if leaves are next to the walls of the terrarium, long periods of sun shining directly through the walls onto the leaves may burn them. An open terrarium is one with an opening equal to half or more of the container's dimensions. For example, a rectangular aquarium or straight-sided cylinder without any top is completely open. A brandy snifter without a cover is considered an open terrarium. A typical glass bubble bowl without a cover may be considered to be about half open.

Closed terrariums may be any of the containers suggested in the previous paragraph with the addition of a clear glass or plastic cover. All bottles and jugs, with or without a cork or plug, are closed containers insofar as the effect of direct sunlight on them is concerned. Closed terrariums are best positioned in strong natural light with little or no sun shining on them. They are ideal subjects for cultivating in fluorescent-light gardens. For brief periods of time, up to a week or two, terrariums cultivated in fluorescent-light gardens may be moved around the house for decorative purposes, but again, not where sun will shine directly on them.

What all this means is that if you want to grow sun-loving plants in a terrarium in natural light, then it will have to be open. This is fine if you have sufficient sunlight and if the plants you want to grow will thrive in the open air of your home. In such a terrarium, there will be slightly more moisture — humidity — in the air immediately surrounding the plants than elsewhere. If you want to grow terrarium plants that require high humidity, the container will have to be closed. This means that if you want to grow them in natural light, your selection will be limited to shade plants. To grow plants that need

some sun in a closed terrarium, a fluorescent-light setup for gardening is necessary.

In the Little Encyclopedia of Terrarium Plants, Chapter 17, you will find an additional discussion of the terms *open* and *closed* as they relate to the selection and culture of various plants.

Selecting a Terrarium Container

The marketplace today is filled with all kinds of terrariums — open and closed. Most of these are excellent. The only fault I find is that occasionally a terrarium only 6 or 8 inches in diameter will be offered with 5 or 6 plants that will soon if not immediately crowd each other to the point of poor health and poor looks.

Which brings up the point that almost any *clear* (not tinted) glass or plastic container may be used as a terrarium. It is merely a matter of fitting plants suitable to each other and to the size and shape of the container.

You do not necessarily have to buy a container in order to have a terrarium. Fruit jars, gallon-size pickle and mayonnaise jars (available for the asking from commercial kitchens), wine and water jugs, decanters and laboratory glassware all make fine terrariums. A 2-inch plastic cube, the top half clear, in which 35mm. color slides are stored, makes a perfect terrarium for a single plant of *Sinningia pusilla* or any other miniature gloxinia. Underwear, pantyhose, and stationery sometimes come in clear plastic containers which are sturdy enough to convert into terrariums.

Terrariums are not limited to table-top and shelf display. Some are ready-made to be hung from the ceiling or from a bracket mounted on the wall. Others are available in the form of tables or as spheres or egg shapes mounted on a pedestal.

LEFT: A hanging bubble bowl planted with dwarf palm, hoya, and young plants of echeveria. A miniature bridge provides a Japanese landscape effect. Use macramè skill to fashion a sling for hanging.

RIGHT: In this bubble bowl terrarium two ceramic butterflies adorn Dracaena sanderiana, *variegated peperomia, aluminum plant,* Philodendron sodiroi *and partridge berry. Keep closed terrariums out of direct sun.*

LEFT, ABOVE: Half-sphere wall-mounted terrarium made of Plexiglas. White marble chips set off plants, which include dark-leaved peperomia, ardisia, miniature African violet and small-leaved English ivy.

LEFT: Small bubble bowl has base filled with black charcoal chips. It holds spotted-leaved Dracaena godseffiana *and cutting of hypocyrta (goldfish plant).*

ABOVE: This six-sided terrarium has its own stand and a built-in light fixture to supplement natural light. Plants include fittonia, aluminum plant, Dracaena sanderiana, *and sansevieria.*

Red partridge berries, rattlesnake plantain (woodland orchid), sphagnum and kelley moss all thrive in this closed terrarium.

By using plate glass, Plexiglas, or Lucite and appropriate epoxy adhesives, it is possible to create your own terrariums as illustrated in some of the accompanying photographs. Thin redwood strips or leaded glass may be used to create elaborate fern and Wardian cases that hark right back to ornate Victorian times. Ob-viously, this business of terrarium gardening can take you almost anywhere — from the kindergarten simplicity of putting a cup of moist soil in a quart jar with a bean seed to the ultimate in sophisticated gardening and such crafts as glass cutting, designing in Plexiglas or Lucite, and wielding a soldering iron to

ABOVE: Materials often used in terrarium/bottle garden plantings: back row, l. to r.: white perlite, sphagnum peat moss, milled sphagnum moss. Front row, l. to r.: vermiculite, sand, packaged terrarium potting soil.

BELOW: To moisten dry planting soil, place desired quantity of soil in small plastic bag; pour in small amount of water; knead the soil-filled bag to distribute the moisture throughout the soil.

create works of art in leaded glass containers. Another craft possibility is the designing and knotting of macramé holders for hanging terrariums.

Terrarium Planting

When it comes to planting a terrarium, those two important words *open* and *closed* take on a slightly different meaning. Consider your terrarium *open* if you can get your hands, one or both, inside to do the planting and maintenance. Consider it *closed* if you cannot reach all the way inside with one hand.

Planting an open terrarium is of course much easier than one that is closed, so let's start at the beginning and work up to the more difficult. No special tools are needed to plant an open terrarium. Besides a selection of plants you will need:

1. Crushed gravel of ⅛-inch size
2. Crushed charcoal
3. Packaged potting soil

You will find both gravel and charcoal available wherever potted plants are sold, or obtain them by mail from terrarium specialists (see Appendix). General purpose potting soils are almost always too heavy in texture for terrarium plantings. Either purchase one labeled specifically for terrariums or alter general-purpose potting soil by mixing it with equal parts vermiculite or perlite (both sold in small bags wherever potted plants are available).

Before you add any ingredients to a terrarium first wash the container in warm water to which a little household detergent has been added. Rinse well in clean water, then dry completely. To begin planting, the basic procedure is to add:

1. A layer of gravel;
2. A layer of charcoal; and
3. A layer of potting soil.

How much of each you add depends on the size and depth of the container. Generally speaking the total depth of the three layers should add up to one-third the height of the

ABOVE: *Use warm, sudsy water to clean thoroughly all terrariums before planting. Rinse with clean water.*

BELOW: *Dry the container inside and out. Let it stand to air-dry completely before beginning planting.*

ABOVE: Add the first layer of material. Here white marble chips are used.

BELOW: After plants are in place, florist's sheet moss is used to provide a carpet all around them.

ABOVE: Then add second layer. Charcoal chips are used here to help keep the soil fresh-smelling.

BELOW: When planting is finished, use soft-bristled brush to remove stray soil from leaves and inside walls.

Curly-top terrarium. The white perlite surface contrasts with the small rocks and stones. Plants are peperomia, ar- *disia, miniature* Gesneria cuneifolia *(almost everblooming), and syngonium.*

container. If the container is 9 inches tall you might add a ½-inch layer of gravel, a ½-inch layer of charcoal, and a 2-inch layer of potting soil for a total of 3 inches. Good gardeners like good cooks develop a sixth sense of what is right in any given situation; some are born with this but most of us develop it by experience.

As you add the layer of potting soil, keep in mind the kind of terrain you want in the finished planting. It can be level like the Texas prairie or gently rolling with hills and valleys. In a fairly large terrarium, chunks of soft pumice rock, in which you can hollow out planting pockets for selected plants, can be used if you want the effect of mountains; or put them into the holes of interestingly shaped, partially decayed wood or driftwood.

Next comes the placement of plants. I find it best generally to add the largest ones first. In some plantings these will represent trees and shrubs in a full scale landscape. In others the

A Japanese figurine gives an Oriental-garden feeling to this pinch-sided covered bowl terrarium. Lining the figure's way are podocarpus, peperomia, ardisia, and pilea.

largest, feature plant may be something like a flowering African violet. Remove each plant from the pot in which it has been growing. Using your fingers, gently work away some of the soil so that the roots are free to nestle into the terrarium soil.

After the larger plants are in place you can add the ground covers — little creepers and carpeters that help give a terrarium a finished appearance.

Next come the finishing touches, and herein lies a world of imagination. If you want the effect of a woodland dell, then you will probably add bits of lichen and mosses, perhaps a few twigs or chunks of weathered bark.

If you are working with cacti and other succulents to create a desertscape, sand is the obvious finishing touch (for the soil, see Chapter 18).

If you want an Oriental landscape in miniature, experiment with rounded, water-polished stones. You might also add an area of sand which can be raked, Japanese-fashion, with the tines of a fork.

One of the simplest ways to complete a terrarium is to carpet any bare soil with pieces of woods moss, florists' sheet moss (available from most local florists), or marble chips.

I have previously given short shrift to the use of animal and human figurines in terrarium plantings. But having seen them used tastefully by my fellow authors Virginie and George A. Elbert, Jack Kramer, and Charles Marden Fitch, I have changed my mind. In fact, as I have been writing my daughter Jeannene returned from vacation with a little keepsake bird fashioned of seashells and placed it immediately in her terrarium. I have to admit the effect is delightful. Now I think of what Jeannene and I might create using dollhouse furniture. Over a patch of green moss, for example, why not spread a tiny picnic cloth complete with doll dishes and a Lilliputian food basket?

This is a marvelous side benefit of terrarium gardening as a hobby. People of all ages enjoy it alone or together. Shopping for the plants is only the beginning. There's the fun of searching through antique and junk shops with an eye for discovering some great container for a

ABOVE: An open globe terrarium with ceramic partridges amid ardisias, pilea, and interesting twigs.

BELOW: Canister terrarium with miniature English ivy, selaginellas, and a rooted tip cutting of Christmas cactus.

ABOVE: Seedling of feathery fine Asparagus plumosus *grows in a bowl with tiny seashells accompanied by one larger shell for accent.*

BELOW: Crystal ball with plastic base forecasts a world of miniature gloxinia, podocarpus, fittonia, and selaginella.

terrarium or an interesting figurine, to mimic the human or animal scale. Collections of stones or seashells can provide the design of a terrarium in a unique display.

A body of water in your terrarium scheme can be simulated by clever placement of a small pocket mirror, or you can actually use a shallow container of water. Which brings me to another suggestion: From time to time insert a small vial of water in your terrarium and place in it some beautiful flower, perhaps picked from your garden indoors or outdoors, or salvaged from a bouquet you are about to throw away. Especially delightful in the spring are a few stems of lily-of-the-valley, wild sweet violets, forget-me-nots, or primroses.

As you shape the placement of plants, remember to check the appearance from the front as well as the top. If a container will be viewed from all sides, your design becomes more complicated than if it will be viewed primarily from only one side. Looking directly into the sides you actually can see the outer edges as a frame for the picture you create inside.

Consider also the appearance of the gravel, charcoal, and potting soil. The different textures and colors are usually attractive, but if you prefer a more subtle appearance, it is possible to work woods moss and florists' sheet moss, green side facing out, between the walls of the container and the various layers of the growing medium.

If you are planting in a tall container you may want to add more than the three layers of gravel, charcoal, and potting soil. You might alternate layers of gravel, sandstone pebbles, charcoal, and sand of various colors, finally topping them with potting soil. Pieces of nylon stocking cut slightly smaller than the dimensions of the container and placed on top of each layer will help keep the different layers unmixed over a long period of time.

OPPOSITE: Plantings in this covered brandy snifter include young sempervivums, maranta (prayer plant), rooted tip cuttings of Zebrina, dwarf palm, and a miniature gloxinia in bloom. Because of moisture, real-feathered bird will eventually deteriorate. Use only figurines of durable materials in your terrariums.

Variegated 'Glacier' English ivy, Dracaena godseffiana, *and podocarpus are handsomely set off by the sandpainting at the base of this candy jar canister terrarium.*

The most recent development in terrarium plantings has been the use of different colored sands to create the effect of a painted desert in the lower part of the container with plants above. Packets of many-colored sand are available wherever terrarium supplies are sold. I feel these sand paintings are more natural in the company of cacti and other desert succulents than with jungle foliage and flowering plants.

Basic Terrarium Maintenance

After all plants and finishing touches are in place, take a soft-bristled camel's-hair brush and remove bits of soil and moss from leaves and the walls of the container. Using a bulb baster from the kitchen, add only enough water to barely moisten the roots in place. Re-member, terrariums have no provision for drainage of excess water. Add a little water in the beginning. The next day poke your finger in the surface soil. It should feel nicely moist; not wet and muddy, not dusty and dry.

If your terrarium with a large opening has a cover, put this in place as soon as you have finished watering. If, after the cover is in place for a few days, the walls of the terrarium are completely clouded with condensed moisture so the plants are not clearly visible, remove the cover overnight; replace the following morning. If, after a few hours, the walls are again clouded with moisture, repeat the procedure. Continue this practice until the walls are mostly free of extensive condensation.

When to add water is one of the most difficult aspects of terrarium gardening. However, in containers with openings you can put your

A sandpainting of a mountainous landscape forms the base of this Plexiglas terrarium "house." Plantings include English ivy, pilea, pteris ferns, and selaginella.

hand through, deciding is somewhat easier. For plants in the *woodsy moist* category (described in detail on page 182), the top inch of potting soil should feel barely moist before you add water. Plants in the *desert* category (see Chapter 18) should have water added if the soil an inch below the surface feels only faintly damp to your finger. The roots of cacti and other succulents are highly susceptible to rot if overwatered, especially immediately after transplanting.

The rest of terrarium maintenance is mostly routine garden work on a miniature scale. Clip and remove any dead leaves or spent flowers. Prune back any plant that is growing too large or rank in height or girth. If a plant dies, or is obviously too large for the container, replace it with another.

Is feeding necessary? Sometimes, but not al-

ways. After a terrarium planting has been growing for about three months, I usually add a little diluted fertilizer three or four times a year, mixing it at one-fourth the usual strength for potted house plants and adding it then as a part of the watering routine.

What about pests inside a terrarium? They're not likely to bother if you have examined and cleaned every plant carefully before placing it inside the terrarium. Even so, you may occasionally discover a slug or snail dining inside. Insects like mealybugs, red spider-mite, cyclamen mite, white fly, scale, and thrips (what a formidable lineup!) require a different tactic. Whatever you do, do not spray an aerosol of house-plant pesticide inside a terrarium; it will coat the walls with an oily film that is difficult to remove. One easy way to eradicate these insects is to cut off an inch-long

A shallow bowl planting with two kinds of hoya (wax plant), ardisia, watermelon-begonia peperomia, and a variegated-leaved peperomia. Tall ardisia is overgrown and should be removed to give remaining plants more room.

piece of a Shell No-Pest Strip and place it inside the terrarium. Fumes given off from the strip (Vapona is the chemical responsible) will kill the bugs without any further effort on your part. The other way is to mix a liquid houseplant pesticide in a small atomizer or plant mister; line the inside walls of the terrarium with paper toweling, then carefully spray the infested plants.

Complete overhaul of a terrarium is generally not needed for at least two years, if you are faithful about grooming and pruning the plants.

What about leaving your terrarium unattended? You are the best person to answer this, for you will discover how frequently each terrarium needs to be watered. Closed containers can be left unattended for weeks, if not months. If they are growing under fluorescent lights, it will be necessary to plug the unit into an automatic timer; 14 to 16 hours of light every day produce excellent results for most plants, although some gardeners reduce light to 12 hours in every 24 while they are absent for extended periods of time.

If you have an open terrarium growing in sunlight, especially if it is filled with plants other than cacti and succulents, they probably require fairly frequent applications of small quantities of water. If the time you will be away is longer than the usual lapse between waterings there are two things you can do: (1) Ask someone to come in and give your terrarium a drink of water — but leave written instructions about how much and how often, otherwise you may return to a bog garden; or (2) place a cover over your terrarium and move it out of direct sunlight.

16
Planting Bottle Gardens

Since you can't reach your hands into that small an opening to plant a bottle or other "closed" container, you will require some special tools. All of these tools you can improvise from materials found around most households:

1. Bulb baster from the kitchen for watering
2. A slender wooden dowel or bamboo plant stake at least 6 inches longer than the height of the bottle, or a planter tool (see page 178)
3. A length of wire coat hanger, bent with a small loop on one end to position plants and materials inside the bottle, with a handle by which to hold it bent on the other end (see shovel tool, page 178)
4. A second length of wire coat hanger with a bottle cork stuck onto one end (the cork must be slightly smaller than the bottle neck) to use as a soil tamper to firm roots in place, or a tamp tool (see page 178)
5. A second piece of wooden dowel with a single-edge razor blade attached to one end, or a pruning instrument (see page 179)
6. A funnel; or, instead, a piece of fairly stiff paper rolled into a funnel shape

In addition to these six bottle gardening tools, I sometimes have taped a demitasse spoon on the end of a long wooden dowel or bamboo stake to serve as a trowel. To remove particles of planting medium from the leaves you can tape a small camel's-hair brush to the same kind of dowel or stake. To remove dead leaves and flowers and growth you have cut with your pruning shears, a mechanic's pickup tool is a great help; you can purchase such tools at an automobile parts supply house or wherever terrarium supplies are sold. Long, slender, wooden terrarium tongs also make a worthwhile investment.

After you assemble your tools, plants, gravel, charcoal, potting soil, moss for ground cover, and any other finishing touches, clean the bottle. First rinse out with warm water to which a little household detergent has been added. Stubborn stains may require soaking for a time in household bleach. Of course, using an aerosol houseplant spray inside a laboratory flask that has a long, slender neck creates an impossible problem of cleaning, as implied in the previous chapter.

Once the bottle is clean, rinse it several times with clean water, then set

ABOVE: Start your bottle terrarium by pouring in, with the aid of a funnel, layers of gravel, charcoal, and potting soil.
BELOW: Position the plant and tamp soil around roots with long-handled tool or heavy-gauge wire.

Remove soil from the roots of the plant (in this case, a peperomia), and drop it through the bottle opening.

aside to dry in a warm place. If the inside walls are wet, every flying particle of planting medium will stick on them. When dry, you will have to use a funnel to add layers of gravel, charcoal, and potting soil. After you add each layer use a piece of dowel, bamboo stake, coat hanger with a loop, or stake with a demitasse spoon attached to shape the terrain.

Before you begin to place plants inside the bottle, set it on a piece of paper and, with a pencil, draw a line around it. Set the bottle aside and experiment with various arrangements of your plants inside the circle (or other shape) you have drawn. Once you have marked out an arrangement that is pleasing, proceed by inserting one plant at a time through the neck of the bottle and settling it in place as nearly as possible to the position it occupied on your paper pattern.

OPPOSITE: A wide mouth jar (opening is large enough for most hands to fit inside). Plants include syngonium, Gesneria cuneifolia, English ivy, selaginella, ardisia, and pteris ferns.

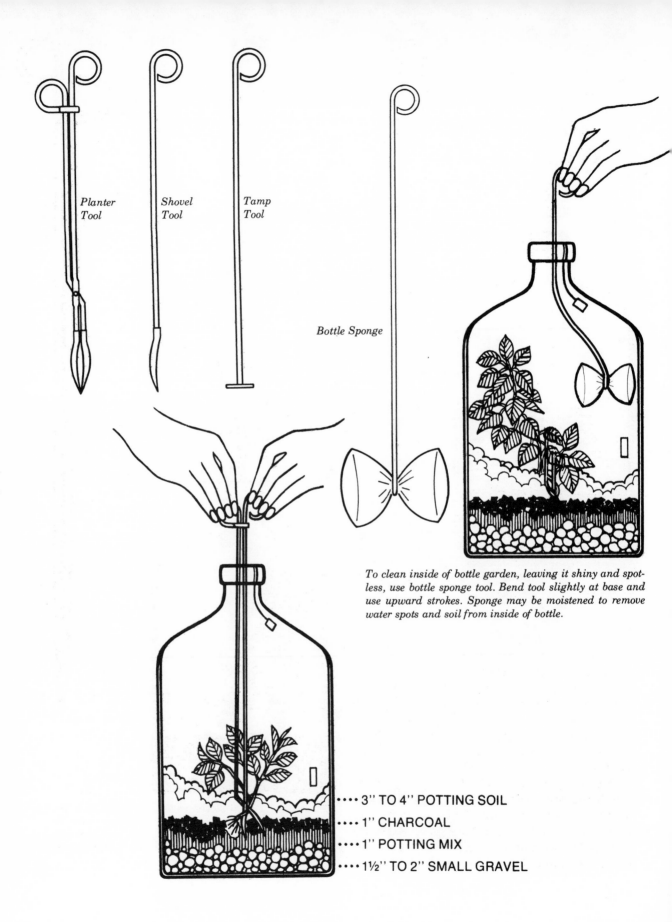

*Planter
Tool*

*Shovel
Tool*

*Tamp
Tool*

Bottle Sponge

To clean inside of bottle garden, leaving it shiny and spot-
less, use bottle sponge tool. Bend tool slightly at base and
use upward strokes. Sponge may be moistened to remove
water spots and soil from inside of bottle.

•••• 3'' TO 4'' POTTING SOIL

•••• 1'' CHARCOAL

•••• 1'' POTTING MIX

•••• 1½'' TO 2'' SMALL GRAVEL

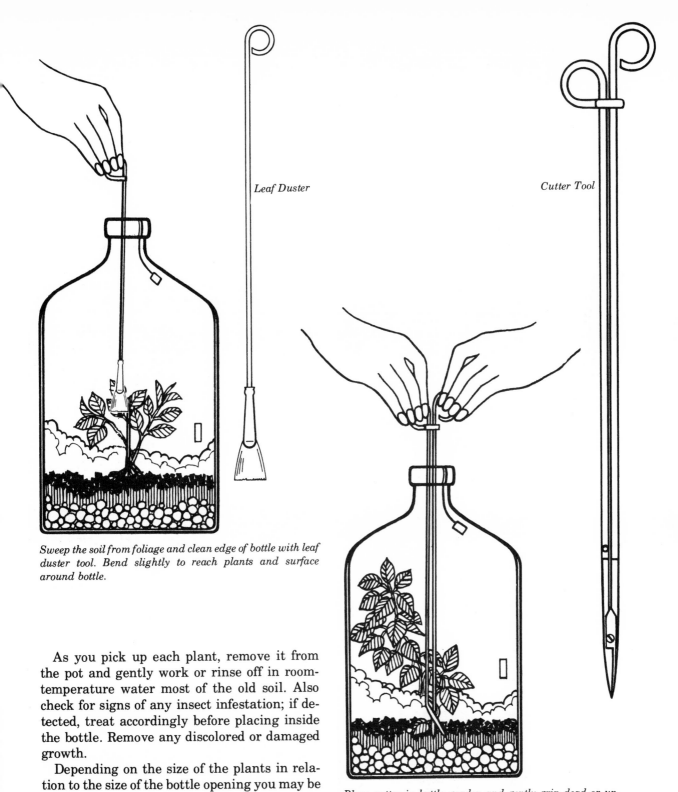

Leaf Duster

Cutter Tool

Sweep the soil from foliage and clean edge of bottle with leaf duster tool. Bend slightly to reach plants and surface around bottle.

As you pick up each plant, remove it from the pot and gently work or rinse off in room-temperature water most of the old soil. Also check for signs of any insect infestation; if detected, treat accordingly before placing inside the bottle. Remove any discolored or damaged growth.

Depending on the size of the plants in relation to the size of the bottle opening you may be able to lower them within the loop of your wire coat hanger tool, or you may have to simply coil the leaves gently around so that the plant alone slips through the neck and drops onto the

Place cutter in bottle garden and gently grip dead or unwanted leaves from plants; lift out of bottle with cutter. To remove plants that have grown too large, clip back with cutter tool at base of root (leave roots intact). Lift trimmings from bottle with tool.

soil surface. Once the plant is inside the bottle use one or more of your long-handled tools and position it and cover the roots with soil.

After all plants are in place you can proceed to add moss ground cover, pebbles, or any other finishing touches. Next, use the camel's-hair brush to clean foliage and flowers and the interior walls of any particles of earth. Finally, draw a little room-temperature water into the bulb baster and rinse down the walls and any leaves or flowers that may have stubborn particles of soil remaining on them. Be very careful about adding too much water to a bottle garden, however.

Maintenance thereafter is approximately the same for a closed terrarium as for one that is open.

An interesting alternative to placing plants inside a bottle is simply to plant a few seeds of one kind of plant, or perhaps several compatible kinds. In a very small bottle you might, for example, drop a few seeds of *Sinningia pusilla* or any other miniature gloxinia. Then you'll have the fun of watching for them to sprout, grow, and eventually reach flowering size. In a gallon to 5-gallon size bottle you might plant a few seeds of hybrid African violets, spores of miniature fern, or whatever small-growing plant appeals to you.

If all this sounds like a lot of trouble, may I assure you that there are terrariums which are practically carefree for months if not years. I have a 2-gallon bottle in my office bookcase that was planted five years ago with one rooted cutting of *Philodendron sodiroi*. Today it has nearly filled the space inside with silvery heart-shaped leaves, yet it receives only a half cup of water once every month or two. It has never been necessary to feed it or even to remove a dead leaf. I have seen similar bottle gardens filled with ferns or with selaginellas that exist beautifully with practically no care.

ABOVE LEFT: White and reddish brown stone chips accent a planting of two kinds of peperomia. Ardisia peeps out of the hand-cut hole.

LEFT: A large water bottle turned on its side with a hole cut in top (available commercially) for easy access. Plants have been planted at different levels for design interest. They include hoya (wax plant), peperomia, and ardisia.

17
Terrarium Plants

In each plant description that follows, you will find a set of cultural terms. To save space these are somewhat abbreviated. Here is the key:

Rooted Cutting: You may plant a rooted cutting in the terrarium, if so designated in the description. *Un*rooted cuttings of most plants placed in the constant warmth and moisture of a *closed* terrarium will promptly form roots and proceed into active growth.

Young Plant: One step beyond a rooted cutting; the sort of specimen shipped by many mail-order specialists, usually in a 2¼-inch pot. Also the kind of plant often found in the garden departments of dimestores, supermarkets, and florists.

Closed: This indicates a plant that tolerates — or needs — the relatively high humidity of a closed terrarium, which may be a container with a large opening that has a glass or plastic cover, or a bottle or jug with a small neck that may or may not have a cork or plug. Plants designated for a closed container that also require sun or half sun are best cultivated in fluorescent light.

Open: Such a plant either requires or will tolerate the open air of the indoor environment. A container is considered *open* if the opening is equal to half or more the dimensions of the container.

Warm: Translate to temperatures that would be comfortable for you, wearing normal at-home clothing. Specifically a range of 65° to 75° F.

Cool: A temperature range of approximately 50° to 60° F. in winter (while artificial heat is being used to warm the house or apartment).

Sunny: A situation that receives direct sunlight; east, south, and west windows generally qualify.

Half Sun: Very bright indirect light most of the day (for example, 5 feet back from a south-facing, sunny exposure), or a few hours direct sun early in the morning or late in the afternoon.

Note: Plants designated for *closed* and *half sun* require careful handling unless you cultivate them in a fluorescent-light garden. Be very careful about letting really hot midday sun shine directly on a closed terrarium or bottle garden. Plants that require some sun in combination with high humidity will generally adapt to a situation where daylight is constantly bright but without much sun shining directly on the leaves.

Fluorescent Light: Illumination for 12 to 16 hours out of every 24 in a fluorescent-light garden. Most terrarium plants do well in a range between 6 and 12 inches below the fluorescent tubes.

Woodsy Moist: This describes a humusy growing medium that is kept evenly moist at all times. Special terrarium planting mixes, sold as such in garden stores and plant shops, qualify as woodsy.

Desert: A sandy growing medium, indicated on the package as being formulated for cacti and other desert succulents. Maintain moisture in a range between nicely moist and nearly dry.

Osmunda and Fir-Bark: Some epiphytic orchids and bromeliads require osmunda or fir-bark as the growing medium. These are available mostly from growers who specialize in orchids and bromeliads.

As you make choices from these plants, keep in mind this basic, good rule of (green) thumb: You'll have best results if you combine plants with the same (or similar) cultural requirements in the same container. However, you can mix something that needs woodsy, moist soil with, for example, an epiphytic orchid or bromeliad that needs moist osmunda as the growing medium simply by raising this slightly above the soil level.

If you have a particular container in mind when you go shopping for terrarium plants, take along its dimensions and a ruler or tapemeasure. In this way you'll be prepared to purchase only plants of suitable size.

Sources for all of these plants are listed in the Appendix, many of them may also be found locally.

Little Encyclopedia of Terrarium Plants

Abutilon: Flowering maple. *A. megapotamicum variegatum* has small variegated leaves on semitrailing stems, yellow flowers. Plant at the crest of a hill, mound, or rock in a large terrarium; stems need room to trail down in a cascade. Rooted cutting or young

ABOVE: *Achimines 'Mexicana Blue.'*

ABOVE: *Ardisia.* BELOW: *Begonia 'Black Falcon.'*

plant. Closed or open. Warm. Sunny to half sun. Fluorescent light. Woodsy moist.

Achimenes: Magic flower. A gesneriad, related to the African violet. Grows from a catkinlike scaly rhizome; plant in spring for summer and autumn flowers. Rest rhizomes in winter in darkness with moderate temperatures; keep nearly dry. During first two months of growth, pinch out growing tips frequently to encourage branching. For fairly large terrarium or case. Closed. Warm. Half sun. Fluorescent light. Woodsy moist.

Acorus: Miniature sweet flag. Select either *A. gramineus pusillus* or *A. g. variegatus.* Clumps of green or green-and-white leaves like 3-inch miniatures of common garden iris. Miniature. Closed. Cool to warm. Half sun to shade. Fluorescent light. Woodsy, very moist.

Actiniopteris: Fern. Miniature. Closed. Warm. Shade. Fluorescent light. Woodsy moist.

Adiantum: Maidenhair fern. Best for terrariums are the species that stay small naturally; for example, *A. bellum, A. diaphanum,* 'Ocean Spray,' and *A. reniforme.* However, a young plant of any maidenhair fern can be enjoyed for a time in cramped quarters and then transplanted elsewhere when it grows too large. Miniature or young plant. Closed. Cool to warm. Shade. Fluorescent light. Woodsy moist.

Aechmea: Bromeliad. Select naturally small-growing types, for example, *A. recurvata benrathii* and *A. tillandsioides,* or young plants of larger kinds. Closed. Warm. Half sun. Fluorescent light. Moist osmunda.

Aerides: Epiphytic orchids. Naturally small-growing kinds such as *A. crassifolium* and *A. japonicum* are best for terrariums. Closed. Warm. Half sun. Fluorescent light. Moist osmunda.

Aeschynanthus: Gesneriad. Lipstick Vine. Eventually becomes a large plant of many cascading stems; however, young rooted cuttings make fine terrarium plants. Excessive growth can be pruned off easily. Closed. Warm. Half sun. Fluorescent light. Woodsy moist.

Agalmyla: A little-known gesneriad, related to the African violet. Red flowers on creeping stems. Miniature. Closed. Warm. Half sun. Fluorescent light. Woodsy moist.

Aglaonema: Chinese evergreen. Superb foliage plants, unfortunately all too large for most terrariums. However, young plants may be enjoyed for some time. Foliage green, usually variegated with white, cream, yellow, or silver. Closed. Warm. Shade. Fluorescent light. Woodsy moist.

Allium: Chives. *A. schoenoprasum,* the chives used in cooking, are easily cultivated in a terrarium. The problem is that the plant tends to be stringy and weak unless it receives an abundance of light and fresh air. However, if you clip it back enough, the results are not all that bad, and besides you will have lots of fresh, tasty snippets to use in the kitchen. Start with seeds or a young, established plant. Open. Cool to warm. Sunny. Fluorescent light. Woodsy moist.

Allophyton: Mexican foxglove. Rosettes of quilted, dark green leaves with clusters of white, lavender, and purple foxglovelike flowers on slender 6-inch stems. Miniature. Closed. Warm. Half sun. Fluorescent light. Woodsy moist.

Alloplectus: Extraordinarily handsome — and large — foliage plants, related to the African violet. They require more warmth and humidity than can be provided in the open air of most homes, but young plants or rooted cuttings can be cultivated quite well in a large terrarium. Closed. Warm. Half sun. Fluorescent light. Woodsy moist.

Alternanthera: Dwarf Joseph's coat. Rooted cuttings or young plants. Shear or clip back regularly to maintain compact growth. Closed or open. Warm. Sunny. Fluorescent light. Woodsy moist.

Ananas: Pineapple. Miniature *A. nanus* is suitable for a fairly large terrarium. Closed. Warm. Sunny to half sun. Fluorescent light. Woodsy moist.

Anoectochilus: Dwarf jewel orchid. *A. sikkimensis* is excellent for terrariums. Closed. Warm. Half sun to shade. Fluorescent light. Woodsy moist.

Anthurium: Related to the philodendron. Species *A. clarinervum* and *A. crystallinum* have green heart-shaped leaves with silvery white veins. Showy in a fairly large terrarium. Closed. Warm. Half sun to shade. Fluorescent light. Woodsy moist.

ABOVE: *Begonia weltonensis*. BELOW: *Begonia 'Iron Cross.'*

BELOW: *Miniature rex begonia.*

Aphelandra: Zebra plant. Rooted tip cuttings are excellent in a terrarium. When an aphelandra begins to outgrow the space, simply chop it back and make new cuttings of appropriate size. Closed. Warm. Half sun. Fluorescent light. Woodsy moist to wet.

Araucaria: Norfolk Island Pine. Seedlings of *A. excelsa* grow slowly and may be enjoyed for up to two years — or even more — in a terrarium. Closed. Cool to warm. Half sun to shade. Fluorescent light. Woodsy moist.

Ardisia: Coralberry. Seedlings and rooted cuttings are popular for terrariums. Nipping out the growing tip will encourage branching. After a few years it will be necessary to root cuttings as older plants become fairly large, woody shrubs. Closed or open. Cool to warm. Half sun to shade. Fluorescent light. Woodsy moist.

Ardisiandra: A miniature relative of the primrose. Closed. Cool to warm. Half sun. Fluorescent light. Woodsy moist.

Ascocentrum: Orchid. *A. miniatum* is especially suited to a terrarium. Closed. Warm. Half sun to shade. Fluorescent light. Moist osmunda.

Asparagus: Young plants of *A. plumosus*, the kind of filmy fernlike leaves you see with a bouquet of roses, may be cultivated in a terrarium. Since this plant has a large and voracious root system, you will find it best to keep it confined in a pot, which you can conceal with rocks or a mound of soil. Closed or open. Warm. Half sun to shade. Fluorescent light. Woodsy moist.

Asplenium: Young plants of the bird's-nest fern (*A. nidus*) and the mother fern (*A. viviparum)* are outstanding for terrariums. Closed. Warm. Shade. Fluorescent light. Woodsy moist to wet.

Aucuba: Gold dust tree. Young, rooted tip cuttings of this plant do well for several months, if not more, in a fairly large terrarium. Green leaves dusted and flecked with golden yellow. Closed or open. Warm. Half sun to shade. Fluorescent light. Woodsy moist.

Begonia: Some of the most beautiful of all begonias grow best in terrariums where they can be surrounded constantly by warmth and high humidity. Some of the best from which to select include: *B. aridicaulis,* 'Baby Perfection,' *B. bartonea* (winter jewel), *B. boweri,* 'Bow-nigra,' 'Chantilly Lace,' 'China Doll,' 'Dawn,' 'Edith M,' *B. hirtella nana,* 'It,' *B. masoniana* (iron cross), 'Medora,' 'Persian Brocade,' *B. prismatocarpa* and *B. rex* cultivars 'Baby Rainbow,' 'Dew Drop,' and 'Silver Dawn.' The exquisite *B. imperialis* and its varieties are also excellent, either alone in a small container (for example, a 12-inch bubble bowl with lid) or in a fairly large terrarium with other plants. Closed. Warm. Half sun to shade. Fluorescent light. Woodsy moist.

Bertolonia: Soft-haired and quilted leaves in colors reminiscent of begonias. Mostly low-growing and miniature. Closed. Warm. Shade. Fluorescent light. Woodsy moist.

Billbergia: Bromeliad. Rooted cuttings or young plants may be small enough to enjoy for a time in a terrarium. Closed. Warm. Sunny to half sun. Fluorescent light. Woodsy moist.

Biophytum: Sensitive life plant. A miniature difficult to obtain except in seed form. Closed. Warm. Sunny to half sun. Fluorescent light. Woodsy moist.

Boea: A flowering, upright, but miniature, relative of the African violet. Difficult to grow except in a terrarium. Closed. Warm. Half sun to shade. Fluorescent light. Woodsy moist.

Bulbophyllum: Orchid. Study current listings of orchid specialists to find miniature species which will be included along with other "botanicals." Closed. Warm. Half sun. Fluorescent light. Moist osmunda.

Buxus: Boxwood. *B. microphylla japonica* is especially useful in fairly large terrariums or trough gardens where a small green shrub is needed. Open. Cool. Sunny. Fluorescent light. Woodsy moist.

Caladium: Miniature *C. humboldtii* (sometimes called *C. argyrites*) is a jewel for terrariums — but difficult to obtain. Closed. Warm. Sunny to half sun; may adapt to shade. Fluorescent light. Woodsy moist.

Calathea: Showy tropical foliage plants. Study growers' listings (see Appendix) for kinds that grow smallest by nature. One of the best for terrariums is *C. micans.* Closed. Warm. Half sun to shade. Fluorescent light. Woodsy moist.

Callisia: Small creeper related to the wandering Jew. Closed or open. Warm. Half sun. Fluorescent light. Woodsy moist.

Callopsis: Like a miniature calla-lily, to which it is related. Closed. Warm. Half sun to shade. Fluorescent light. Woodsy moist.

Carex: Grassy, tufting plants. Closed. Warm. Half sun to shade. Fluorescent light. Woodsy moist to wet.

Carissa: Natal-plum. *C. grandiflora nana* and other dwarf or miniature forms are best for terrariums. Closed or open. Warm. Sunny to half sun. Fluorescent light. Woodsy moist.

Ceropegia: Rosary vine. Dangling vines that become creepers in a terrarium. Do not plant in a bottle as *Ceropegia* requires too much cutting back to keep it in control. Closed or open. Warm. Sunny to shade. Fluorescent light. Woodsy moist to desert.

Chaenostoma: Little Stars. Shrubby, low perennial with flowers in season. Shear or clip back to encourage compact growth. Warm. Open or closed. Sunny or fluorescent light. Woodsy moist to desert.

Chamaedorea: Dwarf palm. *C. elegans bella* is the Neanthe bella of florists. Seedlings are excellent as "trees" in a terrarium planting with tiny creepers like selaginella and miniature flowering plants like *Sinningia pusilla.* Since palms do not lend themselves to pruning back, replacement with a new seedling may be required in a year or two. Closed. Warm. Shade. Fluorescent light. Woodsy moist.

Chamaeranthemum: Ground-hugging creepers with attractively variegated foliage. Miniature to dwarf in size. Closed. Warm. Half sun to shade. Fluorescent light. Woodsy moist.

Chimaphila: Pipsissewa. Princess pine. Ground carpeters found in pine woods. They appear to be seedling evergreens. If you own or have free access to the woods and want to try collecting one or two *Chimaphilas for a* terrarium, fine, otherwise order from a specialist. Closed. Cool. Shade. Fluorescent light. Woodsy moist.

Chirita: A gesneriad, related to the African violet. *C. sinensis* is a showy foliage plant, excellent for terrarium culture. Closed. Warm. Half sun to shade. Fluorescent light. Woodsy moist.

Upright hexagonal with variegated chlorophytum (spider plant), artillery fern, variegated plectranthus, and pellionia.

Chlorophytum: Spider plant. *C. bichetti* is the only form suited to permanent residency in a terrarium. It forms clumps of grassy green leaves with pure white margins. A choice plant. Closed or open. Warm. Half sun to shade. Fluorescent light. Woodsy moist.

Cissus: Young plants of miniature kangaroo vine (*C. antarctica minima*), *C. discolor* (sometimes called the rex begonia vine because of the beautiful foliage coloration), and miniature grape-ivy *(C. striata)* are excellent for large terrariums. Closed. Warm. Half sun to shade. Fluorescent light. Woodsy moist.

Citrus: Seedlings sprouted from pits saved from any citrus fruit — oranges, lemons, limes, grapefruits — make excellent terrarium plants. With a little pruning you can keep them small for many years. Closed or open. Warm. Sunny to half sun. Fluorescent light. Woodsy moist.

Codonanthe: A gesneriad, related to the African violet. Trailing stems set with small hairy leaves and fragrant white flowers. An excellent terrarium plant, especially in fluorescent-light gardens. Start with a rooted cutting or young, established plant. Closed. Warm. Half sun. Fluorescent light. Woodsy moist.

Coelogyne: Study catalogs of orchid specialists for smallest forms of this genus; you'll find them usually in the listings of "botanicals." Closed. Warm. Half sun. Fluorescent light. Moist osmunda.

Coffea: Coffee plant. Dwarf forms of *C. arabica* make fine terrarium plants. The foliage is bright green with a glossy sheen, reminiscent of the gardenia. Seedlings, rooted cuttings, or young plants. Closed. Warm. Half sun to shade. Fluorescent light. Woodsy moist.

Coleus: Persian carpet. This foliage plant tends to outgrow a terrarium quickly. However, tip cuttings will root almost immediately wherever you plant them in a moist growing medium and humid atmosphere. Keep pinching back to cause branching. Start with seeds, tip cuttings, or young, established plants. Closed or open. Warm. Sunny to half sun. Fluorescent light. Woodsy moist.

Columnea: A gesneriad, related to the African violet. Catalogs of gesneriad specialists include long listings of columnea species and hybrids. Best for terrarium plantings are kinds that have an upright or semiupright habit. Use rooted cuttings or young plants. Some columneas tend to be nearly everblooming in a terrarium. Closed. Warm. Half sun. Fluorescent light. Woodsy moist.

Cordyline terminalis minima 'Baby Ti.'

Cordyline: Seedlings or rooted cuttings of the Hawaiian ti plant *(C. terminalis)* or its miniature form *(C. t. minima* 'Baby Ti') are excellent for terrariums. Closed. Warm. Half sun to shade. Fluorescent light. Woodsy moist.

Crossandra: Nearly everblooming with salmon-orange flowers and shiny, dark green foliage like a gardenia. Prune back as necessary to maintain desired size. Start with a seedling, a rooted cutting, or young plant. Closed. Warm. Half sun. Fluorescent light. Woodsy moist.

Cryptanthus: Earth stars. Of all the bromeliads, this genus currently offers the most material for terrarium plantings. They are also well distributed and not at all difficult

ABOVE: Crossandra. BELOW: Ctenanthe oppenheimiana tricolor.

BELOW: Dizygotheca.

to locate in local plant shops; easily obtainable by mail also. Closed or open. Warm. Half sun to shade. Fluorescent light. Woodsy moist to desert.

Ctenanthe: Showy tropical foliage plants. Only young specimens are suited to fairly large terrarium plantings. Closed. Warm. Half sun to shade. Fluorescent light. Woodsy moist.

Cuphea: Delicate appearing woody shrublet with narrow leaves and flowers of pink almost nonstop. Clippings made to maintain proper size and shape may be used for making miniature table flower arrangements. Start with rooted cuttings or a young, established plant. Closed or open. Warm. Sunny to half sun. Fluorescent light. Woodsy moist.

Cyanotis: Teddy-bear plant and pussy ears. Related to the wandering Jew. Succulent creepers. Start with rooted cuttings or young plants. Open. Warm. Sunny. Fluorescent light. Desert.

Cyclamen: Baby cyclamen, *C. neapolitanum,* is suited to a fairly large terrarium or trough garden in coolness only. Closed or open. Cool. Half sun. Fluorescent light. Woodsy moist.

Cymbalaria: Kenilworth-ivy. This creeping ground cover tends to take over a terrarium planting. However, if you keep it clipped and in its place, both the leaves and flowers are attractive. Start with a rooted cutting or young plant. Closed or open. Cool. Half sun. Fluorescent light. Woodsy moist.

Daphne: Small evergreen shrubs with intensely fragrant flowers. Young plants may be used in trough gardens or terrariums. Open. Cool. Half sun. Fluorescent light. Woodsy moist.

Davallia: Rabbit's-foot fern. Species *D. bullata* and *D. pentaphylla* are perhaps best in a terrarium, although a young (small), established plant of almost any species can be enjoyed for a time in a limited space. Closed. Warm. Half sun to shade. Fluorescent light. Woodsy moist.

Dieffenbachia: Dumb cane. This giant of the jungle is sometimes included in commercially planted terrariums and bottle gardens. This is always a mistake for the dieffenbachia has a large, hungry root system and it will almost immediately outgrow all but the largest of terrarium containers. If you receive a terrarium that includes a dieffenbachia, transplant it as soon as possible to a flower pot and replace it with something more suitable.

Diosma: Breath-of-heaven. Small shrub with pine-scented needles. Start with rooted cutting or young, established plant. Clip as necessary to maintain desired size and shape. Closed or open. Cool to warm. Sunny. Fluorescent light. Woodsy on the dry side.

Dizygotheca: False aralia. Seedlings of this plant, sometimes called false aralia or "the one that looks like marijuana," do well in terrariums for a year or two if not more. In combination with miniature creepers and little flowering plants (miniature African violets and gloxinias, for example), it will give the appearance of a palm tree. Closed or open. Warm. Half sun to shade. Fluorescent light. Woodsy moist.

Dracaena: Seedlings and rooted cuttings of many different kinds of dracaenas are widely distributed. Some of them make excellent terrarium plants for a year or two until they outgrow the space. Favorites include *D. godseffiana* (perhaps best of all as a permanent terrarium resident), *D. goldieana* while young (this particular species is difficult to find), and *D. sanderiana* (the striped leaf, bamboolike plant almost always included in commercially planted dish gardens). Closed or open. Warm. Half sun to shade. Fluorescent light. Woodsy moist.

Epigaea: Trailing arbutus. Young plants purchased from a wildflower specialist may be used in terrariums and trough gardens. Closed or open. Cool. Half sun to shade. Fluorescent light. Woodsy moist.

Episcia: Flame violet. A gesneriad, related to the African violet. Beautiful foliage varying from quilted, plain, bright green to all kinds of variegations — white, cream, pink, rose, bronze, and silvery. Flowers may be white, rose, yellow, scarlet, or lavender blue. Seedlings, rooted cuttings, or young plants. Closed. Warm. Half sun to shade. Fluorescent light. Woodsy moist.

Eranthemum: Blue sage. The species *E. nervosum* has bright blue flowers above dark green leaves. Seldom seen but very worthwhile. Start with a young plant which you will probably have to obtain by mail from a

ABOVE: Dracaena godseffiana *'Florida Beauty.'*

ABOVE: Dracaena sanderiana. *BELOW: Episcia hybrid.*

ABOVE: Episcia 'Harlequin.' BELOW: Episcia 'Pink Brocade.'

BELOW: Episcia dianthiflora.

specialist. Closed. Warm. Half sun. Fluorescent light. Woodsy moist.

Erythrodes: Jewel orchid. Exquisite foliage plants with small flowers in season. Available by mail from orchid specialists. Closed. Warm. Shade. Fluorescent light. Moist mixture of osmunda and unmilled sphagnum moss.

Euonymus: This common garden shrub is surprisingly useful in terrarium plantings, especially *E. japonicus microphyllus* and its variegated form. Closed or open. Cool to warm. Half sun to shade. Fluorescent light. Woodsy moist.

Exacum: Start these plants from seeds, which may be sown directly on the surface of moist soil in a terrarium. They bloom while quite young, especially well in a fluorescent-light garden. You'll have to constantly clip and remove dead flowers, but as new starry lavender-blue ones open, you will decide the upkeep is worthwhile. Closed or open. Warm. Half sun to shade. Fluorescent light. Woodsy moist.

Festuca: Blue fescue. Fine-textured blue-green leaves in clumps. Start with seeds or young plants. Open. Warm. Sunny. Fluorescent light. Woodsy moist to desert.

Ficus: Creeping fig. *F. pumila* and its smaller version, *F. p. minima*, make excellent carpeters for terrariums of all kinds. Start with rooted cuttings or young plants. Closed. Warm. Half sun to shade. Fluorescent light. Woodsy moist.

Fittonia: More or less ground-hugging foliage plants, green with white veins or green with rosy pink. Start with rooted cuttings or young plants. Closed. Warm. Half sun to shade. Fluorescent light. Woodsy moist.

Gesneria: This gesneriad, and African violet relative, is perhaps the best of all everblooming plants to grow in a terrarium. Kinds include *G. cuneifolia,* 'El Yunque,' 'Quebradillas,' 'Lemon Drop,' and the hybrid *G. pedicellaris* x *citrina.* Start with seeds, rooted cuttings, or young, established plants (available from gesneriad specialists). Keep dead flowers clipped off and removed from the terrarium. Closed. Warm. Half sun to shade. Fluorescent light. Woodsy moist.

Hexagonal terrarium with one panel removed for visibility in the photograph—and to facilitate planting and routine maintenance. Plants include fittonia, artillery fern, Victo-rian table ferns (Pteris), miniature English ivy, and one rooted cutting of jade plant.

Goodyera: Rattlesnake Plantain. A dwarf terrestrial orchid. Start with a young, established plant. Beautiful foliage for a terrarium. Closed. Cool to warm. Shade. Fluorescent light. Woodsy moist.

Guzmania: Bromeliad. Young plants of almost any species may be enjoyed for a time in a fairly roomy terrarium. Among the best is naturally small *G. lingulata minor flammea striata.* Closed. Warm. Half sun. Fluorescent light. Woodsy moist.

Hedera: English ivy. Small-leaved varieties are great to plant in all kinds of terrariums. Start with rooted cuttings or young plants. Miniatures tend to be upright, little bushes; others will trail or climb, depending on how you train them. Closed or open. Cool to warm. Half sun to shade. Fluorescent light. Woodsy moist.

Helxine: Baby's-tears. This little ground carpeter grows with abandon in terrariums — almost too well. Start with cuttings or young

This domed environment—called Terra-pet by the manufacturer—contains a ceramic turtle amid small-leaved *English ivy,* Helxine *(baby's-tears), pilea, moss, and a young fern.*

plants. Closed or open. Cool to warm. If open, best situated in half sun. If closed, best cultivated in a fluorescent-light garden. (Lack of sufficient light causes helxine to grow weak, stringy, and unattractive; in ample light it forms a dense mat on the surface of the ground.) Woodsy moist.

Hemigraphis: Red or flame ivy. The sort of foliage plant mostly overlooked in greenhouses and nurseries, but in the right terrarium setting it can be a beauty. Leaves metallic green with rosy or burgundy suffusion. Start with rooted cutting or established, young plant. Keep clipping back to encourage compact growth. Closed or open. Warm. Half sun to shade. Fluorescent light. Woodsy moist.

Hoya: Wax plant. Rooted cuttings and young plants of any *Hoya* may be used in terrarium plantings. Closed or open. Warm. Sunny to shade. Fluorescent light. Soil may be in a range from woodsy moist to dry (desert).

Hypocyrta: Gesneriad, related to the African violet. Study listings of gesneriad specialists and order only named hybrids such as 'Rio,' 'Mardi Gras,' and 'Tropicana.' Start with rooted cuttings or young, established plants. Closed. Warm. Half sun. Fluorescent light. Woodsy moist.

Hypoestes: Pink polka dot. Freckle Face. Olive-green leaves with pink spots and splashes. Start with a rooted tip cutting. Keep nipping and snipping or it will quickly outgrow the terrarium. Closed or open. Warm. Half sun. Fluorescent light. Woodsy moist.

Impatiens: Sultana. Any of the tender perennial *Impatiens* may be cultivated for a time as terrarium plants. The annual garden balsam is not suited to indoor culture. Of special note are the newer *Impatiens* from New Guinea which have highly colored foliage as well as flowers. Start with seeds, rooted cuttings, or young plants. Keep pruned back as necessary to maintain desired size. Closed or open. Warm. Sunny to half sun. Fluorescent light. Woodsy moist.

Iresine: Bloodleaf. Rosy red and reddish-purple leaves. Start with a young, rooted tip cutting. Tends to grow rampantly in a humid terrarium, but attractive if kept pruned. Also drops old leaves on the soil surface, so you'll have to do some raking. Closed or open. Warm. Sunny to half sun. ·Fluorescent light. Woodsy moist.

Jacobinia: In window gardens, greenhouses, and outdoors, this plant tends to be a gangly half shrub. Tip cuttings rooted in a terrarium often flower splendidly. When growth exceeds available space, remove and plant in a flower pot in the open; replace with a healthy tip cutting. Closed or open. Warm. Half sun. Fluorescent light. Woodsy moist to slightly dry.

Jasminum: Jasmine. *J. sambac* variety 'Maid of Orleans' makes an interesting trailer with fragrant white flowers for a fairly large terrarium. Start with a rooted cutting or young, established plant. Closed. Warm. Half sun. Fluorescent light. Woodsy moist.

Koellikeria: Small-growing member of the gesneriad family; culture is similar to that of the related *Achimenes* in that this plant also grows from a scaly rhizome. Closed. Warm. Half sun to shade. Fluorescent light. Woodsy moist.

Kohleria: This member of the gesneriad family grows from a scaly rhizome, as does the related *Achimenes.* Smaller growing *K. amabilis* and *K. lindeniana* have beautiful foliage as well as flowers in season. Tip cuttings of all

ABOVE: Variegated Euonymus japonicus microphyllus.

ABOVE: Ficus pumila. *BELOW: Fittonia.*

ABOVE: English ivy 'Glacier' (Hedera).

ABOVE: Ludisia *(jewel orchid). BELOW: Maranta.*

root fairly easily inside a terrarium, which means if the old plant grows too large, you simply remove it and replace with healthy cuttings. Closed. Warm. Half sun. Fluorescent light. Woodsy moist.

Lagerstroemia: Crape-myrtle. The dwarf crape-myrtlette introduced recently by the George W. Park Seed Company makes an excellent terrarium plant. Start with seeds or a young plant. Closed or open. Warm. Sunny to half sun. Fluorescent light. Woodsy moist.

Lobularia: Sweet-alyssum. This common garden annual is sometimes useful in a trough or tray garden, especially the double-flowered *L. maritima florepleno.* Start with seeds or young plants. Open. Cool. Sunny. Fluorescent light. Woodsy moist.

Lockhartia: Study catalogs of orchid specialists to find this attractive foliage and flowering plant for a terrarium. Start only with a flowering-size, established plant. Closed. Warm. Half sun to shade. Fluorescent light. Moist osmunda.

Ludisia: Jewel orchid. Sometimes listed by the name *Haemaria discolor dawsoniana.* Exquisite foliage is bronzy green with vivid pink veins. Obtain young plant from an orchid specialist. Closed. Warm. Shade. Fluorescent light. Woodsy moist.

Lycopodium: Club moss. Unusual green carpeters found on northern forest floors. Neither true mosses nor ferns, but sometimes confused with both. If you have your own woods and an abundance of club moss, try transplanting some to a terrarium. Otherwise, buy a young, established plant from a wildflower specialist. Closed. Cool. Shade. Fluorescent light. Woodsy moist.

Majorana: Sweet marjoram. Fragrant gray-green leaves on low, bushy plants. Start from seeds or purchase a young, established plant. Cut back as necessary to maintain desired size and shape; use clippings for seasoning. Open. Cool or warm. Sunny. Fluorescent light. Woodsy moist.

Malpighia: Miniature holly. *M. coccigera* forms a little twiggy shrub covered with miniature hollylike leaves. In season there are pink flowers. Start with a young plant. Prune it to shape as necessary. Closed or open. Warm. Sunny. Fluorescent light. Woodsy moist.

Neoregelia carolinae *'Tricolor.'*

Maranta: Prayer plant. Tropical foliage, beautifully colored and patterned that folds up at night. In high humidity and insufficient light, marantas tend to grow too rangy for a small terrarium. Start with healthy, young, established plants. With age, older leaves naturally turn brown, curl up, and die. Clip them off and remove from the terrarium to avoid problems of disease. Closed. Warm. Half sun to shade. Fluorescent light. Woodsy moist.

Mimosa: Sensitive plant. *M. pudica* folds up its leaves at the slightest touch. Start from seeds. Remove from terrarium when the plant ceases to be attractive. Closed or open. Warm. Sunny to half sun. Fluorescent light. Woodsy moist.

Mitchella: Partridge-berry. Evergreen creeper often found growing wild in northeastern woodlands. Obtain established plants from a wildflower specialist. Closed. Cool. Half sun to shade. Fluorescent light. Woodsy moist.

Myrtus: Myrtle. *M. communis microphylla,* the dwarf myrtle, is especially suited to terrarium plantings. It can be clipped into miniature topiary shapes. Start with rooted cuttings or young, established plants. Closed or open. Cool to warm. Sunny to half sun. Fluorescent light. Woodsy moist.

Nautilocalyx: Primarily foliage plants of the gesneriad family, and related to the African violet. Start with small rooted cuttings; pinch back to encourage branching. When plant outgrows space, remove and start over with a cutting. Closed. Warm. Half sun to shade. Fluorescent light. Woodsy moist.

Neoregelia: Bromeliad. Almost any young neoregelia may be enjoyed for a time in a terrarium planting. In time it will outgrow the

A terrarium—called Terra-dome by the manufacturer—that provides perfect growing conditions for baby spider plant, syngonium (trileaf wonder), a very young Boston fern (Nephrolepis), selaginella, and miniature rex begonia.

space and you will have to replace it with something else. Closed. Warm. Half sun. Fluorescent light. Woodsy moist.

Nephrolepis: Boston fern. Young plants may be enjoyed for several months, if not a year or more, in a terrarium. Best suited for long-range, small-space culture are the more delicate kinds such as *Whitmanii* and *Norwoodii.* Start with small, young, established plants. Closed. Warm. Half sun to shade. Fluorescent light. Woodsy moist.

Nertera: Coral bead plant. Ground carpeting creeper covered in season by orange-red berries. Start from seeds. Closed. Cool. Half sun. Fluorescent light. Woodsy moist to wet.

Ocimum: Sweet basil. Sow a few seeds of either the green or purple leaf type. Or purchase young, established plants. Constantly pinch and clip to encourage bushy, compact growth; use what you cut off for seasoning. Open. Warm. Sunny. Fluorescent light. Woodsy moist.

Oncidium: Check listings of orchid specialists for miniature *Oncidiums.* Like many epiphytes, ideally they need an atmosphere of fresh, very moist air, but more and more growers are reporting success with miniature *Oncidiums* in terrarium conditions. Closed or open (with high humidity). Warm. Half sun. Fluorescent light. Moist to dry osmunda.

Ornithocephalus: Orchid. Species fairly easily obtainable from specialists grow only 1 to 3 inches tall. Ideal for terrarium culture. Invest only in established plants. Closed. Warm. Half sun. Fluorescent light. Moist osmunda or firbark.

Osmanthus: Sweet-olive. A young, established plant of *O. fragrans* makes an unusual tall shrub or treelike addition to a fairly large terrarium. In the right light it will be nearly everblooming, each small creamy-white flower intensely fragrant. Closed or open. Cool to warm. Half sun. Fluorescent light. Woodsy moist.

Oxalis: Fire fern. *O. hedysaroides rubra* makes a beautiful foliage plant in a terrarium. If it outgrows the space, prune excess growth. Start with a rooted cutting or young, established plant. Closed or open. Warm. Sunny to half sun. Fluorescent light. Woodsy moist. Ground-carpeting *O. martiana aureo-reticulata*

Oncidium macranthum, *an orchid.*

Oxalis hedysaroides rubra *(fire fern).*

ABOVE: Assorted Paphiopedilums (ladyslipper orchids).

ABOVE: Peperomia rubella. BELOW: Peperomia 'Silver Ripples.'

has typical four-leaf clover leaves, remarkably veined in bright yellow. Best suited to fluorescent-light culture. This oxalis increases by bulblets and spreads quickly in a terrarium. Closed or open. Warm. Sunny to half sun. Fluorescent light preferable. Woodsy moist.

Paphiopedilum: Ladyslipper orchid. Check listings of orchid specialists for low-growing *Paphiopedilums.* Buy established, flowering-size plants. Closed. Warm. Shade. Fluorescent light. Woodsy moist or moist osmunda.

Pelargonium: Geranium. Varieties of miniature geranium are the right size for a terrarium but almost impossible to grow well in the average house because winter temperatures are too high, especially inside a terrarium. Keep yellowing and dead leaves and flowers removed. Start with young, established plants or rooted cuttings. Open. Cool. Sunny. Fluorescent light. Woodsy moist to nearly dry.

Pellaea: Small-growing ferns. Start with young, established plants. Closed. Cool to warm. Shade. Fluorescent light. Woodsy moist.

Pellionia: Ground-carpeting creepers with handsomely variegated foliage. Start with rooted cuttings or young, established plants. Closed. Warm. Half sun to shade. Fluorescent light. Woodsy moist.

Peperomia: Dozens of foliage plants for terrarium plantings. Like begonias, they tend to be touchy about over- and under-watering. They usually do well in soil that varies between nicely moist and just slightly dry. Start with rooted cuttings or young, established plants. Closed or open. Warm. Half sun. Fluorescent light. Woodsy moist to slightly dry.

Petrocosmea: Little-known gesneriad, a relative of the African violet. White and cream-colored flowers set amidst the softly furred leaves. Start with a young, established plant. Closed. Warm. Half sun to shade. Fluorescent light. Woodsy moist.

Petroselinum: Parsley. Buy started plants or sow a few seeds. Open. Cool to warm. Sunny. Fluorescent light. Woodsy moist.

Phalaenopsis: Moth Orchid. Dwarf species and new dwarf hybrids are outstanding for terrarium culture, especially in a fluorescent-light garden. Invest only in established plants.

Closed. Warm. Shade. Fluorescent light. Moist osmunda or fir-bark.

Philodendron: In a small terrarium, *P. sodiroi* makes an excellent plant. It has silvery green, heart-shaped leaves and can be kept small almost indefinitely. In a larger container you can plant almost any small-leaved, trailing philodendron or enjoy one of the rarer climbing sorts by providing a tree-fern bark totem on which it can climb. Start with rooted cuttings or young, established plants. Closed. Warm. Half sun to shade. Fluorescent light. Woodsy moist.

Phinaea: A gesneriad, related to the African violet. Miniature with furry grayish leaves and white flowers. Start with a young, established plant. Closed. Warm. Half sun. Fluorescent light. Woodsy moist.

Pilea: Artillery fern. Aluminum plant. Panamiga. Creeping Charlie. English Baby's-tears. All of these popular names represent different species of *Pilea*, a very useful terrarium plant. Also to consider are the newer varieties, 'Black Magic,' 'Moon Valley,' and 'Silver Tree.' Start with rooted cuttings or young, established plants. Nip back growing tips frequently to encourage compact growth. From time to time you may find it necessary to prune more severely to keep growth within space limitations. Closed or open. Warm. Half sun to shade. Fluorescent light. Woodsy moist.

Platycerium: Staghorn fern. Young plants of this fern grow beautifully in large terrariums. Remove when they begin to crowd. Closed. Warm. Half sun to shade. Fluorescent light. Woodsy, moist osmunda.

Plectranthus: Swedish ivy. This plant tends to be rampant in a terrarium, yet nothing is so easy to obtain and to grow. Be prepared to do a lot of pruning and pinching to maintain compact growth of desired size. Start with cuttings, rooted or unrooted. Closed or open. Warm. Sunny. Fluorescent light. Woodsy moist.

Pleurothallis: Orchid. Select from true miniature species, listed in catalogs of specialists. Start with established plants. Closed. Warm. Shade. Fluorescent light. Moist osmunda or fir-bark.

Podocarpus: Young, rooted cuttings of this popular outdoor hedge plant and tree are excel-

ABOVE: *Jumbo terrarium with its own pedestal. Plants are* piggyback (Tolmiea), *dwarf palm, aluminum plant,* Philodendron sodiroi, *and silver-leaved Chinese evergreen* (Aglaonema).

BELOW: *Pellionia.*

Pilea microphylla, *the artillery fern.*

lent for terrariums. Closed or open. Cool to warm. Sunny to half sun. Fluorescent light. Woodsy moist.

Polypodium: Fern. Young plants of many species may be cultivated in terrarium gardens. Naturally small kinds like *P. lycopodioides* and *P. piloselloides* may be kept indefinitely in a terrarium. Closed. Warm. Half sun to shade. Fluorescent light. Woodsy moist.

Polyscias: Aralia. Rooted cuttings can be kept to terrarium size for months if not years by pruning now and then. Unusual crinkled, parsleylike foliage and gnarled, corky gray bark. Closed or open. Warm. Half sun to shade. Fluorescent light. Woodsy moist.

Polystichum: Various species of this fern may be enjoyed in a terrarium while they are young, but the best of all is a miniature, *P. tsus-simense,* which is a truly great fern. Start with a young, established plant. Closed. Warm. Shade. Fluorescent light. Woodsy moist.

Pteris: Victorian table fern. These are avail-

Podocarpus.

Pilea 'Moon Valley.'

Polystichum tsus-simense *and* Davallia *ferns.*

ABOVE: Silver-and-green Pteris *fern. BELOW: Plain green* Pteris *fern.*

BELOW: Miniature African violet (Saintpaulia) *'Pixie Blue.'*

able in almost countless forms. As young plants, all are useful in terrariums. Closed. Warm. Shade. Fluorescent light. Woodsy moist.

Punica: Pomegranate. *P. granatum nana,* a dwarf version, is fun to cultivate in a terrarium as a young plant. Prune as necessary to maintain desired shape and size. Beautiful flowers in season. Closed or open. Warm. Sunny. Fluorescent light. Woodsy moist.

Pyrola: Shinleaf. Beautiful green leaves grow in low rosettes. The flowers are tiny waxy bells, in season. If you have your spot of woodland, you may be able to find a spare *Pyrola* to transplant, otherwise purchase an established plant from a wildflower specialist. Closed or open. Cool. Half sun to shade. Fluorescent light. Woodsy moist.

Ramonda: A gesneriad, related to the African violet, but nearly cold-hardy in up-North gardens. Under the right conditions, it makes a fine terrarium subject. Start with seeds or a young, established plant. Closed or open. Cool. Half sun to shade. Fluorescent light. Woodsy moist to on the dry side.

Rechsteineria: A gesneriad, and related to the African violet. Tuberous-rooted, like the gloxinia (known botanically as *Sinningia),* which is also related. Rechsteinerias make fine plants for a large terrarium where the constantly warm, moist atmosphere will help flowers develop properly. Closed. Warm. Half sun to shade. Fluorescent light. Woodsy moist.

Rhipsalidopsis: A jungle cactus that resembles Thanksgiving and Christmas cactus. Start with a rooted cutting or young, established plant. Closed or open. Warm. Half sun. Fluorescent light. Moist fir-bark.

Rosa: Miniature rose. Start with a young, established plant. Prune back as necessary to maintain proper size. Best for a fairly large terrarium. Open. Cool to warm. Sunny. Fluorescent light. Woodsy moist.

Rosmarinus: Rosemary. The herbalists' *R. officinalis* makes an excellent terrarium plant. Start with a rooted cutting or young established plant. Save for seasoning the parts you clip back to maintain desired size and shape. Closed or open. Cool to warm. Sunny to half sun. Fluorescent light. Woodsy moist.

Ruellia: Tropical foliage and flowering plants. Start with rooted tip cuttings or compact, young, established plants. Closed. Warm. Half sun. Fluorescent light. Woodsy moist.

Saintpaulia: African violet. Miniature varieties make excellent flowering terrarium plants. In slightly larger quarters almost any African violet can be cultivated for a year or two. The species are also interesting for terrarium plantings. Start with seeds, rooted cuttings, or young, established plants. Closed or open. Warm. Half sun to shade. Fluorescent light. Woodsy moist.

Sansevieria: Common snake plant and the bird's-nest types may not be of much interest to you, but study listings in catalogs of specialists (see Appendix) for unusual species. Mostly they are fairly large growing and more suited to dish or bowl gardens than to confinement in a terrarium. Start with young, established plants. Open. Warm. Sunny to shade. Fluorescent light (for suitably low-growing types). Woodsy moist to dry.

Saxifraga: Strawberry-geranium. Strawberry-begonia. Plain-leaved *S. stolonifera* and the white-rose-green *S. s. tricolor* are outstanding for terrarium plantings. Start with young, established plants. Closed. Cool to warm. Half sun to shade. Fluorescent light. Woodsy moist.

Scilla: The tender *S. violacea* is a beautiful foliage plant all year, with spikes of tiny flowers in season. Start with a young, established plant. In a terrarium it will multiply so that within a year you will have several, which may be left as one clump or divided. Closed or open. Warm. Half sun. Fluorescent light. Woodsy moist.

Scindapsus: Pothos. This trailing philodendronlike plant is often included in commercially planted terrariums and dish gardens. Rooted cuttings may be confined to a small space for a few weeks, or possibly months, but this is not an ideal terrarium plant. Closed or open. Warm. Half sun to shade. Fluorescent light. Woodsy moist.

Seemannia: A gesneriad, related to the African violet. Miniature to 6 inches tall with bright green leaves and orange-red flowers. May be nearly everblooming in a fluorescent-

ABOVE: Saxifraga stolonifera *(strawberry-begonia).*

ABOVE: Saxifraga stolonifera tricolor.*BELOW:* Scilla violacea.

ABOVE: Selaginella kraussiana. BELOW: Siderasis fuscata.

BELOW: Sinningia (miniature gloxinia).

light garden. Closed. Warm. Fluorescent light. Woodsy moist.

Selaginella: Sweat plant (*S. emmeliana*), spreading club moss (*S. kraussiana*), dwarf club moss (*S. k. brownii*), and *S. uncinata* are among the best of all terrarium plants. Although miniature by nature, they tend to spread and even climb (in very high humidity), so that some pruning and training is necessary from time to time. Start with rooted cuttings or young, established plants. Closed. Warm. Shade. Fluorescent light. Woodsy moist.

Serissa: Small shrublet with dark green leaves and tiny white flowers. An interesting form for terrarium plantings, especially in combination with rocks. Start with an established, young plant or rooted cutting. Closed or open. Warm. Half sun to shade. Fluorescent light. Woodsy moist.

Siderasis: This relative of the wandering Jew forms low rosettes of furry leaves that are olive-green, silvery, and burgundy colored. From time to time there are lavender-blue flowers. Excellent in a fairly large terrarium. A tidy plant that only occasionally needs to have one of the older, yellowing leaves removed. Closed or open. Warm. Half sun to shade. Fluorescent light. Woodsy moist.

Sinningia: Gloxinia. *Sinningia pusilla,* the miniature gloxinia, and any of its hybrids, along with *S. concinna* and its offspring, are superb flowering plants for all kinds of terrarium plantings. You can even plant one of these in a 2-inch clear plastic cube for a miniature terrarium. They tend to be nearly everblooming. Start with established, young plants purchased from a specialist. Many of these seed themselves, eventually forming colonies of plants in a terrarium. Closed. Warm. Half sun to shade. Fluorescent light. Woodsy moist.

Smithiantha: Members of the gesneriad family, related to African violets and gloxinia. Beautiful foliage and breathtaking flowers in season. Too large except for a sizable terrarium. Closed. Warm. Half sun. Fluorescent light. Woodsy moist.

Sonerila: Delicate foliage plants with flowers in season. Excellent miniatures. Start with established, young plants. Closed. Warm. Half sun to shade. Fluorescent light. Woodsy moist.

ABOVE: Sonerila margaritacea argentea.

Streptocarpus: A gesneriad, related to the African violet. Until recently most were too large for terrariums. However, recent hybrids like 'Mini-Nymph' and 'Netta Nymph' are excellent. They grow about a hand spread across and the flowering stems to 6 inches high. Start with young, established plants. Closed. Warm. Half sun. Fluorescent light. Woodsy moist.

Thymus: Thyme. Available in both creeping and upright forms. Start from seeds or purchase young, established plants. Shear back as necessary to maintain desired size and shape; use clippings for seasoning. Open. Cool to warm. Sunny. Fluorescent light. Woodsy moist to slightly dry.

Tillandsia: This genus of bromeliads contains many plants that may be enjoyed in a terrarium while they are young — and therefore small enough. There are also some that mature and flower as miniatures. Check with mail-order specialists in bromeliads to see what is currently available. Spanish moss, *T. usneoides,* is sometimes successfully cultivated in a terrarium that has high humidity. Closed. Warm. Half sun. Fluorescent light. Woodsy moist.

Tolmiea: Piggyback. Pickaback. This foliage plant grows much too large for most terrariums, but baby plants may be rooted and grown for some months in this manner. Closed. Cool to warm. Half sun to shade. Fluorescent light. Woodsy moist.

Tradescantia: Wandering Jew. A large grouping of foliage plants best cultivated as hanging baskets in open air. Tip cuttings root almost overnight in a terrarium and may be cultivated in this manner, but unless you constantly clip them back they will crowd out the other plants. Closed or open. Warm. Sunny to half sun. Fluorescent light. Woodsy moist.

Viola: Violet. *V. odorata,* the sweet violet, is fun to try in a terrarium. Transplant from your garden or purchase a young, established plant from a wildflower specialist (who may list other tiny violets you'd like to try — but stay away from larger kinds known popularly as violas and pansies). Closed or open. Cool. Half sun to shade. Fluorescent light. Woodsy moist.

Zebrina: Wandering Jew. See comments and culture for *Tradescantia* (also called wandering Jew).

ABOVE: Miniature Tillandsia. *BELOW:* Tolmiea.

A desertscape of miniature cacti and succulents planted in an 8-inch diameter clay saucer.

18
The Desert in Miniature

If cacti and other succulents appeal to you, try growing them in open terrariums, low dishes, trays, and pottery bowls. Keep in mind that as house plants most of them require full, direct sun for as many hours as possible each day. If you have no sunny windows, then a fluorescent-light garden can make a fairly successful substitute for the real thing.

Also remember that most of these containers have no drainage hole to allow the escape of excess water. Strive for a happy medium between dusty, bone dry (which is too dry even for desert plants) and wet.

The one problem you may have in planting cacti in any terrarium or dish garden is in handling the thorny bodies. The painless way is to take a sheet of newspaper and fold it over and over into a thick strip about 1 inch wide. Loop this around each cactus to lift, position, and hold it in place until the soil is firmed about the roots.

In the Little Encyclopedia of Desertscape Plants which follows, you will notice that each has the designation "Desert." This refers both to the composition of the planting medium and the amount of moisture it receives. Basic planting steps for a desertscape are the same as for an open terrarium (see Chapter 15). Instead of using packaged potting soil or special terrarium soil, purchase a kind labeled specifically for cacti and other desert succulents. Or mix 1 part *each* of packaged potting soil, peat moss, and perlite to 3 parts clean sharp sand.

Study all of Chapter 15, review the cacti and other succulents described and illustrated in this chapter, then proceed to create your own desert in miniature. For further information, see Part II, of this book.

ABOVE: Young aloe in flower.

ABOVE: Bishop's cap (Astrophytum). *BELOW: Young* Cereus *cactus.*

Little Encyclopedia of Desertscape Plants

Acanthocalycium: Globe cactus. Seedling or young plant. Open. Cool. Sunny. Desert.

Adromischus: Clustering succulents. Many with beautifully variegated foliage. Miniature or young plant. Open. Warm. Sunny. Fluorescent light. Desert.

Aeonium: Rosette-forming succulents. Some are naturally miniature; others can be used as young plants. Open. Warm. Half sun. Fluorescent light. Desert.

Agave: Century plant. Mostly giant rosettes of succulent leaves, but interesting subjects for containerized desertscapes while they are very young. Open. Warm. Sunny. Fluorescent light. Desert.

Aloe: Mostly large rosette-forming succulents useful in containerized desertscapes only as young plants. Open. Warm. Sunny. Fluorescent light. Desert.

Aloinopsis: Miniature succulent. Open. Warm. Sunny. Fluorescent light. Desert.

Anacampseros: Small succulents, often matforming. Rooted cuttings or young plants. Open. Warm. Sunny. Fluorescent light. Desert.

Apicra: Small succulents which may remind you of the better known aloe and haworthia. Use rooted cuttings or young plants. Open. Warm. Sunny to half sun. Fluorescent light. Desert.

Aptenia: Trailing succulent with gray and white heart-shaped leaves. The little flowers are purple. Rooted cuttings or young plants. Open. Warm. Sunny. Fluorescent light. Woodsy moist.

Argyroderma: Small, clustering succulents. Mostly of a miniature nature and excellent for containerized desertscapes. Open. Warm. Sunny. Fluorescent light. Desert.

Astrophytum: Sand dollar, bishop's cap, and other spherical succulents. Excellent for small desertscapes. Open. Warm. Sunny. Fluorescent light. Desert.

Beaucarnea: Pony-tail. Elephant's-foot. Succulent member of the lily family with a swollen base that protrudes above the soil line. Only seedlings or young plants are suited to containerized desertscapes as the *Beaucarnea*

A desert microcosm, this fishtank planting of cacti/succulents receives supplementary night light from a table lamp.

grows eventually to giant size. Open. Warm. Sunny. Fluorescent light. Desert.

Cheiridopsis: Clustering, mat-forming, or tufting succulents. Open. Warm. Sunny. Fluorescent light. Desert.

Conophytum: Miniature succulent bodies. Open. Warm. Sunny. Fluorescent light. Desert.

Coryphantha: Globe cactus. Open. Warm. Sunny. Fluorescent light. Desert.

Crassula: Jade plant. Creepers to low uprights to tree form jade plant (*C. argentea*). There are dozens of different crassulas; in fact, you might create an entire containerized des-

ertscape using only these succulents. Use seedlings, rooted cuttings, or young plants. Open. Warm. Sunny. Fluorescent light. Desert.

Delosperma: Mostly small-growing succulents. Start with rooted cuttings or young plants. Open. Warm. Sunny. Fluorescent light. Desert.

Echeveria: Succulent relatives of the crassula. Seedlings and rooted cuttings of almost all make interesting subjects for containerized desertscapes. Open. Warm. Sunny. Fluorescent light. Desert.

Echinocereus: Globe and other growth

ABOVE: Crassula tetragona. BELOW: Crassula argentea (jade plant).

shapes associated with cacti. Seedlings and rooted cuttings are useful in small desertscapes. Open. Warm. Sunny. Fluorescent light. Desert.

Echinofossulocactus: Unusual members of the cactus family. Seedlings and rooted cuttings may be used in desertscapes. Open. Warm. Sunny. Fluorescent light. Desert.

Euphorbia: Christmas poinsettia. The Christmas poinsettia is *E. pulcherrima,* but it is like the tip of an iceberg for this genus includes hundreds of fascinating succulents for containerized desertscapes. Most grow large eventually, but not before you have had years of pleasure from them. Study catalogs of cacti/succulent specialists. Start with seedlings, rooted cuttings, or young plants. Open. Warm. Sunny. Fluorescent light. Desert.

Fenestraria: Baby toes. Clustering, tufting succulents. Start with seedlings, rooted cuttings, or young plants. Open. Warm. Sunny. Fluorescent light. Desert.

Frithia: Purple baby toes. Clustered, windowed succulent. Open. Warm. Sunny. Fluorescent light. Desert.

Gasteria: Fairly large group of succulents worthy of cultivating for their handsome foliage. Start with seedlings, rooted cuttings, or young plants. Open. Warm. Half sun. Fluorescent light. Desert.

Gibbaeum: Cluster-forming succulent bodies. Start with seedlings or young plants. Open. Warm. Sunny. Fluorescent light. Desert.

Graptopetalum: Ghost plant. Interesting succulent with rosettes of silvery white leaves. Start with rooted cuttings or young plants. Open. Warm. Sunny. Fluorescent light. Desert.

Greenovia: Rosettes of blue-green succulent leaves; related to the crassula. Start with rooted cuttings or young plants. Open. Warm. Sunny. Fluorescent light. Desert.

Gymnocalycium: Globe cactus. Outstanding for desertscaping in containers. Start with seedlings or young plants. Open. Warm. Sunny. Fluorescent light. Desert.

Haworthia: A large group of rosette-forming succulents of the lily family. Start with seedlings, rooted cuttings, or young plants. Open. Warm. Half sun. Fluorescent light. Desert.

Huernia: Fascinating small succulents.

Barrel cactus (Echinocactus grusonii).

Gymnocalycium delaetii.

Gymnocalycium leeanum.

Gymnocalycium denudatum.

Gymnocalycium quehlianum.

ABOVE: Lithops in flower.

BELOW LEFT: Kleinia articulatus.

Lithops in tray garden.

Start with seedlings, rooted cuttings, or young plants. Open. Warm. Half sun. Fluorescent light. Desert.

Kalanchoe: A large genus of interesting succulents for containerized desertscapes. Some grow small naturally, others can be kept reasonably small by pruning. Start with seedlings, rooted cuttings, or young plants. Open. Warm. Sunny. Fluorescent light. Desert.

Kleinia: Succulent members of the daisy family. Start with rooted cuttings or young plants. Open. Warm. Sunny. Fluorescent light. Desert. ‛

Lampranthus: Succulent creepers, mostly with gray-green leaves and many with showy flowers in season. Open. Warm. Sunny. Fluorescent light. Desert.

Lithops: Stoneface. Living stone. Miniature succulents. Hundreds of different kinds are in cultivation. They are superb for small desertscapes. Start with seeds, seedlings, or young plants. Open. Warm. Sunny. Fluorescent light. Desert.

Lobivia: Globe cactus. Some naturally small, others suited to a small desertscape only while young. Start with seedlings or young plants. Open. Warm. Sunny. Fluorescent light. Desert.

Mammillaria: A vast grouping of succulents from the cactus family. Start with seeds, seedlings, rooted cuttings, or young plants. Open. Cool to warm. Sunny. Fluorescent light. Desert.

Melocactus: Globe or turk's cap cactus. Start with young plants. Open. Warm. Sunny. Fluorescent light. Desert.

Monanthes: Miniature succulents. Start with young plants. Open. Warm. Sunny. Fluorescent light. Desert.

Nananthus: Miniature succulents. Start with young, established plants. Open. Warm. Sunny. Fluorescent light. Desert.

Notocactus: Globe cactus. Some naturally small, others grow large with age. All are useful while young in desertscapes. Start with seedlings or young, established plants. Open. Cool to warm. Sunny. Fluorescent light. Desert.

Opuntia: Prickly-pear. Pad cactus. Mostly large succulents, but useful in containerized

ABOVE: Mammillaria euthele.

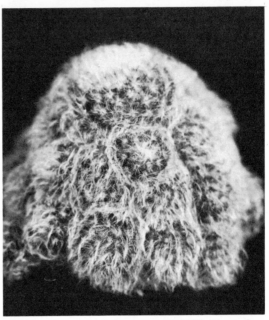

ABOVE: Mammillaria bocasana. *BELOW:* Monanthes.

Opuntia vistata.

Senecio haworthii.

desertscapes while young. Open. Warm. Sunny. Fluorescent light (only while quite small). Desert.

Pachyphytum: Beautiful foliage succulents related to the crassulas. Start with rooted cuttings or young, established plants. Open. Warm. Sunny. Fluorescent light. Desert.

Pachyveria: Hybrid succulents resulting from crosses of *Pachyphytum* and *Echeveria.* Young plants excellent for desertscapes. Open. Warm. Sunny. Fluorescent light. Desert.

Parodia: Globe cactus. Small-growing and excellent for desertscapes. Start with young plants. Open. Warm. Sunny. Fluorescent light. Desert.

Pleiospilos: Mimicry plant. Fascinating miniature succulents. Start with young established plants. Open. Warm. Sunny. Fluorescent light. Desert.

Portulacaria: Elephant bush. Young plants are easily shaped and trained to give the appearance of desert shrubs in miniature. In fact, this succulent is often used as a bonsai. Start with a young, established plant or rooted cutting. Open. Warm. Sunny. Fluorescent light. Desert.

Rebutia: Clustering miniature cacti. Outstanding for containerized desertscapes. Start

with seeds, seedlings, or young, established plants. Open. Cool to warm. Sunny. Fluorescent light. Desert.

Sedum: This group of succulents is rich in materials for desertscapes of almost all sizes. Start with rooted cuttings or young, established plants. Open. Warm. Sunny. Fluorescent light. Desert.

Sempervivum: Hen-and-chicks. Houseleek. Rosette-forming succulents of many sizes and colors for desertscapes. Open. Cool to warm. Sunny. Desert.

Senecio: This genus includes the popular florist gift plant, cineraria, but there are several succulent types you may find in the catalogs of cacti/succulent specialists. Start with rooted cuttings or young, established plants. Open. Warm. Sunny. Fluorescent light. Desert.

Stapelia: Clambering or spreading succulents with star-shaped flowers that give off a foul odor. Interesting addition to a fairly large containerized desertscape, preferably one that can be kept out of doors most of the year. Open. Warm. Sunny. Desert.

Titanopsis: Miniature succulents. Start with young, established plants. Open. Warm. Sunny. Fluorescent light. Desert.

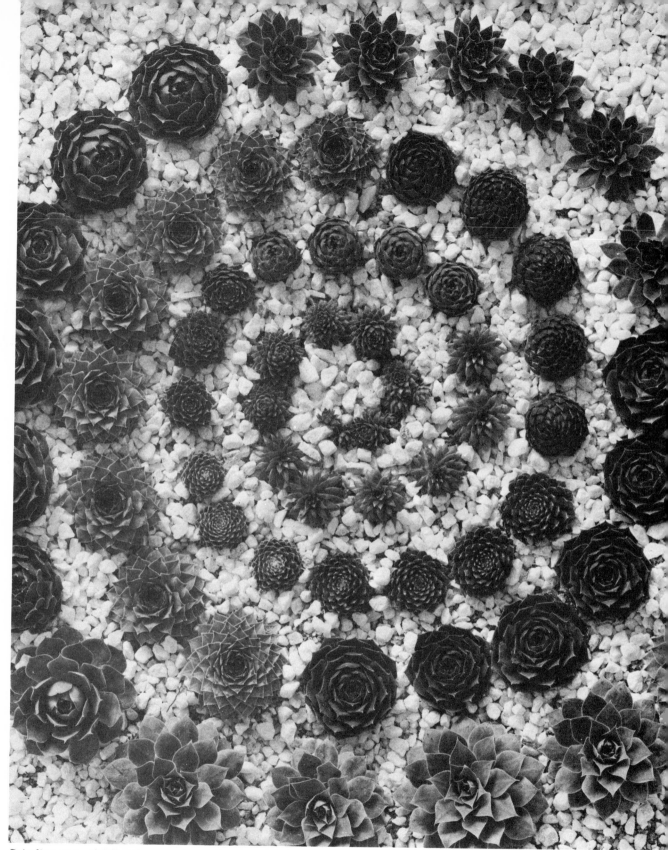

Spiraling array of different sempervivums (in tray garden with marble chip mulch) emphasizes their beauty.

19
Carnivorous Plants, Aquariums, Vivariums

Three kinds of miniature, glassed-in gardens are suggested in this chapter: terrariums of carnivorous plants, aquariums with underwater plants, and vivariums that combine plants with pets. Actually, they appeal to persons of all ages, but especially to children. They make great classroom projects, but each or all may be enjoyed even more when pursued together by an adult and a child at home.

Carnivorous Plants

Insect-eating plants are truly among the most fascinating of all living things. A closed terrarium is the only feasible way to cultivate these plants as house plants, and even then most need coolness in winter. Children can catch small live insects and place them inside the terrarium. Slowly the plants go into action, enticing and trapping the unsuspecting victims.

The list that follows includes all of the carnivorous plants commonly available and suited to terrarium culture. It is best to obtain these from specialists, not as the highly commercialized packaged products sometimes offered by mail-order houses of questionable repute.

Pinguicula: Butterwort. Carnivorous. Miniature. Start with established, young plants. Closed. Cool to warm. Shade. Fluorescent light. Woodsy wet.

Darlingtonia: Cobra Plant. Carnivorous. Strange hooded growth. Not beautiful in the usual sense but truly fascinating. Start with a young, established plant obtained from a specialist. Closed. Cool. Shade. Fluorescent light. Woodsy moist to wet.

Sarracenia: Pitcher plant. Huntsman's horn. Carnivorous. Purchase young, established plant from wildflower specialist. Closed or open. Cool. Sunny to half sun. Fluorescent light. Woodsy with unmilled sphagnum moss and wet.

Drosera: Sundew. Carnivorous. Various miniatures, all fascinating to watch in a terrarium. Start with young, established plants. Closed. Cool. Fluorescent light. Woodsy wet.

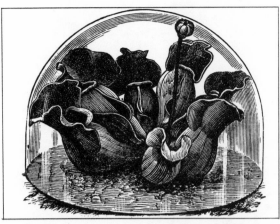

Woodcut of Sarracenia *(pitcher plant).*

Dionaea: Venus's-flytrap. Carnivorous. Miniature rosettes of spoon-shaped leaves with long teeth along the edges. If a fly stays too long on the leaf surface, it will fold together

Woodcut of Dionaea *(Venus's-flytrap).*

with the teeth interlocking like fingers clasped. Start with a young, established plant. Closed. Cool. Fluorescent light. Moist to wet unmilled sphagnum moss.

Aquarium Plants (with or without Fish)

The prettiest fresh-water aquariums with the healthiest fish are usually those well planted with aquatic plants. Some are surprisingly beautiful. Specialists stock a variety of suitable plants, but some you are likely to find

include anacharis (or elodea), eichornia, and vallisneria. Anchor the roots of these plants in an ample mound of coarse sand.

Underwater plants require relatively little light in order to thrive. A medium size aquarium with one 15- or 20-watt fluorescent over it will grow a fascinating collection of thriving aquatic plants.

Anacharis: Water-thyme. An excellent plant for the spawn of fish. The stems are covered with small leaves not unlike those of culinary thyme although the two plants are not related. Submerge in water.

Cabomba: Fanwort. Fans of threadlike leaves, reminiscent of dill foliage. Delicate in appearance but easily cultivated. One of the best oxygenators and widely distributed. Grows quickly and the color is a bright, refreshing green. Submerge in water.

Echinodorus: Amazon sword plant. Bright green spear-shaped leaves spread out in fans. Bold, tropical appearance. Submerge in water.

Hydrocleys: Water-poppy. This small plant floats on the surface of the water and produces lovely poppylike flowers in season. *H. commersonii* is the species most often cultivated in aquariums. Plant roots in a pocket of soil submerged in water.

Hygrophila: Pale green leaves have silvery undersides. Cuttings root easily. Not as well known as most other aquarium plants, but certainly worth growing. Submerge in water.

Ludwigia: This aquatic plant has rounded red and green leaves. Although it grows mostly submerged, some of the leaves will appear on the surface of the water, and in sunlight these turn coppery and red.

Myriophyllum: Two species of this plant are commonly cultivated in aquariums. *M. proserpinacoides* is almost always called parrot's feather with reference to the feathery light green leaves that grow in whorls about the stems which tend to grow out of the water and cascade attractively from the container. *M. heterophyllum* (and sometimes *M. pinnatum* and *M. rubrifolium*), also called water-milfoil, resembles cabomba but is more delicate in appearance. An excellent oxygenator. Submerge in water.

Plants submerged in water make a fascinating aquascape in this crystal temple jar.

Vivariums:
Plants and Pets Together

Mostly this book is about plants and people living together; now we add the possibility of including such creatures as chameleons, frogs, toads, and salamanders to a terrarium with a fine screened covering.

A standard rectangular fish aquarium makes an ideal container for a vivarium. At the pet store, where you can also purchase the aquarium, you will find suitable animals to place inside it. What you want to create is a natural home for the animals so that both you and they will not think of them as caged but rather in a hospitable habitat.

Before you place different kinds of animals in the vivarium, be sure that they are compatible. Generally speaking, frogs of the same size can be placed together with toads of the same size and turtles. Geckos of the same size may be placed together, along with lizards. Most lizards may be placed with other lizards of the same size and turtles. The common chameleon is compatible with horned toads.

Salamanders of the same size may be housed together, along with small frogs. Skinks and small lizards are acceptable companions. Place toads of the same size together or with lizards. Turtles do well together and with lizards.

What to Feed Your Pets

When you purchase the animals for your vivarium, ask the shopkeeper for advice about diet, care, and handling. The following suggestions will give you a general idea of what to expect.

Chameleons: Small grasshoppers, houseflies, mosquitoes, caterpillars, fruit flies, meal worms (available at your pet shop). As with the terrarium of carnivorous plants, children will often be interested in catching their food. Provide water by dropping it onto the leaves of plants.

Frogs and Toads: Cockroaches, grasshoppers, worms, plant insects (aphids, for example). Provide land and water in the vivarium.

Salamanders and Newts: Plant insects (aphids, mealybugs, for example) and worms. Provide land and water, preferably with a kind of diving-board rock jutting out over the water.

Geckos: Meal worms or live insects. Supplement this diet with a mixture of equal parts cod liver oil, honey, molasses, and a little orange juice. Provide dry land and water.

Lizards: Ants and small insects, also plant leaves. Provide a terrain that is mostly sandy and dry; stones and rocks are to their liking.

Skinks: Insect larvae, worms, grubs. Provide dry land and water.

Turtles: Best choices are land turtles or land/water turtles. Provide dry land and water. Change the water often enough to keep it clean and clear. Some turtles carry the disease salmonellosis; so it is best to purchase them with a guarantee that they are disease free. Wash hands after handling. It is a good idea not to pet them anyway — for your sake and theirs. Most turtles will eat very small bits of *raw* chicken or lean beef; also meal worms and earthworms as well as bits of carrots, lettuce, and fresh fruit. They also eat plants.

As you plan and plant your vivarium, be sure to leave plenty of open space so that the animals can move about freely.

Vivarium container with screen top and light.

*In a large terrarium or Wardian case it is possible to grow
exotic tropicals like this showy Calathea.*

20
Window Greenhouses, Wardian Cases, and Enclosed Light Gardens

You'll find on the market today a variety of large glass or plastic enclosures for growing plants. Some depend on natural light, others come equipped with fluorescent fixtures.

Table-top greenhouses are really just modern-day versions of Victorian Wardian cases. One presently on the market, available both by mail and through department and garden stores, measures 18 inches deep, 15 inches high, and 24 inches wide. The frame is made of masonite and it has 22 windows of clear plastic. One side of the roof swings open for easy access to the plants and to allow for ventilation and humidity control. This unit might be used in natural light, or a fluorescent reflector fixture with two 20-watt tubes might be suspended over it.

You can also build a table-top greenhouse, using strips of redwood for the framing and either glass, Plexiglas, or Lucite for the windows.

Inside a table-top greenhouse you can set it up as a replica in miniature of a working greenhouse, complete with benches, a narrow walkway, and thumb pots of Lilliputian plants. Add diminutive hanging baskets of tiny creepers and vines to complete the picture.

Or, you can plant the entire table-top greenhouse as a miniature landscape, the theme for which might be Japanese, complete with a footbridge, tiny stone lanterns, and a meandering stream; or an English perennial border with clumps and tufts of leafy, grassy, and flowering plants; or a woodland dell with ferns, mosses, lichen, bits of weathered bark, and some lofty trees reaching toward the greenhouse roof.

Prefabricated window greenhouses vary from small units that extend out from the window, and are installed in the same manner as an air-conditioning unit, to larger window greenhouse units, designed to cover — or extend slightly beyond — an entire window, with one or more shelves on which you can display a number of terrariums. In north light these can be open or closed; if the window greenhouse receives direct sun, place only open terrariums inside. The space inside one of these is excellent for planting a miniature landscape. Select plants according to the amount of light the window greenhouse receives.

*An empty aquarium with a 20-watt fluorescent placed over
it and burned 14 hours daily, makes a propagator.*

Decorative fluorescent unit with one 20-watt tube.

One of the most recent introductions to home greenhouses is a greenhouse terrarium 60 inches tall, 39 inches wide, and 20 inches deep. It has a white plastic frame, clear plastic covering, and a door for easy access to the two shelves inside. In this unit you might grow any number of terrariums, open or closed in north light, open if the unit receives direct sun.

In the accompanying illustrations you will also see several kinds of growth chambers, which come equipped with fluorescent light fixtures. Although the humidity inside these is too high for most cacti and other desert succulents, you can grow almost any other terrarium plants in them. These units give you complete control over all growth factors except temperature; inside these closed units with the fluorescent lights burning, temperatures are approximately 10 degrees higher than the room in which they are placed. In the average home

This plastic-covered greenhouse, designed to be placed in-doors in a sunny window, makes a large terrarium.

The Plantarium shown on these pages is available with or without fluorescent lighting.

ABOVE: African violets and Dracaena godseffiana 'Florida Beauty' thrive in the warmth and high humidity assured by this kind of growth chamber. These plants would thrive in a bright east or west window, or in a southern exposure with noonday shading.

LEFT: The same Plantarium unit is shown here planted as a large-scale terrarium with rocks, a pool of water and the soil formed into a fascinating landscape design. The plants include (from left to right) aluminum plant, aphelandra, rex begonia, maidenhair fern, and a flowering episcia.

OPPOSITE: With the addition of a fluorescent fixture with two 40-watt tubes burned 14 hours out of every 24, the Plantarium can be used to nurture flowering and foliage plants in a dark corner or hallway where no natural light reaches.

Fluorescent-lighted china cabinet holds rare plants.

this means that they are ideally suited to tropical foliage and flowering plants such as African violets, episcias, miniature gloxinias, calatheas, marantas, rex begonias, and certain exquisite orchids (any referred to as "jewel orchids").

If you have a full-scale home greenhouse, terrariums of all kinds can be cultivated to perfection. Situate the closed ones in shade; provide an appropriate amount of direct sun, depending on the kinds of plants you are growing, for the open terrariums. A home greenhouse is also a potential gold mine for propagating hundreds of different terrarium plants. One home greenhouse gardener of my acquaintance, Sandra Mauro, brings classes of school children into her greenhouse and teaches them how to make cuttings, then how to plant terrariums and bottle gardens. She uses gallon-size pickle and mayonnaise jars because they are available at no charge from commercial kitchens and the large openings make planting relatively easy for youngsters.

A greenhouse is ideal for growing miniature gardens.

Fluorescent light illuminates terrarium in a fireplace.

Miniature orchids like these cattleya hybrids will thrive in a terrarium that receives some fresh air.

*Look for the telltale spots of powdery mildew on begonia
leaves; fresh air helps avoid mildew.*

*Arrow points to coleus leaves and stems that have rotted for
lack of air circulation.*

21
Terrarium Trouble
Signs – and What to Do

If you do your homework well, more often than not a terrarium will be the most trouble-free of all gardening endeavors. However, just in case something goes wrong, here are some fairly common symptoms and suggestions for what to do about them.

Plants Tall, Lanky, Weak-Stemmed; Leaves Frail or Pale: The terrarium needs more light. The plants you are trying to grow may need more fresh air, or less water. Take this problem firmly in hand. Start over, either by removing all plants and cutting them back or by purchasing compact new ones.

Walls of Container Constantly Fogged Over Entirely with Moisture: Too much water inside. Remove cork or cover until walls are clear, then replace. If they quickly cloud over again, repeat the same procedure. Do this until they remain mostly clear, but not entirely. It is healthy for some moisture to condense on the walls and trickle back into the soil.

Leaves Wilt and Develop Yellow or Brown, Burned Spots: Too much hot sun shining directly through the walls of the terrarium onto tender leaves. Reduce amount of sun or switch to a fluorescent-light garden.

Leaves Wilt or Look Pale; Moss Ground Cover Turns Pale or Brown: The terrarium is too dry. Add a little water and mist the foliage with an atomizer.

Water Stands on Surface of the Soil; Soil and Plants Floating on Water: You've watered too much. To solve this problem in an open terrarium, take a bulb baster and draw off the excess water. In a closed terrarium, such as a bottle garden, you may find it necessary to siphon off the water by using a length of small rubber or plastic tubing.

Insects Visible on Leaves and Stems: Cut off an inch-long piece of a Shell No-Pest Strip and place it inside the terrarium. (Fumes given off by the strip [Vapona is the chemical] will kill the bugs.) In an open terrarium you can treat insect pests by mixing a liquid house-plant pesticide in a small atomizer or plant mister; line the inside walls of the terrarium with paper toweling, then carefully spray the infested plants. Under no circumstance should you spray an aerosol of house-plant pesticide inside a terrarium; it will coat the walls with an oily residue that is difficult to remove.

Leaves or Stems Rotted Off; Mold or Mildew Forms. Too much moisture; lack of air circulation. Some plants are not suited to a terrarium that is always

Arrow points to worm that has been chewing leaves.

closed. Angel-wing and semperflorens begonias, for example, will quickly develop powdery mildew in such a container.

Leaves and Stems Fill the Terrarium in a Tangled Mass of Undefined Growth: Complete replanting is in order. Completely clean out the terrarium and start over from Step 1, which is to wash it in warm soapy water, rinse, and dry. Use fresh gravel, charcoal, and potting soil. Cut back old plants, make cuttings of them (which may be rooted directly in the terrarium), or use new plants.

One Plant is Growing Rampantly, Climbing Over and Crowding Out the Others: Cut it back drastically, or remove entirely and replace with a better choice.

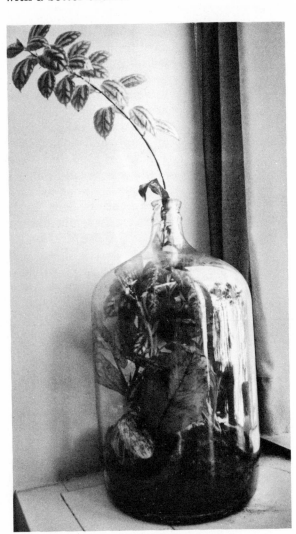

This bottle garden is badly in need of replanting.

Brown scale can be removed with tip of knife blade.

Part IV
Gardening in Containers

BY ELVIN McDONALD

22
The Movable Plants

Cleopatra did it on her barges. King Louis XIV did it at Versailles. But it is the modern-day Californians who have made container gardening our new national pastime, which may, depending on your personal interests, serve as a hobby, a sport, an avocation, or merely a pleasurable chore to make your surroundings more attractive.

Container gardening is many-sided. It is house plants and patio flowers and much more. The whole idea is based on having plants of all kinds and sizes whose roots grow in a mobile home. Mobility is the word. Indoors this means you can grow container plants where the indoor climate is to their liking, but for decorative effect you can move them around. Outdoors you can bring plants to the bud stage in a utilitarian nursery or growing-on area. When leafed out or flowering, wheel or carry them off to display at the front door or around your patio.

Besides mobility, climate is another important part of container gardening. Even in the coldest of up-North gardens you can enjoy tropicals outdoors while the weather is warm and bring them inside when cold or frost threatens. If you have a place indoors that is sunny and pleasantly warm and moist, many kinds can be kept in active growth all winter. For example, Chinese hibiscus and dwarf citrus will continue flowering. If you do not have sufficient good growing space indoors for all of your tropicals, you can maintain them in a kind of "hold" situation in any cool but frost-free place, like an unheated but light porch, until the arrival of warm weather the following summer. The key to success with this technique is to withhold all fertilizer and to keep the soil just barely moist while the plants are in a state of semidormancy.

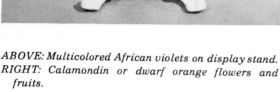

ABOVE: Multicolored African violets on display stand.
RIGHT: Calamondin or dwarf orange flowers and fruits.

Influence of the African Violet

The major influence of California gardeners on container gardening in this country had a parallel development in the rest of the country that is still very much felt today. It is traceable to one single plant, the African violet or *Saintpaulia*. By the time the African Violet Society of America was founded shortly following the end of World War II, thousands of people were growing—or trying to grow in all sorts of conditions and places—the little plant with violetlike flowers from Usambara in what was then known as East Africa. By the 1950s African violets had become a major force popularizing indoor gardening, no longer a pastime of the wealthy alone. If someone's collection outgrew window space, the problem had an instant solution in fluorescent light. In fact, fluorescent light grew such flower-covered and perfectly symmetrical plants it immediately became apparent that in the competitions staged by the African Violet Society

it was unfair to judge plants grown in natural light with those from a fluorescent-light garden.

So the African violet paved the way for tremendous development in all that houseplants and indoor gardening represent. There was exploding interest and activity to justify the development of products designed specifically for growing better plants indoors, and dozens of single plant societies and gardening clubs sprang up.

It was not long before the roof garden, the patio, the terrace, the deck and the inside garden created special problems for plants that could be moved around, inside the house and out, in season and out.

Before you can enjoy container gardening, there are certain supplies you will want to acquire. Obviously, containers of one kind or another are necessities. These, whether to buy, build or find, are discussed throughout this book, according to the various kinds of plants and situations. Remember these general rules about pots and other containers: scrub and rinse them clean before using for planting; and when a plant outgrows a container, move it to the next size larger and immediately scrub and rinse clean the outgrown container. Then you can store it away or use it for another plant.

FAR LEFT: In space 2 by 4 feet a 3-level fluorescent-light stand provides 24 square feet of growing space.

LEFT: Mobility is the advantage of container gardening, here facilitated by a plant caddy.

ABOVE: Flowers, shrubs, and trees grow in redwood planters in this spacious outdoor living area.

BELOW: Grow containers of flowers in any convenient place, then wheel them to where you want blooms.

RIGHT: Could these be Cleopatra's potted roses?

ABOVE: *Bushy young philodendrons fill this contemporary planter situated in bright light, but no direct sun.*
LEFT: *Potted succulents, marigolds, roses and geraniums bring flowers into this living area.*
BELOW: *Calathea (shown in color on the cover) thrives indoors in low-light areas; requires no direct sun.*

23
What Do Plants in Movable Containers Need?

Psychologists tell us that having plants in our environment is vital to a healthy state of mind. In an earlier, more agrarian age, this was taken for granted. Now we have a much greater awareness of every individual's need for living with living plants. This appears to be universal. It has the power to bridge every communications gap known to the human race.

Adopting one plant whose roots are confined to a pot is the first step in getting back to nature. Especially a potted plant kept indoors, where you are solely responsible for providing it with all that makes a growing environment: light, temperature, moisture and food. Outdoors a potted plant may receive some natural moisture, but indoors you are totally responsible.

Becoming involved in container gardening is something every person can do. There is no such thing as a green thumb, a purple thumb, a brown thumb, or any other color thumb except skin-colored. Every person can grow plants. The only way to fail is not to try at all. No one who really tries can be the kiss of death to flora. Even if you've tried and failed, you have to be willing to try again.

Climate. Whether you want to grow a container plant in a clay pot, a Japanese jardiniere, or an elaborate planter box, as in a Florida room, indoors or outdoors, you must first evaluate the climate where that plant will grow. Climate is a word we tend to associate with vast geographical areas. We think of vacationing in or retiring to a "warm climate." On television we watch forecasters predicting the effects of widespread winter snowstorms and we think "cold climate." But actually we live indoors and outdoors in countless mini- or microclimates. To be aware of this is the first positive step toward becoming a successful gardener.

Light, Temperature, Humidity

Let's say you want to grow a pot plant on your desk—at work or at home. Before you can determine which plant is most likely to be

*Arranging container plants in ever-changing displays
is one of the great pleasures of gardening this way.*

the right choice, think about the climate that exists on your desk. Make a checklist like this:

Light. Amount of light that reaches the surface of the desk at various times during the day. It may receive direct sun in the morning, during midday or in the afternoon. It may receive no direct sun at any time but bright daylight for several hours daily. Or it may receive no natural light at all, in which case a desk lamp may provide enough illumination to nurture a small-leaved English ivy or trailing philodendron. Full sun from an unshaded east- or west-facing window is usually referred to in most writings about house plants as *semisunny* or *semishady.* Full sun from an unshaded south-facing window translates to *sunny* or *semisunny.* Any bright exposure that receives no direct sun or only an hour or two, even a north-facing window, may be referred to as *semishady, shady,* or as bright indirect light.

Light evaluation is perhaps the most difficult part of determining the climate for a particular container plant. Generally speaking, if there is enough natural light by which to read or do needlework, there is enough light to grow certain plants that grow naturally in the shade. Throughout this book you will find discussions of various kinds of plants and with each a suggestion as to light requirement indoors or out. Since most plants are rather demonstrative about receiving too much light (leaves wilt and develop yellow, burned spots) or too little (leaves become pale, new stems are spindly and weak), don't be afraid to try a plant in questionable light. Just watch it, and if the plant's sign language indicates more or less light, try to accommodate it.

Temperature. This is much easier to evaluate than the amount of light. Generally speaking, if the temperature range is comfortable for you, it will also be comfortable for most container plants. There are exceptions, of course: tropicals that always want a toasty warm place or essentially cold-climate, outdoor plants that will survive indoors only in temperatures too chilly for human comfort. In books about houseplants or greenhouses, you will find the term *cool* used to describe a temperature range of approximately 40 to 60 degrees F. *Moderate* suggests a range of 55 to 70 degrees F. *Warm* represents average house temperatures, or a range of 62 to 75 degrees F. during that time of the year when artificial heating is required.

The greatest temperature problems have to do with too much heat. Cacti and other succulents from the dry, arid deserts of the world don't seem to mind drafts of artificial heat. Most leafy plants —Boston fern and asparagus-fern, for example—find it difficult to thrive directly over a radiator or other source of heat. Cacti and other succulents that grow wild in the jungle, as opposed to the desert—Christmas cactus and the *Epiphyllum,* or orchid cactus, for example— prefer moderate to warm temperatures with some moisture in the atmosphere instead of a hot, dry place.

Interestingly e n o u g h, many indoor plants do quite well with summer air-conditioning. In my office, in a sunny west window, I have many plants that thrive with the pots resting directly on the heating/air-conditioning unit. In winter warm air rustles the leaves all day long; in the summer it is a chilly breeze. One good rule of thumb to remember is that most container plants resent being at the same time either hot and dry or cold and dripping wet.

Humidity. Closely related to temperature is humidity, the amount of moisture in the air surrounding a container plant. Most indoor environments are painfully dry during that part of the year when artificial heat is required. In this day of fuel shortages and attendant high prices, it is amazing that public buildings continue to be overheated, and this holds

ABOVE: *Small plants grouped together grow better.*
BELOW: *Rex begonia enjoys humidity by bathroom sink.*

ABOVE: Fountain in indoor garden increases humidity.
BELOW: Lath shade for plants also helps cool bedroom.

true of many homes as well. Excessive heat robs the air of all moisture and sets up a vicious cycle: the drier the atmosphere, the higher the temperature has to be for human comfort. In a lower temperature there tends to be more humidity —or at least it is easier to raise the humidity—and the result is greater human comfort and healthier plants.

Measuring the amount of humidity in a given space indoors is fairly simple if you invest in a hygrometer (available at hardware stores). This instrument will give you a readout in terms of the amount of humidity expressed in percentages from 0 to 100 percent. Anything up to 20 percent may be considered as *dry*; from 20 to 40 percent as *medium*; and from 40 percent up as *moist*.

Without a hygrometer it is fairly easy to determine if your indoor environment is *dry* because your respiratory system and dry skin will tell you. And, at the opposite, you can feel and smell a really *moist* atmosphere. It is in-between where evaluation is more difficult without an instrument to tell you.

If the soil in a pot is kept nicely moist at all times, most common houseplants will tolerate a dry atmosphere, but a *medium* amount of humidity is much more desirable, not only for plants but for the human occupants and fine wooden furniture as well, including the piano. It is almost impossible to have a medium amount of humidity indoors in artificial heat unless you use some kind of humidifier. If your home has a furnace, an automatic humidifier can be installed into that existing system. Otherwise, as in an apartment or office building, a portable humidifier will probably be the answer. For the treatment of respiratory illness, virtually every neighborhood drugstore and pharmacy sells room-size cool-vapor humidifiers that hold about two gallons of water. These vaporize up to four gallons of water in every 24 hours and thus require twice-a-day filling. There are also larger cool-vapor units sold for general humidification of several rooms in a dwelling. These hold about six gallons of water and need filling every two or three days.

Many times I sense a certain reluctance from individuals when I recommend the use of these humidifiers. I know they are thinking the atmosphere will smell dank and musty, but this is definitely not the case when the humidity is combined with some fresh air. In my own apartment the wintertime humidity ranges from 40 to 60 percent, combined with a little fresh air from windows kept open slightly even in cold weather. No one who has entered my apartment for the first time has ever complained of a musty, overly damp smell. Rather they comment on the lush greenery and the feeling of being revived by the pleasantly moist atmosphere.

Adding up your climate. Light, temperature, humidity: How much did you find on and around your desk—or whatever part of your environment where you want to grow plants? Once you have these facts firmly in mind, you can decide to find a plant uniquely suited to the environment you have, or you can alter that environment to fit the needs of a special plant you want to grow.

The rest of growing a plant in a clay pot or other handsome container indoors is relatively simple—you can provide and control water and nutrients in the soil or other growing medium simply by using common sense. If the surface soil feels dry to your fingers, give the plant a good drink of water. If it feels moist, additional water is probably not yet needed. If it is really wet, or if water is actually standing on the surface, check to be sure excess can drain properly. Very few container plants like to stand in water for more than an hour or two at a time.

Applying fertilizer to container plants is far less critical than watering. If you are growing in a medium based on real soil, earth—or dirt, as we used to say when I was a child—it will contain enough nutrients to sustain fairly good plant growth with or without a precise program of supplementary feeding. However, if you are growing in one of the newer soil-less mediums (based on a mixture of peat moss, perlite and vermiculite), regular feeding is a necessity. The possibilities of growing container plants in various soils or in a soil-less medium are discussed more fully in Chapter 34.

There are other factors involved in growing container plants. Bugs, for example. And diseases, though infrequently. And also plenty of other problems. To help you cope with these inevitabilities, I have prepared a section of symptoms and what to do about them. This you will find also in Chapter 34.

Getting Started with Container Gardening

If you've never before tried growing a plant in a pot, or if you've tried and failed, some easy projects that require little or no investment of money can give results that are almost sure to build confidence.

Bean and pea gardens. Take a five- or six-inch flowerpot and fill it with potting soil, either from your garden or the kind you purchase in a bag wherever plants are sold. Add enough soil to the pot so that when you firm it down with your fingers the surface is one inch below the top of the pot. Take about six dried beans or peas (but not split peas) from your kitchen cupboard and scatter them over the surface soil. Cover them with about a half inch of potting soil; pat this down with your fingers. Add water until the entire pot of soil is moist. Place the pot in bright light or direct sun where temperatures would be comfortable for you. Within two or three days the seeds will begin to sprout. Add more water when the surface soil begins to feel dry as you pinch a little of it between your fingers.

This pot of beans or peas makes an

ABOVE: Jeannene McDonald plants beans in pottery bowl.
BELOW: From avocado pit to tree takes about two years.

almost instant garden of healthy green foliage. Children are often fascinated by this and can do it with some help. If you keep the pot always nicely moist in good light, the plants will grow well for several weeks, but since these are really for growing outdoors, don't expect too much of them. As soon as the growth ceases to be interesting and attractive, discard the plants. You can use the same pot of soil to grow another batch of peas or beans, or you can try something else. Incidentally, if you have a pet cat in your house, it may eat the bean or pea sprouts almost before the leaves have a chance to open.

Avocado tree or bush. Take the seed pit from a full-size ripe avocado. In clean water rinse off the seed, then dry it with a towel. Snuggle the bottom half, the larger part, of the pit about an inch deep into a pot of moist soil—perhaps the same you have used for a bean or pea sprout experimental garden described above. Keep the soil evenly moist at all times—not ever bone dry and not dripping with excess moisture for more than a few hours. When you see a sprout of growth, provide the young avocado with bright light and some direct sun shining on it if possible.

Once your avocado pit has sprouted, you have the beginnings of what can be a very fine houseplant that will last for as long as you like. If you want a bushy or shrublike plant, it will be necessary to pinch or cut out the top inch of tip growth after three or four leaves have opened out fully. This pinching or cutting will encourage two branches to grow where before there was only one. When these two branches each have three or four healthy leaves, again pinch or cut out the tip growth of each. Soon you will have one main stem, two secondary branches, and four growing points. Continue this pinching-branching-pinching procedure for as long as you have the plant.

If you want your avocado to form an

indoor tree with branches that spread out from a trunk, the procedure is slightly different in the early stages of growth. To form a single straight trunk, do not pinch out the main growing tip until you want branching to begin. If the avocado starts branching of its own accord, and some do, nip out any but the single strongest, hardiest, most vigorous growing tip. You may have to insert a sturdy bamboo stake in the pot and loosely tie the avocado stem to it, using half-inch-wide strips of plastic cut from a green garbage bag or plastic plant tie to do the tying. Once a trunk of sufficient height has grown, you can begin the pinching-branching-pinching routine the same as described for a bushy avocado plant.

Indoor avocados will adapt to various kinds of light, from shade (as in a north-facing window) to sun, but one thing they won't tolerate is being terribly hot and dry at the same time. This will cause all the older leaves to turn brown and crisp along the edges; some will have dry, dead areas within the leaves; and some leaves will die and drop off almost immediately.

Water gardening indoors. If you want to get into container gardening without so much as touching soil, you can grow cuttings in water. Take any clean glass vase or bottle and fill it with water. Ask friends who have container plants to give you some cuttings. Some good plants to root in water include wandering Jew, wax plant (*Hoya carnosa* and its varieties), trailing philodendron, English ivy, wax begonia, angel-wing begonia and Chinese evergreen (species or cultivar of *Aglao-nema*). Before you put the cuttings in water, cut off any leaves from that part of the stem which will be submerged. The cuttings will form roots in water, and many will exist this way for weeks and months, if not years. For best results keep the containers filled with water, adding fresh from time to time. Once a month pour out all the old water, rinse

ABOVE: Coleus is an easy plant to grow in water.
BELOW: Hoya. Remove submerged leaves of stem in water.

out the container, then refill it with fresh water to which you have added a little houseplant fertilizer. To mix the fertilizer in water to the proper strength, read directions on the fertilizer box, then add fertilizer to water at one-fourth to one-fifth the strength recommended for feeding plants in soil. For example, if the label says to add one teaspoon fertilizer to one quart of water for soil, then add only one-fourth teaspoon of fertilizer to each quart of water you are going to use for your water-grown cuttings.

Experimenting with plants for containers. Beyond these suggestions for getting into container gardening without spending a lot of money or risking the loss of an established, purchased plant, you will find literally thousands of possibilities for container gardening indoors and outdoors. The photographs accompanying this chapter have been selected to give ideas for how to use and enjoy container gardens of all kinds. In subsequent chapters you will find photographs of specific plants along with guides telling precisely how to grow different kinds of plants in pots and other containers.

Once you get the feel for growing any plant in a container, indoors or outdoors, you will realize that almost anything is fair game. Even if a garden catalog or book says nothing about growing a particular plant in a container, don't be afraid to try. If you can provide the plant's requirements of light and temperature, then the rest is mostly a matter of giving the plant a container of sufficient size to support its root system, in combination with a thoughtful feeding and watering program. Half the fun is in the experimenting.

If you want containers of flowering plants outdoors in a shady place in the summer, then you'll grow impatiens at first because they're sure to perform well. Eventually, however, you'll begin to search the catalogs for other plants that flower in the shade because they'll make your garden more interesting.

It's the same indoors. If, for example, you want a beautiful foliage plant to grow in a corner where light is bright enough for you to read a name in the telephone book, but there is no direct sun, you might wisely select that Chinese evergreen, but in time you will want to experiment with other foliage plants to see if they will adapt to less than ideal lighting conditions.

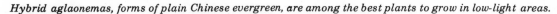

Hybrid aglaonemas, forms of plain Chinese evergreen, are among the best plants to grow in low-light areas.

ABOVE: *Sanseverias, top; bromeliads and small Norfolk Island pines, middle; two dracaena species, bottom.*

BELOW: *Blooming aphelandra (two zebras) and a jade plant.*

Indoor Gardens without Natural Light

If you have no light indoors sufficient to sustain plants, then some means of artificial illumination is the answer. Fluorescent light is the most efficient way to grow plants where natural light is not available. Ceiling fluorescents used for general illumination in most offices are too far away from plants to benefit much; they do supplement weak natural light. However, it is simple and fairly inexpensive to rig up a fluorescent unit specifically for growing plants. Here's how:

Take a standard industrial fixture that contains two 20-watt or two 40-watt tubes. Suspend it about 18 inches above a shelf or other surface on which you will place flowerpots. Ordinary fluorescent tubes may be used for growing plants, or you can invest in some of the special agricultural growth tubes such as Gro-Lux Wide Spectrum. One proven combination is to use one Cool White and one Warm White tube in each fixture. Burn the tubes 12 to 16 hours out of every 24; you'll find it more convenient to use an automatic timer so that day length is uniform regardless of your schedule and whether or not you're at home.

Where only leaf growth is desired, and no flowering plants are being cultivated, days of fluorescent light longer than 16 hours may be beneficial. In fact, in recent experiments I have done with leaf lettuce, 20-hour days of light—up to continuous illumination—have produced the makings of fresh-picked salads more quickly than with shorter daylight.

It is never necessary to combine incandescent light with fluorescent for growing plants. However, incandescent alone can be beneficial. In its simplest form this may mean a table or desk lamp burned 12 to 16 hours out of every 24, with a small plant or two placed within the range of brightest light. Small-leaved English ivies and trailing philodendrons do espe-

ABOVE: Fluorescent unit supplements light at dim window.
BELOW: Light unit and tray are suspended from ceiling.

cially well in this kind of illumination as do small terrariums planted with shade-loving plants.

More recently, indoor gardeners have discovered that certain kinds of incandescent floodlights can be used to supplement or to entirely replace natural light for maintaining and growing large foliage plants indoors. It is important to use floodlights, not spotlights. Spots concentrate the light so much that it tends to burn the foliage. Floodlights—for example, General Electric's Cool Beam and Sylvania's Cool-Lux—are available in sizes from 75 to 300 watts. Smaller ones can be placed in a range of 12 to 24 inches from the foliage; larger ones may need to be 24 to 36 inches away from the leaves. After a flood has been burning over a plant for about an hour, feel the leaves. If your fingers tell you that the leaf is warm, move the flood back or up another 12 inches. If an incandescent flood is a plant's sole source of light, burn it 12 to 16 hours out of every 24; if it is merely a supplement to some natural light, 6 to 8 hours daily will probably suffice. Floodlights for plant growth should be used in ceramic sockets. Suitable fixtures and stands are available from electrical and photographic supply houses, and also from lighting-fixture departments in some department stores. Ceiling track lighting systems offer an excellent means of housing floodlights for plant growth.

Special Environments for Container Gardens

One of the easiest ways to be successful with plants indoors is to grow them in a special, glassed-in environment—a terrarium or bottle garden, for example. For greatest success with this kind of miniature garden, group plants together that share similar requirements—for example, kinds that need moisture and shade are especially suited to a bottle garden or closed terrarium. Kinds that need sun and more dryness—cacti and other succulents, for example—are better choices for an open terrarium or dish garden.

One step beyond a terrarium or bottle garden is the indoor planter, often built along a glass wall section at floor level or raised, just as they are outdoors.

Some homes have glassed-in gardens beneath a skylight. You'll find these available by mail and at local garden centers. The window greenhouse is a special pleasure for the container gardener. Some of the smaller ones are installed in exactly the same manner as a window air-conditioning unit. The larger window greenhouses are attached to the window frame outdoors, or they can extend some inches wider and higher than the dimensions of the window, provided you have access to all parts of the greenhouse by reaching through the open window which the greenhouse covers.

Full-scale greenhouses are the dream of nearly every person who gardens, and, interestingly enough, to some who've never gardened at all but want to. If you are serious in your desire to have a greenhouse, send away for the catalogs of manufacturers suggested in the Appendix. Prefabricated greenhouses continue to be one of the best buys around. You'll find a variety of architectural styles available in sizes to suit almost any conceivable situation. Many are designed in a modular fashion so that you can add on units with relative ease at a later date.

If the cost of heating a standard greenhouse worries you, consider building a sun-heated pit. By this approach, solar energy provides the heat at no cost to you—or to our environment. The procedure is surprisingly simple. For example, if you want a sun-heated pit greenhouse 8 feet wide by 12 feet long, dig a pit in the ground 4 to 5 feet deep and slightly larger than the dimensions, siting it from east to west. Add concrete or concrete block walls with a sill plate at the top on which you will mount an A frame with glass or plastic windows facing toward the south and an insulated roof wall facing the north. On cold nights and cloudy, cold days, cover the glass or

ABOVE: *Window greenhouse attaches like an air conditioner.*
BELOW: *Standard window greenhouse with ventilator top.*

This prefabricated lean-to greenhouse has glass to the ground, a feature that increases growing space and reduces construction costs. Often, heating can be provided by the dwelling's existing system.

to run a sun-heated pit as a moderate-temperature greenhouse, and then you can grow anything save tropicals like philodendron, gloxinia and African violet. For example, in a moderate temperature range of nighttime lows between 45 and 55 degrees, and daytime temperatures perhaps edging up to 75 degrees on a sunny day, you can grow all kinds of geraniums, fragrant sweet-olive, winter sweet peas and pansies, and good crops of leaf lettuce, parsley, other herbs and flowering bulbs.

Besides studying the catalogs of greenhouse manufacturers, I would suggest also that you send 25¢ to the Superintendent of Documents, U.S. Government Printing Office, Washington, D.C. 20402, for a copy of Bulletin No. 357, "Building Hobby Greenhouses." For further reference I suggest also these publications:

Eaton, Jerome A., *Gardening Under Glass,* The Macmillan Company, 866 Third Ave., New York, N.Y. 10022.

Acme Engineering and Manufacturing Corp., *The Greenhouse Climate Control Handbook: Principles and Design Procedures,* Acme Engineering and Manufacturing Corp., Muskogee, Okla. 74401, $2.00.

Courtier, J. W., and Curtis, J. O., *A Simple Rigid Frame Greenhouse for Home Gardeners,* Cooperative Extension Service, Circular 880, University of Illinois, College of Agriculture, Urbana, Ill. 61801. Out of State, 10¢.

Courtier, J. W., and Curtis, J. O., *Home Greenhouses for Year-round Gardening Pleasure,* Cooperative Extension Service, Circular 879, University of Illinois, College of Agriculture, Urbana, Ill. 61801. Out of State, 10¢.

U.S. Department of Agriculture, *Plastic Covered Greenhouse Coldframe,* Miscellaneous Publication 1111, Washington, D.C. 20250.

plastic with heavy straw mats, old carpeting or sheets of lightweight plastic foam. These serve as insulation to keep the heat in and the cold out. On sunny winter days, remove the insulation materials as early as possible to allow maximum penetration of solar energy—which stores up heat against nighttime cold.

Built and managed as I have just described, a sun-heated pit greenhouse can be maintained in cold climates without any supplementary heat. Granted, in the dead of winter average temperatures may range only slightly above freezing to perhaps 50 degrees F., but in this environment it is still possible to grow an incredible variety of beautiful flowering plants—camellias, primroses, spring bulbs, azaleas and acacia, to name a few. By adding a little auxiliary heat, it is possible

24
Containers to Buy or Build

Containers for growing plants are all around us. You can buy clay or plastic flowerpots from thumb size to 20 inches in diameter—or larger. You can make do with household castoffs, for example, tin cans, cutoff milk cartons and gallon-size (or larger) plastic bottles. You can buy ready-made tubs and boxes of redwood or cypress (both moisture-resistant), or you can build your own planters using these woods, marine plywood or wood salvaged from shipping crates (which will not last more than a season or two unless you first treat the wood with a preservative). In the pages that follow, you will find photographs and diagrams depicting a number of handsome containers you can build for gardening indoors and outdoors.

What Size Container?

It's easy to fit plants to pots. For one thing, when you put a plant together with a pot, it should look right to your eye. You may be surprised to discover that what looks right to your eye, however inexperienced you may be as a gardener, will probably be right in a cultural sense. This has to do with esthetics which we learn by association and, for some persons, a natural sense of proportion and scale.

If you'd like a more precise guide, here is a general rule: For a plant that is growing mostly upright, the diameter of the pot should be one-third to one-half the height of the plant. By this rule of thumb a dieffenbachia (dumbcane) 18 inches tall needs a pot six to nine inches in diameter.

If the plant grows mostly in a horizontal plane, the same rule holds. For example, an African violet with a leaf span of nine inches will look right—and grow well—in a pot that measures from three to five inches across the top.

These two rules work fairly well for small or young plants. However, large bushes, trees and vines are not so easily defined. For example, a weeping fig tree six feet tall does not need a pot two to

Burro's-tail sedum in standard clay pot with saucer.

Climbing philodendron in woven terra-cotta pot.

three feet in diameter. It will do nicely in a pot or tub 12 to 14 inches in diameter and of about the same depth. Perhaps the general rule that can be applied here is that in addition to looking right to the eye, the container has to be large enough to balance the physical weight of the plant so that it stands firmly without danger of tipping over under average circumstances. For any large plant, whether it grows as a bush, a tree, a climbing or trailing vine, the container should also hold enough soil so that it is not constantly dry at the roots. If a container is too small, the soil will dry out so rapidly and so often that you will find it impossible to water often enough to sustain healthy root and leaf growth.

Although all of these rules are generalities and are to be taken as such, if you will consider them along with the visual sense you can develop just by studying all of the photographs in this book, you should have no problem either esthetically or culturally in fitting plants to suitable pots.

Clay or Plastic?

Both clay and plastic pots have advantages and disadvantages. Clay flowerpots are such classics in terms of design that they look right in virtually all settings—period, traditional or contemporary, elegant or casual. From a cultural viewpoint, unglazed clay pots have porous walls that transpire air and moisture. Consequently they dry out more rapidly than glazed pottery or plastic. Unglazed clay saucers seep enough moisture to damage wood floors and carpeting. To avoid this problem, cut a piece of half-inch cork to fit under each saucer. Excess

Young bird's-nest fern growing in white plastic pot.

Fiberglass cylinder pots and pedestal for plant display.

moisture evaporates through the cork, and under normal circumstances should never build up sufficiently to harm either carpeting or wood floors.

Glazed pottery containers and plastic pots require less watering than unglazed clay. The matching saucers are waterproof.

Containers without drainage holes require special attention to watering. Growing a plant successfully in a container without any drainage provision is not easy. A skilled workman may be able to drill a drainage hole for you in such a jardiniere. You can do it yourself in a metal container. I recommend planting in any utilitarian container that has drainage—even a tin can with holes punched in the bottom—and then slipping this inside of the decorative container that has no drainage. If you wish to plant directly in such a container, first add a good lay-er of pebbles, broken clay flowerpot or chipped charcoal, then proceed with planting. But whether you plant directly in a container without drainage, or indirectly by using a utilitarian liner, be cautious about applying too much water at any given time. If a container is to be used outdoors where rainfall reaches it, drainage is a necessity.

Glazed ceramic and plastic containers are easily kept clean in very much the same way you wash dishes. After prolonged use, a layer of mineral salts may build up along the edge or lip of the pot, and this should be removed by scrubbing with a soap pad or wire brush. Unglazed clay pots also build up this layer of mineral salts along the edges as well as the exterior walls. Again, all of this can be removed by scrubbing with a soap pad or wire brush and then rinsing in clear water.

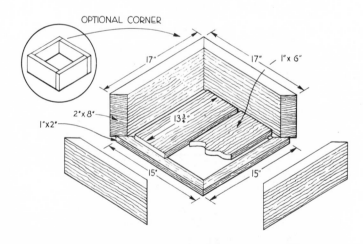

Containers to Build

Severe demands are made on the wood from which a planter box is built. Direct contact with soil and periodic watering provide an ideal medium for decay and destructive insects. The use of redwood heartwood for planter-box construction will eliminate this problem. Redwood's preservatives are present throughout the heartwood. Therefore, minor surface checks and splits, which appear in all woods, will not affect redwood's interior resistance. These same conditions, which are ever present in planters, can lay open a surface-preserved wood's interior to insect and decay attack.

Redwood heartwood's durability is the result of a combination of chemical extractives which, occurring naturally, make applied preservatives unnecessary: every cell and fiber is naturally repellent to insects and decay-producing fungi.

Redwood is dimensionally stable. When kiln dried, it results in a lumber product that resists shrinking, swelling, checking and cupping. Dimensional stability means redwood planters will keep their shape despite extreme variations of moisture and temperature.

But it is probably redwood's beauty and versatility that have made redwood planters as popular as they are today. Redwood needs no finish. Weathering will turn the unfinished wood to an attractive driftwood gray—a pleasing backdrop for all flora. Or redwood may be finished with a variety of water repellents and light- or heavy-bodied stains to achieve almost any effect. And redwood's easy workability means it can be shaped to any specification.

All heartwood grades of redwood lumber are recommended for planters containing soil. These are *Clear All Heart,* for applications where a clear, knot-free wood is desired; *Select Heart* and *Construction Heart,* where knots are of little or no consequence. Containerized planters used indoors may be constructed of heartwood or sapwood-containing grades.

Redwood heartwood's extractives can cause initial stains on concrete patios. To avoid this, the inside of the planter can be coated with a tar substance or lined with polyethylene film. A water repellent will discourage extractive staining, but allow two weeks before planting to let toxic agents become harmless. Another alternative is to set a new planter in a metal pan or similar container for the first two or three waterings to avoid stains.

Redwood planter boxes, whatever their design, require two preliminary precautions to make them maintenance-free. First, be sure to drill holes or leave narrow spaces between the bottom boards for water drainage necessary with any planter. Second, be sure that nails and metal fasteners are corrosion resistant. That is, the metal used in contact with redwood should be stainless steel, aluminum alloy or *top-quality*, hot-dipped galvanized. Otherwise, the chemical reaction that occurs when redwood extractives encounter iron and water will cause black streaks on the wood. More complete information on fasteners and finishes is available by writing the California Redwood Association, 617 Montgomery Street, San Francisco, California 94111.

Depending on your interests, you may wish at the same time to ask the California Redwood Association for any of a series of data sheets on garden uses of redwood. These include:

Building a Redwood Fence (3C2-2)
Building a Redwood Garden Shelter (3C2-3)
Redwood Garden Work Centers (3C2-4)
Redwood Deck Construction (3C2-5)
Patio Paving with Redwood (3C5-1)
Redwood Exterior Finishes (4B1-1)

Fir and other less expensive woods can also be used to construct containers, but they must be specially treated if they are to last.

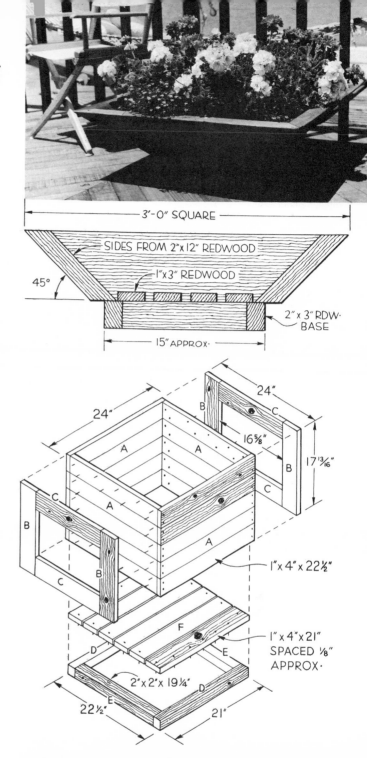

A garden within a garden: primroses, pansies, and emerging bulbs grow in handsome redwood planter boxes.

25
Flowering Plants

Regardless of where you live, most flowering plants for container gardening indoors and out can be classed as *tender perennial* or *annual*. "Tender perennial" means that the plant cannot survive freezing temperatures. The geranium of window gardens and boxes (actually a form of *Pelargonium*) makes a perfect example. Like many tender perennials, it can be grown from seed to bloom in a single growing season. In any climate where freezing occurs, the geranium—or any other tender perennial—will die unless brought indoors before frost in autumn. Plants in this category can be maintained all year in a coldframe, or indoors in a suitable environment, or they can be wintered indoors and summered out of doors. Where freezing temperatures never occur, these plants can be cultivated all year in the garden. In such a climate many tender perennials, geraniums included, may become large shrubs or even trees unless they are pruned back regularly.

An annual is a plant that grows from seed to bloom and produces seed with which to perpetuate itself all within a single growing season, then it dies. The zinnia is a good example.

Flowers

Group 1. Interestingly enough, the plants in the list below are members of the same family. They are gesneriads. All have fuzzy or hairy foliage that tends to become unsightly when subjected to

Group 1

Tender Perennial Flowers for Indoor Containers All
Year or Outdoors in Warm Weather with Protection from Rain

LATIN NAME	POPULAR NAME
Part sun to shade	
Episcia	flame violet
Saintpaulia	African violet
Sinningia	gloxinia
Smithiantha	temple bells

Episcia dianthiflora *has fringed white flowers.*

ABOVE: Tuberous begonia.
BELOW: Assorted achimenes.

wind and rain outdoors. They do make fine porch plants, however, during warm weather. The easiest way to get started with all of them is to buy established plants. These are available from many local florists and greenhouses, or you can send away to some of the specialists listed in the Appendix.

These gesneriads all need a warm, moist atmosphere and part sun to bright open shade. They grow to perfection in fluorescent-light gardens.

Hybrid sinningia (gloxinia) tubers available in the winter may be started into growth inside, then placed outdoors in a protected area when the weather is thoroughly warm. They will then flower all summer.

Hybrid gloxinia four months after planting tuber.

Group 2. Among these tender perennials are some of the best of all flowering plants for container gardens, both indoors and out. According to their uses and growth habits, they can be further categorized as follows:

Tender bulbs. Those needing a good half day of sun include agapanthus, anemone, canna, crinum, dahlia, galtonia, hippeastrum, hymenocallis, lycoris, mont-

bretia, nerine, oxalis, ranunculus, spre-
kelia, tigridia, zephyranthes; for a place
with some shade, especially at midday,
achimenes, tuberous begonia, clivia, cyclamen, eucharis, eucomis, gloriosa, hae-
manthus, vallota and zantedeschia. Of
these, agapanthus and clivia are evergreen and can be kept growing year
round. All the others make leaf growth
and bloom, the foliage matures, and then
they require a period of dormancy during
which time the soil is kept nearly dry, no
fertilizer is applied, and the pots can be
stored in a dark but frost-free and mouse-
proof place. All may be planted in winter
or spring.

Hanging baskets. Almost any plant can
be put in a hanging container, but some
of the best cascaders and trailers require
some direct sun: *Abutilon megapotamicum variegatum*, antigonon, felicia, helio-
tropium, lantana, nierembergia, oxalis,
pelargonium (ivy-leaf types), petunia,
plumbago, verbena and vinca. For a place
protected from midday sun: achimenes,
aeschynanthus, tuberous begonia, browallia, columnea, fuchsia, hoya and impatiens.

Hot and dry. It is sometimes required
that outdoor container gardens be tolerant of hot, dry weather. Some of the
best ones from this list are: agapanthus,
Begonia semperflorens, canna, gazania,
lantana, pelargonium, tigridia and verbena. I do not mean to imply you can be
careless about watering these—only that
they won't die from being dry for a day
or two.

Availability. Although the Latin names
may not be familiar to you, if you will
read down the list of popular names I
am sure you will find many old acquaint-
ances. Most of these plants are commonly
available at local garden centers and
greenhouses. Some better and less common kinds and varieties may be found in
the catalogs of mail-order suppliers (see
listing of these firms in the Appendix.

ABOVE: *Hybrid amaryllis.* BELOW: *Impatiens 'Huck-
abuc.'*

Calla-lily semperflorens begonia has some white leaves.

Group 2

Tender Perennial Flowers for Outdoor Containers in Warm Weather, Indoors During Winter

LATIN NAME	POPULAR NAME
Full sun	
Abutilon	flowering maple
Agapanthus	Lily of the Nile
Alstroemeria	Lily of Peru
Anemone	windflower
Antigonon	coral vine
Begonia semperflorens	wax begonia
Canna	canna
Capsicum	ornamental pepper
Clianthus	glory pea
Clitoria	butterfly pea
Crinum	milk-and-wine lily
Cytisus	butcher's broom
Dahlia	dahlia
Datura	angel's trumpet
Dianthus	carnation; pink
Felicia	blue marguerite
Galtonia	Cape hyacinth
Gazania	gazania
Haemanthus	blood-lily
Heliotropium	heliotrope
Hibiscus	hibiscus
Hippeastrum	amaryllis
Hymenocallis	ismene; Peruvian daffodil
Jacobinia	king's crown
Lantana	lantana
Lycoris	spider lily
Montbretia	montbretia
Nerine	nerine
Nicotiana	flowering tobacco
Nierembergia	purple cups
Oxalis	oxalis
Oxypetalum	southern star
Pelargonium	geranium
Pentas	Egyptian star cluster
Petunia	petunia
Plumbago	plumbago
Phygelius	Cape fuchsia
Ranunculus	buttercup
Solanum	Christmas cherry
Sprekelia	sprekelia
Strelitzia	bird of paradise
Tigridia	tiger flower
Vallota	Scarborough lily
Verbena	verbena
Vinca	periwinkle
Zephyranthes	rain lily

Part sun to shade	
Achimenes	magic flower
Aeschynanthus	lipstick vine
Anthurium	Valentine flower
Aphelandra	zebra plant
Begonia semperflorens	wax begonia
Begonia tuberosa	tuberous begonia
Bletilla	Chinese orchid
Browallia	Browallia
Clivia	Kafir lily
Columnea	columnea
Crossandra	crossandra
Cyclamen	shooting star
Eucharis	Amazon lily
Eucomis	pineapple lily
Fuchsia	fuchsia
Gesneria	gesneria
Gloriosa	climbing lily
Hoya	wax plant
Impatiens	patience plant
Orchidaceae	orchids
Streptocarpus	Cape primrose
Zantedeschia	calla-lily

Eucharis has fragrant white flowers.

26
Foliage Plants

Plants included in this chapter are cultivated primarily for attractive foliage and often used in terrarium and bottle-garden plantings and as tabletop and window-sill decorations. Most can be kept indefinitely as small bushes or hanging-basket plants. The woody shrub-types are discussed in Chapter 27; foliage plants of tree size are in Chapter 28.

Foliage without Direct Sun

If you have a place that receives bright light, but no direct sun, here are some of the best plants from which to choose; these are the toughies that survive, even thrive, in the average house or office environment:

LATIN NAME	POPULAR NAME
Aglaonema	Chinese evergreen
Aspidistra	cast-iron plant
Beaucarnea	pony-tail
Brassaia	schefflera
Bromeliad	bromeliad
Ceropegia	hearts entangled
Chlorophytum	spider plant
Cissus	grape-ivy; kangaroo vine
Dieffenbachia	dumbcane
Dizygotheca	false aralia
Dracaena	corn plant
Fatsia	aralia
Filicineae	ferns
Hedera	English ivy
Hemigraphis	Red or flame ivy
Hoya	wax plant
Maranta	prayer plant
Pandanus	screw-pine

Rex begonia leaves are like quilted brocade. This one combines silver, green, and burgundy coloring.

ABOVE: *Cryptanthus, miniature relative of the pine-apple.*

BELOW, LEFT: *Maranta foliage.* RIGHT: Anthurium clarinervum.

BELOW: *Miniature rex begonias have such colorful leaves, they can take the place of flowers in terrariums.*

Pellionia	pellionia
Peperomia	peperomia
Philodendron	philodendron
Pilea	artillery fern
Pilea	aluminum plant
Plectranthus	Swedish-ivy
Polyscias	aralia
Rhoeo	Moses in the cradle
Sansevieria	snake plant
Scindapsus	pothos
Spathiphyllum	peace-lily
Syngonium	nephthytis

In moderate to high humidity of 40 to 60 percent, you might grow any of the plants in the preceding list, plus these, many of which have beautiful multicolored foliage:

LATIN NAME	POPULAR NAME
Acorus	miniature sweet flag
Alocasia	alocasia
Anthurium	anthurium
Asparagus	asparagus-fern
Begonia rex	rex begonia
Bertolonia	bertolonia
Calathea	calathea
Caladium	caladium
Chamaeranthemum	chamaeranthemum
Cordyline	Hawaiian Ti
Ctenanthe	ctenanthe

Ctenanthe has leaves of many colors.

Cyperus	umbrella plant
Euonymus	euonymus
Ficus	creeping fig
Fittonia	fittonia
Gynura	purple passion
Hoffmannia	corduroy plant
Homalomena	homalomena
Hypoestes	pink polka dot
Ligularia	leopard plant
Ophiopogon	lily-turf
Rhektophyllum	rhektophyllum
Saxifraga	strawberry-begonia
Scilla violacea	scilla
Selaginella	sweat plant
Sonerila	sonerila
Tolmiea	piggyback
Xanthosoma	xanthosoma
Zingiber	ginger

Best Foliage for Terrariums

From the two preceding lists, my favorite foliage plants for terrariums and bottle gardens are the ones that stay fairly small naturally. These include: **cryptanthus (a bromeliad), miniature spider plant** (*Chlorophytum bichetti*), many ferns, small-leaved English ivies, pellionia, peperomia, *Philodendron sodiroi,* acorus, *Anthurium clarinervum,* miniature varieties of rex begonia, berto-*lonia,* small varieties of calathea, chamaeranthemum, euonymus, creeping fig, fittonia, saxifraga, *Scilla violacea*, selaginella and sonerila.

For a terrarium or bottle garden that receives bright reflected light most of the day—but little or no direct sun—or one cultivated in a fluorescent-light garden, you might add to my list of foliage plants these little plants that also flower: *Allophyton mexicanum* (Mexican foxglove), *Begonia prismatocarpa,* 'Cygnet' episcia, *Gesneria cuneifolia* and its hybrids, miniature African violets, *Seemannia latifolia* and *Sinningia pusilla* and other miniature gloxinias.

27
Shrubs

Virtually all shrubs and vines with more or less woody stems can be cultivated in container gardens. If the plant grows outdoors in the ground year round in your climate, then you can also try it in a good-sized tub or wooden planter box. Where freezing temperatures occur, it is vital that soil in the container go into winter freeze-up in a moist condition. It follows that pottery containers should not be left out in the winter, because frozen soil expands and the result will be cracked pottery. Often concrete containers do not break, owing to their strength and bowl-shaped bottoms.

If you have an outdoor garden in the North, I am going to assume you have all the common shrubs like lilacs and forsythia you want growing in the ground, and that your interest in container shrubs will be for more exotic tropicals. However, if you have only a terrace or rooftop garden in the North, there is no reason not to try your most favorite woody shrubs, evergreens and vines as part of a container garden.

Cold-sensitive (Below 45°) Shrubs for Containers

The plants in this category are mostly common and everyday in the tropics, but the only way to really enjoy them in up-North gardens is to take advantage of container plantings. In warm weather they can be wheeled outdoors, but when frost threatens they need a warm place inside. This doesn't have to be a greenhouse or sun porch, although either place makes a fine winter home for these plants. You can keep them in any cold-free space—perhaps a garage or basement, or simply within the light range of a bright window. Hot, dry heat in the winter is not to the liking of any of them.

Availability. In the South you will find most of these at your local nursery or garden center. In the North you may or may not. The widespread popularity of container gardening has encouraged Northern nurserymen to stock more and more tropical shrubs.

Young plants of most of these are also available through mail-order specialists whose names and addresses are listed in the Appendix.

LATIN NAME	POPULAR NAME
Allamanda	golden trumpet
Ardisia	coral berry
Bambusa	bamboo
Begonia, cane or angel-wing	begonia
Bougainvillea	paper flower
Calliandra	powderpuff
Callistemon	bottlebrush
Camellia	camellia
Carissa	natal-plum
Clerodendrum	Bleeding-heart vine
Clerodendrum	**Cashmere** bouquet
Codiaeum	croton
Daphne	daphne
Dipladenia	dipladenia
Eugenia	Surinam cherry
Fatshedera	fatshedera
Gardenia	gardenia
Hibiscus	hibiscus
Ixora	ixora
Jasminum	jasmine
Ligustrum	ligustrum
Mahonia	mahonia
Malpighia	Barbados cherry
Nerium	oleander
Osmanthus	sweet-olive
Passiflora	passion flower
Pittosporum	pittosporum
Podocarpus	podocarpus
Stephanotis	stephanotis vine
Tecomaria	Cape honey-suckle

ABOVE: Golden allamanda. BELOW: Pots of fragrant jasmine.

ABOVE: Vivid bougainvillea. BELOW: Sweet Daphne odora.

'Mrs. Roeding' oleander flowers readily in containers.

How to Grow Potted Camellias

The year-round schedule for growing camellias in pots or tubs is partly like that for other cold-sensitive shrubs. There are some distinct differences, however, and since camellias are among the most beautiful of shrubs to grow in containers, specific instructions are included here. The suggestions that follow, prepared by the U.S. Department of Agriculture, tell how best to succeed with camellias, but also give ideas for how to handle other tender shrubs in containers.

Camellias can be grown in containers indefinitely if they are given the proper care. Their requirements are essentially the same as for plants grown outdoors—partial shade, adequate moisture, rich soil and good drainage.

If the plant you buy from the nursery is container-grown, you need not transplant it unless you want a more attractive container. Nursery plants are usually potted in good soil. If your plant out-grows its container, you can transplant it at any time of the year.

Use a potting soil made of one-fourth woods leaf mold, one-fourth sand and one-half peat moss. Place a one-inch layer of gravel at the bottom of the new container to provide drainage.

Water the plants heavily, then allow the soil to dry moderately before watering again. The critical period in watering occurs in spring, when the plants are growing rapidly. They need much more water then than at any other time of the year.

During the hot summer months, spray the leaves with water every afternoon. Spraying keeps the air humid around the plants.

Fertilize potted plants monthly throughout the year. For monthly feedings from March through July, use a liquid fertilizer, analysis 15-5-5. In August through February use a 7-6-19 liquid fertilizer. Do not overfertilize; it is better to feed too little than too much. Never fertilize a dry plant.

Potted camellias may be pruned any time of the year to control their size and maintain their shape. When cutting a bloom, take two or three leaves with it. This will help to maintain the shape of the plant.

You may want to disbud your plant to obtain large specimen blooms. The best time to disbud is when you are able to distinguish the flower bud from the growth bud. For early blooming varieties, disbudding is best done in September or October.

To disbud, use a large pin or a shingle nail to pierce a hole from the tip of the bud downward. This allows air to enter the bud so it will dry and fall off naturally, thus eliminating possible injury to the adjoining bud that you want to keep.

In some parts of southern California, southern Texas and Florida, potted camellias can be left outdoors all winter. In other areas it is best to move them

ABOVE: Crape-myrtlette flowers profusely in pots.

ABOVE: Azaleas grow well in pots. BELOW: Clematis.

in winter to some place where their roots will be protected from freezing.

They can be taken indoors and will bloom there if the room temperatures can be kept between 35 and 50 degrees F. and the humidity held reasonably high.

Hardy Shrubs for Containers

In this category, please take the designation "hardy" with a grain of salt. If the shrub grows well in your community without special winter protection, then you will probably have no difficulty growing it outdoors all year in a container, providing the soil about the roots goes into winter freeze-up in a well-moistened condition. If the shrub is of doubtful winter hardiness in your climate when planted in a desirable spot in the ground, then you cannot hope to bring it through winter as a container plant in the open. Move it to an interior space where it will have some protection—for example, a garage, basement or cool room where there is light.

Availability. Most if not all of these shrubs may be found already growing in containers in local nurseries and garden centers. For unusual varieties you may find it best to send away to a specialist; see names and addresses in the Appendix.

LATIN NAME	POPULAR NAME
Aucuba	golddust plant
Campsis	trumpet vine/bush
Clematis	clematis vine
Cotoneaster	rockspray
Ilex	holly
Juniperus	juniper
Lagerstroemia	**crape-myrtle**
Nandina	heavenly bamboo
Pyracantha	firethorn
Rhododendron	rhododendron
Rhododendron	azalea
Rosa	rose
Viburnum	viburnum
Wisteria	wisteria

Trees 28

One of the nicest influences of container gardening has been the widespread planting of trees in large tubs and planters. At first we saw them greening and shading open public spaces, but gradually they have moved inside. A few years ago it was unusual to see a tree indoors, spreading its branches out and upward to the ceiling. Now no living space seems quite finished without a tree-size plant. The idea has been nurtured along by environmentalists, architects, decorators and by young people seeking to get closer to nature. It is now universally accepted as the right and good thing to do, indoors and outdoors.

The best trees for growing year round as houseplants tend to be relatively expensive, however. The one exception is an avocado, which you can grow to tree size in two years for practically no investment at all. After all, you bought the avocado to eat; the seed pit is a true bonus. For how to start an avocado, see Chapter 22.

The Best Indoor Trees

All of the tree-size plants cultivated in containers as houseplants are incapable of withstanding freezing temperatures or even cold exposed sites. You can move them outdoors in warm weather, but they should be brought back inside well ahead of frost in autumn.

Araucaria excelsa. Norfolk Island pine. This cold-tender needle evergreen is available in all sizes from a two-and-a-half-inch pot seedling to a real ceiling pusher (the latter for quite a high price, incidentally). It needs bright light, preferably with a little direct sun. Keep the soil evenly moist. It can't stand being hot and dry at the same time.

Norfolk Island pine makes a graceful indoor tree.

Brassaia actinophylla. Schefflera. Available in all sizes from seedlings and rooted cuttings to towering trees. Little schefflera plants grow rapidly in the right conditions; no matter how small one appears, it is a mistake to plant it in a terrarium or dish garden. Schefflera grows well in bright light, although a little direct sun won't hurt indoors. Water the soil really well, then not again until the surface feels almost dry to your fingers.

Chamaedorea erumpens. Bamboo palm. A graceful palm with strong vertical lines; it may well remind you more of a clump of bamboo than a palm. It tolerates low light, but does best in light you might read or do needlework by. Keep the soil evenly moist. The related, and more common dwarf or Neanthe bella palm, *Chamaedorea elegans,* seldom grows taller than four feet indoors, but one of this size placed on top of a stool or pedestal can give the effect of a tree indoors.

Chamaerops humilis. European fan palm. This tree is wider-spreading than the bamboo palm. In fact, the specimens most often available in Northern shops seem to be widest in girth right at eye level. You can solve this problem by elevating the pot on a footstool, low table or some other kind of pedestal so that the branches spread high enough for you to walk under them. This palm needs as much light as possible. Keep the soil evenly moist.

Dieffenbachia amoena. Dumbcane. This big tropical plant is not really a tree with spreading branches, but in terms of leaf volume, you can buy a lot of green for relatively little money when you invest in a large dieffenbachia. Give it medium light, preferably a little direct sun indoors. Water well, then not again until the surface soil feels almost dry.

LEFT: Brassaia (schefflera) grows to ceiling height.
ABOVE: Dwarf palm grows to four feet tall indoors.
BELOW: Pale green dieffenbachia and large philo-
dendron.

Loquat tree in tub will survive winters indoors if it receives some sun outdoors in warm weather.

Dizygotheca elegantissima. Spider aralia. This is the plant with leaves that look like marijuana; in fact, people have been known to ask shopkeepers for "the one that looks like marijuana." It thrives in as much light as you can give it, but direct sun is not required. The dizygotheca, like most related plants in the aralia family, resents being moved. It will lose some leaves, but if you care for it properly and leave it in one place, it will adapt. Keep the soil evenly moist at all times.

Dracaena fragrans. Corn plant. Like the dieffenbachia, this dracaena tends to be more of a big bush than a tree. However, it does give a mass of fresh green foliage, and this plant is one of the most tolerant of all of low light and neglect. For best results, keep the soil in a range from evenly moist to wet; however, it won't keel over and die if you forget to water it for a few days.

Dracaena marginata. Dragon tree. This plant is characterized by tall, slender trunks or branches that often curve and zigzag in an interesting if not bizarre fashion. These are topped by tufts or plumes of narrow green leaves banded in dark red. Give it medium light; direct sun is not needed. Keep the soil in a range from evenly moist to wet. Each time you forget to water and the soil dries out severely, many of the older leaves will turn yellow and fall off.

Eriobotrya japonica. Japanese loquat. This plant has rather coarse leaves, but it makes an excellent indoor tree. In the Northeast, at least, I have never seen it offered in a plant shop, but it is widely cultivated in the Los Angeles area. It needs some direct sun indoors. Keep the soil evenly moist.

Ficus benjamina exotica. Weeping Java fig. Probably the most popular of all indoor trees, especially among designers and decorators. It is always graceful and

ABOVE: Characteristically bizarre Dracaena marginata.
BELOW: Ficus benjamina exotica, *the weeping fig tree.*

Ficus elastica decora, *an improved rubber tree.*

Ficus lyrata, *fiddleleaf fig, is an excellent tree.*

tends to develop wide-spreading branches which you can sit under indoors and easily make believe you are resting under a marvelous old shade tree outdoors. It needs strong light indoors, but direct sun is not necessary. Keep the soil evenly moist.

Ficus elastica decora. Rubber plant. This fig has much bolder leaves than *F. benjamina,* and it is never as graceful, especially in a relatively small space. However, it is not terribly expensive nor is it temperamental. Give it medium light but little or no direct sun (which tends to burn holes in the leaves). Keep the soil evenly moist.

Ficus lyrata. Fiddleleaf fig. This fig is

even bolder in appearance than the rubber plant, but it often succeeds in being more graceful. Culture is the same.

Other. tree-size figs to grow indoors include *Ficus philippinensis* (Philippine fig), *F. retusa nitida* (Indian laurel), which lends itself well to training and clipping into a formal tree, and *F. triangularis,* which has triangle-shape leaves and has only recently begun to appear in commerce.

Howea forsteriana. Kentia palm. If you want a big Victorian-looking palm, this is the one to search out. It is in great demand and is apparently somewhat difficult to propagate. Therefore, expect to pay more than you would for the ubiquitous and temperamental areca palm.

Ficus triangularis *has triangular leaves.*

A young kentia, perhaps the best large indoor palm.

However, the kentia is worth every penny. It grows beautifully and easily indoors if you give it half a chance. Provide low to medium light; little or no direct sun is needed. Keep the soil evenly moist.

Ligustrum lucidum. Waxleaf privet. Like *Ficus retusa nitida,* this is amenable to training and trimming into a neat, rather formal appearance. Give it medium light. Water well, then not again until the surface soil begins to feel dry. However, don't expect this privet to thrive indoors in winter in hot, dry heat.

Podocarpus macrophylla maki. Podocarpus. This is a handsome evergreen tree for indoors, with older leaves a dark green, the newer ones pale chartreuse. It will tolerate light indoors from sunny to shady. Keep the soil evenly moist. In the winter, try not to situate it where hot, dry heat blows on the branches.

Rhapis excelsa. Lady palm. This graceful palm makes a beautiful indoor tree. Give it medium light; little or no direct sun is needed. Keep the soil in a range from evenly moist to wet.

Fitting Trees to Containers

Any of the indoor trees suggested here will grow in a 12- to 14-inch pot or tub until it is about six feet tall, then it will need an 18-inch container for best growth. If an indoor tree really does become a

ceiling pusher, prune out the top and re-pot in the same container in which it has been growing; simply remove part of the old soil, clip away some of the old roots, and add fresh soil.

One problem you may experience with large indoor trees is keeping the foliage clean. If you can put one in the bathtub and give it a shower of tepid water, you have no problem. Or if you can put it outdoors for a shower from the hose in warm weather, the leaves can be cleaned with relative ease. Otherwise, you can take a damp cloth and clean individual leaves if they are large enough to make this feasible, or you can use a feather duster for small leaves like those of *Ficus benjamina exotica.*

Chamaedorea erumpens, *or bamboo palm, is an attractive tree for the indoors.*

29
Vegetables, Herbs and Fruit

Herbs have been grown in containers for hundreds of years, but only recently have we realized that not only can vegetables be beautiful but they too can be grown in pots, tubs, plastic-lined fruit baskets, garbage pails and even in hanging baskets. Among fruit, strawberries, dwarf citrus and dwarf peaches of the Bonanza variety in particular are especially suited to container gardening.

To grow herbs indoors you will need a window that receives full sun for at least half of the day. With this same amount of sun, but in cooler temperatures—preferably not over 60 degrees F.—you can also grow a fairly decent crop of leaf lettuce. If you have no sun, then a fluorescent-light garden will give you a place to grow herbs and a few salad greens. Dwarf citrus can be a fine houseplant, but strawberries and dwarf peaches are best left to the outdoor garden.

Herbs Indoors and Outdoors

Some herbs are grown primarily for seasoning, others for good scents. Among the favorites for culinary purposes are sweet basil, chives, dill, oregano, parsley, rosemary, thyme, sage, various mints, savory, sweet bay and tarragon. Others you may want to try include anise, borage, caraway, chervil, Florence fennel and sweet marjoram.

Herbs cultivated primarily—or entirely—for the good scents they give off, especially when a leaf is squeezed, include lavender, catnip (used, of course, for making tea), and scented geraniums. Besides the fairly common rose-scented geranium there are varieties with the fragrance of nutmeg, apple, lemon, coconut, pineapple, orange and pungent.

Young plants of all these herbs may be found at some local nurseries and garden centers in the spring. Occasionally they may also be found in autumn. Mail-order herb specialists (listed in the Appendix) will ship plants almost any season the weather permits. You can also grow many fine herbs from seeds. Some of the easier ones to start this way include basil, chives, dill, parsley, anise, borage, caraway, marjoram, fennel and summer savory.

If you're a good container gardener who never forgets to water, you should be able to keep sweet bay, rosemary and lemon-verbena indefinitely. As container plants, they should not be left out of doors in freezing weather, however. The best place for them in the winter is a cool, sunny place where temperatures seldom go above 68 degrees F. Hot, dry artificial heat is not to their liking.

Whether you are growing herbs in natural or fluorescent light, keep snipping them back, both for seasoning and to promote more compact growth.

Herbs used alone, or in combination with pots and other planters of flowers, make handsome container gardens outdoors in warm weather. Foliage colors vary from silvery gray to dark green to burgundy, in texture from filmy and feathery to broad and bold.

Young potted herbs ready for first clippings. Left to right: chives, sweet basil, rosemary, and oregano.

Vegetables in Containers, Indoors

Vegetables are not exactly superstars among houseplants, but there are a few with which you may be successful in a sunny window or in a fluorescent-light garden.

Perhaps the best is Curlycress, which will grow from seed packet to salad and sandwich garnish in ten days. Make sowings at any season approximately every two weeks. The dark green, finely cut and curled leaves are similar to parsley. If you have a cool window, try watercress. It is a slower crop (allow about 50 days from planting) and should be cultivated in a large, shallow container of soil with the saucer kept filled with water at all times.

Lettuce would make a fine houseplant were it not for the fact that it loves cool weather. If you have a cool, sunny room, or can build a fluorescent-light garden in a cool room or basement, you may be successful with any of the leaf lettuces such as Ruby, Green Ice and Oak Leaf. If you are growing only lettuce and seasoning herbs in a fluorescent-light garden, you may wish to experiment with continuous lighting. Although this procedure will not work where flowering plants are involved (they need properly balanced periods of light and dark within every 24 hours), it is definitely worth trying where leaf growth is the only kind desired.

Small hot peppers and cherry tomatoes are also sometimes cultivated indoors in a sunny place or under fluorescent lights burned 16 hours out of every 24. They are naturally warm-weather plants, so the indoor environment is no great challenge for them.

In an indoor environment suited to lettuce, you might also try a few pots of radishes. Planted in pots of a spongy

ABOVE: *Patio Pik hybrid cucumber in hanging basket.*
BELOW: *Patio hybrid tomato thriving in large pot.*

ABOVE: Fruit baskets and boxes lined with polyethylene plastic and filled with potting soil provide a ready and inexpensive place for growing vegetables. Kinds include lettuce, radishes, cabbage, scallions, and colorful rhubarb chard. Containers of marigolds and flowering sage complete the picture.
LEFT: Sweet pepper thrives as a container plant.

soil-less medium (see Chapter 34). and fed lightly with each watering, they will do nicely.

If the container is large enough, you can grow any. vegetable this way outdoors. All of them need at least a half day of sunlight and generous watering and feeding.

In terms of their decorative appearance and edible harvest, some of the most rewarding vegetables to grow in containers outdoors are rhubarb chard, Swiss chard, eggplant, dwarf or patio type cucumbers and tomatoes, leaf lettuce, okra (in climates with a long, warm

season), peppers, Malabar spinach and zucchini.

The only real problem with vegetables in containers is letting the soil dry out between waterings. If the plants wilt, then you've waited too long to give them a drink and the harvest will be nonexistent or of poor quality. If you are growing any vegetable in an individual pot 12 inches in diameter or smaller, you may find it advantageous in really hot weather to place the pot inside a larger container and then fill the space between with moist peat moss. This will help keep roots cooler and also prevent the soil from drying out so rapidly.

Dwarf citrus flower and fruit are in these planter boxes.

Spider plant makes a graceful subject for hanging-basket culture indoors and outdoors.

30
Hanging Baskets, Window Boxes and Urns

The plants that naturally trail, creep, cascade or climb are ideal choices for hanging baskets, urns and other pedestal-displayed containers and. outdoor window boxes. In recent years hanging baskets have all but replaced draperies and curtains in many houses and apartments.

Indoors, brackets for holding hanging baskets can be mounted on walls or frames near the window, or the baskets can be suspended from ceiling hooks. Indoors the major problems with hanging baskets are lack of light and winter heat—which naturally rises to the ceiling, where it tends to dry out basket plants, especially kinds that prefer temperatures on the cool side.

Outdoors, hanging baskets can be suspended from hooks installed in overhanging eaves, from tree branches and porch ceilings. Some arbors are built solely for them. Brackets can be mounted on walls, fences and posts. The main problem with hanging baskets outdoors is too much exposure to hot, dry winds.

Of major concern for basket gardening indoors and outdoors is hanging them so they are absolutely secure. There is nothing quite so disappointing as to find that the wind has blown a perfectly beautiful hanging tuberous begonia from its perch and left it strewn about the terrace or porch. And indoors it is not a pleasant chore to clean up the mess left by a basket that has fallen from a poorly installed ceiling hook or other means of display.

Containers for Hanging Plants

The best hanging baskets for indoors are those with some means of catching excess moisture. Outdoors, where dripping water is of little concern, the time-honored wire baskets make excellent containers, as do redwood boxes and cradles. At your local garden center you will also find a variety of plastic hanging containers. The white hanging pots with an attached saucer have been sold by the millions in recent years. If your color scheme includes white, they may be fine. Otherwise, you may wish to cover them with inexpensive woven baskets.

To suspend hanging containers you can use nylon cord, wire or special macramé holders.

If you want an almost-instant effect from hanging-basket plants, you may prefer to buy established specimens. However, many of the ones sold by local florists have reached peak growth and will be difficult to keep in good condition. The best way is to grow your own basket plantings, starting from seeds, cuttings or young plants.

For planting a hanging container, use only a growing medium that is light and spongy and holds moisture well. You might use a mix composed of two parts sphagnum peat moss to one part each of garden loam and sand. Or you can use a mixture of equal parts garden loam, sphagnum peat moss and vermiculite. In recent years the soil-less mixes have become popular for hanging-basket plantings. These are marketed under such names as Vita-Bark University Mix, Jiffy Mix, Redi-Earth and Supersoil. If you grow in soil-less, however, be prepared to feed a little with almost every watering (see Chapter 34).

If you are using a porous basket, for example, a container constructed of wire or wooden slats, or an open-work plastic container, line it completely with unmilled sphagnum moss or florist's sheet moss before you add potting soil. After you finish planting such a container, immerse it in a pail, sink or tub of water for a good soaking; remove, allow to drain; then hang it in the growing place. If a hanging basket of this type is never allowed to dry out severely, you will not need to remove it for soaking. However, if such a basket dries out severely, remove it, soak in a container of water, allow to drain, and then hang it back up.

Hanging baskets indoors will need to be turned a quarter or half turn once each week in order for all growth to receive a uniform amount of light.

Whether indoors or outdoors, hanging-basket plants will grow best if you are attentive to pinching back tips. This encourages compact, full growth. Rapid-growing indoor basket plants such as Swedish-ivy and wandering Jew in particular need almost weekly pinching back in order to keep them dense and healthy.

One word of caution: plants suspended in the air tend to dry out much more rapidly than those resting on the floor, a window sill or a surface outdoors. Baskets that receive full sun outdoors in the summer may need to be watered well twice a day, once in the morning, once in the evening.

Best Houseplants for Hanging Baskets

In the lists that follow I have divided the best and most popular hanging-basket plants according to their light requirements. Some are so adaptable, I have listed them in more than one category. Also light is tremendously variable from climate to climate, according to the time of the year and many other factors. If any hanging-basket plant wilts daily or develops burned, yellowed leaves, you will know it needs less direct sun. If, on the other hand, a basket plant looks pale, drops a great many older leaves, and new growth is weak, more direct sun is probably needed.

Burro's-tail Sedum morganianum *as a hanging basket.*

Baskets for sun

LATIN NAME	POPULAR NAME
Abutilon megapotamicum	flowering-maple
Aeschynanthus	lipstick vine
Asparagus	asparagus-fern
Begonia	begonia
Bromeliad	bromeliad
Campanula isophylla	star of Bethlehem
Ceropegia	hearts entangled; rosary vine
Chlorophytum	spider plant
Cissus	grape-ivy
Coleus	coleus
Columnea	columnea
Epiphyllum	orchid cactus
Episcia	flame violet
Helxine	baby's-tears
Hoya	wax plant
Hypocyrta	goldfish plant
Ipomoea	sweet potato
Kalanchoe	kalanchoe
Mahernia	honeybells
Maranta	prayer plant
Orchidaceae	orchids
Oxalis	oxalis
Passiflora	passion flower
Pilea	pilea
Plectranthus	Swedish-ivy
Polypodiaceae	ferns
Rhipsalis	rhipsalis
Schizocentron	Spanish shawl
Schlumbergera	Christmas cactus
Sedum	donkey-tail
Streptosolen	orange browallia
Tradescantia	wandering Jew
Zygocactus	Thanksgiving cactus

Baskets for sun/shade

LATIN NAME	POPULAR NAME
Achimenes	magic flower
Aeschynanthus	lipstick vine
Bromeliad	bromeliad
Calathea	calathea
Ceropegia	hearts entangled; rosary vine

Pellionia makes a beautiful basket in a shady place.

Chlorophytum	spider plant
Cissus	grape-ivy
Columnea	columnea
Cymbalaria	Kenilworth-ivy
Episcia	flame violet
Ficus pumila	creeping fig
Hoya	wax plant
Hypocyrta	goldfish plant
Manettia	manettia
Maranta	prayer plant
Pellionia	pellionia
Peperomia	peperomia
Philodendron	philodendron
Pilea	pilea
Polypodiaceae	ferns
Schizocentron	Spanish shawl
Scindapsus	pothos
Selaginella	sweat plant
Senecio	German ivy
Syngonium	trileaf wonder
Tradescantia	wandering Jew

The dwarf pomegranate is one of the best of all bonsai subjects for cultivating all year indoors.

31
Bonsai and
Other Art Forms

Container plants offer exciting possibilities beyond the rewards of flowers, foliage, fragrance and fruit. They can become living art forms that offer endless hours of pleasure. Some of these specialized techniques are described in illustrations here.

Miniature Trees the Bonsai Way

In recent years the ancient Oriental art of bonsai has swept this country. In fact, while keeping the time-honored traditions and techniques, enterprising American growers have applied them to hundreds of new and different plants, even in fluorescent-light gardens. For material in this chapter I am indebted to Henry M. Cathey, head of ornamentals research for the U.S. Department of Agriculture. In fact, a bulletin prepared under his direction, called *Growing Bonsai*, makes an excellent introduction to the art; it is available for 35¢ from the Superintendent of Documents, U.S. Government Printing Office, Washington, D.C. 20402. Request Home and Garden Bulletin No. 206.

Dr. Cathey writes: "The aim of bonsai culture is to develop a tiny tree that has all the elements of a large tree growing in a natural setting. This look is achieved, principally, by branch and root pruning and shaping. Bonsai require daily watering during their growing season, and, because the plants are rooted in shallow pots, careful pruning.

"Bonsai are kept outdoors most of the year, but from time to time these miniaturized versions of nature are brought indoors for display. Only certain tropical trees, shrubs and vines can be kept continuously indoors as bonsai.

"Not all plants are equally effective as bonsai. To produce a realistic illusion of a mature tree, look for plants with these characteristics:

ABOVE: Japanese maples trained as bonsai.
BELOW: Long-needled pine makes picturesque bonsai.

- Small leaves or needles
- Short internodes or distances between leaves
- Attractive bark or surface roots
- Branching characteristics for good twig forms

"All parts of the ideal bonsai—trunk, branches, twigs, leaves, flowers, fruits, buds, roots—should be in perfect scale with the size of the tree. Plants used for bonsai should have small leaves, or leaves that become small under bonsai culture. Plants with overly large leaves such as the avocado will look out of proportion if chosen for bonsai. Among the plants with suitable small leaves and needles are spruce, pine, zelkova, pomegranate and certain oaks and maples."

Among the houseplants suited to bonsai culture, Dr. Cathey suggests woody types native to the tropics and subtropics of the world. These include: *Acacia baileyana,* aralia (*Polyscias* species *balfouriana, fruticosa* and *guilfoylei*), bird's-eye bush (*Ochna˙ multiflora*), camellia, *Gardenia jasminoides radicans, Citrus* species (calamondin, kumquat, lemon, lime, orange and tangerine), *Eugenia uniflora,* Arizona and Monterey cypresses, *Ficus diversifolia, Cuphea hypssopifolia, Hibiscus rosa-sinensis cooperi, Malpighia coccigera, Jacaranda acutifolia, Crassula arguetea* (jade plant), *Jasminum parkeri, Murraea exotica, Trachelospermum jasminoides, Ficus retusa, Myrtus communis, Quercus suber, Nicodemia diversifolia, Grevillea robusta, Bauhinia variegata, Olea europaea, Oxera pulchella, Schinus molle, Pistacia chinensis, Carissa grandiflora, Delonix regia,* dwarf pomegranate, *Leucaena glauca, Calliandra surinamensis, Serissa foetida* and *Cassia eremophila.*

In addition to nursery stock, plants for bonsai can be collected from the wild or propagated from plants in your garden. You can also purchase trained bonsai plants in this country or import them from Japan (but only deciduous varieties ship well).

Dr. Cathey advises that the best method for a beginner to obtain bonsai is to buy nursery stock and develop his own:

These plants come in 1- to 5-gallon cans and their root systems have become adapted to cramped conditions.

Buy only young, healthy plants when purchasing nursery stock. Look for plants that are well rooted and well branched. Inspect the overall plant and then push back the foliage and examine the base from all sides. See if the foliage is full enough to be shaped into an interesting bonsai. Check to see if branches are where you will need them.

Do not thin the root system excessively all at once when placing the plant in a smaller container. By thinning the roots gradually and reducing the root system safely over a period of years, you will not damage the plant. If you prune and shape first and neglect thinning the roots, some plants may die.

Strive for flowing form when shaping bonsai. Visualize the overall theme and try to get a three-dimensional effect. Remember to select the front, back and sides of your bonsai before pruning, and don't forget to examine the roots that will influence the growth of these areas.

Use your pruning shears judiciously to make changes that benefit your bonsai. Fine adjustments are made by wiring and bending and thinning (removal of branches).

Before shaping a plant into a bonsai, decide whether the best attitude of the tree is upright, slanted, cascaded or semi-cascaded. Examine the general form of the tree and note whether it is straight or twisted. Match the potential of a tree to the style that fits it best. Decide whether the base will rise from the soil level or whether you will expose some bare roots.

You will need the following basic tools: a pair of sharp hook-and-blade pruning shears; a garden trowel; blunt sticks; a pair of sturdy wire cutters; copper wire of various lengths; and a sprinkling can. Also useful are scissors for trimming leaves, tweezers for nipping and brushes for cleaning the top soil.

Nursery plants are often overgrown and need much pruning to establish their best form. Through pruning you control growth and form by removing excess foliage and ugly limbs.

When pruning make all cuts above a bud, a side branch, or a main fork of the tree. Remove all buds except those on the outside of the trunk to force the growth outward and upward. Leave stubs flush with stem; long stubs serve as an entry for insects (and besides, they are ugly). Avoid cutting back so far that you weaken the main branches.

When pruning, keep branches growing toward an open space instead of toward each other or the trunk. Do not shear bonsai as you would cut a hedge.

After deciding on the foliage form for your bonsai, remove all crossed branches and any dead branches. Then thin other branches until the tree takes on the form you have selected.

If you want to slant a tree that has been growing in an upright position and insure that branches take a normal shape, prune it in an upright attitude, and then tip it to where it should be and work on it that way.

Next, cut back new growth and thin out excess branches. When pruning an upright style, remove unneeded side branches and leave the center ones that will fill out as they grow.

A tree usually requires only one heavy pruning in its life to establish its basic form. After this initial pruning, shaping is done by nipping or pinching back to shape and develop the trunk and to control the overall size of the plant. Nipping controls new growth before it becomes so dense that it must be pruned.

Nipping is done not only to shape a plant but to develop more luxuriant foliage. As the new growth tips show up, nip them with your fingers, twisting rather than cutting or pulling. Also nip off tiny spurs that appear on the trunk or along heavy branches. These may develop into unsightly suckers that will leave scars when removed. Do not overdo this removal; be careful not to damage the foliage you leave on the plant.

After the top of a bonsai is pruned, trim the roots. Try to keep all fibrous roots and maintain a balance, if possible, of one branch for one root. Remove any roots that were damaged in digging. Leave the surface root system intact and make it appear as if the roots cling to the soil surface. Prune roots with sharp, sloping cuts to avoid damaging them.

The wiring and bending of branches that give bonsai its shape is unique to the art. Wiring is done after pruning when the tree has been thinned to essential branches.

Copper wire is usually used for shaping bonsai because it is flexible. The sizes of copper wire that are best for bonsai work are: 10, 12, 14, 16 and 18. Wire as light as No. 16 should be used for very thin branches and for tying rather than bending.

Wire evergreen trees only during their dormant period when the branches can be shaped without damaging growth. Wire deciduous trees only during their growing season.

The day before you wire a plant, do not water it; this will make the branches more flexible. Once a branch has taken on its trained form, remove the wire, straighten out its twists and flatten it with a mallet for reuse.

Wiring and shaping should begin at the lowest point on the tree, working upward. Do the following when wiring:

1. Anchor the end of the wire at the base of the tree before winding it. Push the end of the wire deep into the soil.

2. Wire from the trunk to the main branch. Use a foam pad under the wire to prevent damaging the bark. Keep the turns about 1/4 inch apart and spiral upward at a 45-degree angle. Do not wire too tightly, and do not damage leaves or stems.

After wiring, the plant is shaped or bent by hand. The trunk and main branches are gradually bent in the planned direction. Never try to straighten a branch that has been bent; this may split the bark.

Branches sometimes snap, even when carefully wired and bent. If the branch is not completely broken rejoin the broken ends, and wind some garden tape around the break. These fractures often heal quickly. If a branch snaps off, prune back cleanly at the first side branch.

Wire should be kept on the plant for not more than one year. Remove the wire before the bark becomes constricted; ridges will form if the wire is left on too long. When removing a wire, start at the outermost end of branches, and take care not to harm leaves, twigs or bark.

Other Garden Art Forms

If the idea of training a plant appeals to you, consider the techniques of topiary and espalier.

Classic topiary is represented by great old specimens of boxwood or privet artfully pruned into squares, balls, spirals, even animal and human forms. Today it is possible to buy ready-made topiary frames or armatures and with these you can have a lot of fun creating almost "instant" specimens by using small-leaved varieties of English ivy, creeping fig or any other vining or trailing plant. Three-dimensional forms are usually first filled and stuffed with unmilled sphagnum moss that has been soaked in water to which

LEFT: Small-flowered chrysanthemums may be trained as standards like this one. They can also be espaliered or trained into magnificent cascades. The secret lies in starting the training process early in the season and continuing until the flowers open. Never allow the soil to dry out.
ABOVE: Stylish topiaries like these two privets growing in Versailles tubs can be cultivated indoors or outdoors in large or small sizes, depending on the plant materials used and the shape desired.
RIGHT: To make a bromeliad tree you will need a good-sized piece of driftwood anchored in plaster of Paris. Wrap roots of assorted bromeliads in moist sphagnum moss, then tie securely into the crotches formed by the driftwood branches. Keep bromeliads happy by misting frequently with water.

fertilizer has been added. Then rooted cuttings of the selected plant are positioned as thickly as possible over the form.

A two-dimensional form for a topiary— for example, a wire coat hanger bent into a circle and anchored in a pot of soil—is in effect also a form for espaliering a plant. If you anchor that circle in the center of a pot filled with a long-stranded small-leaved English ivy, you can immediately tie it around the wire. Nip off wayward branches. Continue nipping and shaping in order to maintain a tidy, well-

defined shape. By using galvanized wire or strips of redwood, you can create longer-lasting espalier frames in any pattern or design that pleases you, for example, classic trelliswork or treillage, a single trunk with one or more "U" shapes above it—in a stylized, flattened tree.

For containerized espaliers, you can use any of the tropical and subtropical plants suggested earlier in this chapter for bonsai training. Vines such as passiflora, clematis and dipladenia can also be trained in this manner.

32
Calendar Planting Guide for Tender Flowering Plants

NOTE: The temperature following the name of each plant suggests optimum nighttime temperature indoors during that part of the year when artificial heat is used. Most plants will adapt several—if not many—degrees above or below this optimum.

As these are tender plants—of tropical or semitropical origin—their time of flowering in the United States indoors or outdoors is often a mystery to the gardener.

January

BROWALLIA—65°—For plants to use outdoors in the spring and summer, start seeds now. They will grow slowly the first two months. Tip cuttings made now or in February will also provide flowering plants for spring planting out of doors.

CALENDULA—40°—Sow seeds now for May-to-hot-weather flowers. Varieties recommended include Sensation, Lemon King Select, Ball Orange Improved and Ball Gold. A sunny, cool, airy atmosphere is needed by calendulas.

CLERODENDRUM—60°—Now is the time to take 6-inch cuttings of half-ripened wood in order to have vigorous young plants of flowering size the coming season. Few flowers equal the fragrance of *C. fragrans pleniflorum*. The bleeding-heart vine (*C. thomsonae*) is a shrubby vine easily kept in bounds as a container plant. Trim back and repot old clerodendrum plants now.

DIDISCUS—50°—For blue-lace flowers beginning in April, sow seeds now in a 5-inch-deep flat. Thin to stand about 3 inches apart. Discard at the end of the flowering season.

FELICIA—50°—The blue daisy flowers of this plant (sometimes called agathea) are always welcome. Sow seeds now for blooming plants next winter. Pinch back several times until September to encourage branching.

GERANIUM—55°—Bedding plants cut back and brought in last fall can take a little more water as the days get longer. Feed lightly every two weeks. Cuttings of half-ripened wood made now will make excellent planting-out material next spring. Try some of the new seed-grown geranium varieties.

GYPSOPHILA—60°—Sow seeds of baby's-breath now in deep flats, or an 8-inch standard flowerpot. Be sure to purchase seeds of the annual type so you will have flowers this year.

IMPATIENS—60°—Sow seeds now for an abundance of flowering plants at planting-out time this spring. There's a wealth of beauty in the new dwarf impatiens hybrids. Check your seed catalog for descriptions. For full shade to semishade indoors or outdoors, few plants can equal the flower crop given by impatiens. If you have old plants of favorite impatiens, tip cuttings can be started now.

LOBELIA—55°—For baskets, window boxes, edging and pots, it's hard to have enough lobelia plants. Start seeds now indoors so the plants will be blooming at planting-out time. Even if summer heat takes its toll of these cool-loving plants, you'll still reap a big flower show early in the season if you start seeds now.

MARIGOLD—55°—Most of today's hybrids will bloom in about 90 days from seeds. The Spun Gold and Spun Yellow types are especially nice for a bold block of color in a sunny place indoors during April and May; then you can transplant them outdoors.

SALPIGLOSSIS — 55° — These fascinating plants with spectacular trumpet flowers need an early start. Sow seeds now; transplant later to individual 3-inch pots if you plan to put them outdoors after frost danger is past. If you have a greenhouse, transplant three

seedlings to each 8- or 10-inch pot. Stake and tie as necessary.

SCHIZANTHUS—55°—Sow seeds now for a late-spring-into-summer showing of butterfly flowers. Transplant first to 3-inch pots, then finish at a 6-inch size. Pinch twice to induce branching. I transplant three seedlings to each 3-inch pot. Two of these I pinch, one I don't. The one not pinched blooms earlier than the other two, thus providing a longer season. The same technique will work with other plants that get pinched—snapdragons, for example.

February

ABUTILON—60°—If you have established flowering maples, now would be a good time to repot. Trim back branches that are too long, or which make the plant unshapely. Trimmings may be rooted to have compact, flowering plants for indoors, or you can use these outdoors this spring. For "wow-some" large-size flowers in rich colors—varying from yellow and orange to dark red, paling to pink—plant seeds of Thompson and Morgan's Large-Flowered Mixed hybrids. Sown in January or February, they will start flowering about the end of July. By pinching out the leading shoot, their height can be kept to about 18 inches.

ACALYPHA—60°—Now is the time to root 4-inch tip cuttings of the chenille plant, as well as the variety called "copper leaf." Root in a warm, moist place; provide high humidity and keep shaded until rooting occurs.

ACHIMENES—60°—Now is the time to plant the scaly rhizomes of this popular summer-blooming gesneriad, a relative of the African violet and gloxinia. Six rhizomes will make a big show in a 6-inch pot. Warmth, high humidity and evenly moist growing medium will encourage rapid growth, with flowers beginning in late spring. If you have a greenhouse going in summer, achimenes can be the stars of the show. Outdoors in warm weather, they are as desirable for shady gardens as impatiens.

AGAPANTHUS—45°—Now is a good time to divide and repot large, crowded specimens. To grow a plentiful supply of this "lily of the Nile," sow seeds in a warm, moist place. First blooms can be expected in three years.

BEGONIA—65°—Divide, cut back and repot large wax or semperflorens begonias. If you take cuttings, make them of base growth that shows an indication of branching. Cuttings made from vigorous tip growth often root poorly if at all, and then they may not branch properly. There's still time to sow seeds, too, for flowering plants next summer, and real specimens next fall and winter. Try some of the newest dwarf hybrids, but also try Red and Rose Butterfly—magnificent new semperflorens with flowers to 2½ inches across! At a short distance away these appear to be tuberous begonias.

CALADIUM—60°—For specimen plants in full foliage by June, start the tubers now in warmth and moisture. You can start a quantity of tubers in a deep flat of vermiculite, transplanting later to individual 6- to 8-inch pots. Or start individual tubers in 6-inch pots. Planting caladium tubers upside down results in more shoots, and thus more but smaller leaves.

CAMPANULA—45°—Make cuttings now of C. isophylla and similar types in order to have a plentiful supply of blooming plants next fall. Keep warm, moist and in high humidity, with shade, while roots are forming.

CESTRUM—60°—If you like fragrant flowers, try some of the cestrums. C. nocturnum is the plant I grow for its creamy white flowers that give off a fragrance like Chanel No. 5 every evening in the summer. If you have a cestrum already, now is the time to root 3-inch tip cuttings.

COLEUS—60°—This month take 3-inch tip cuttings of your favorite plants. Sow seeds of selected strains, or named varieties, in order to have an abundance of plants this spring. Check every coleus plant in your collection for signs of mealybug infestation. Coleus and mealybugs have such an affinity for each other, if you find them together, discard both. Start over with seeds.

FREESIA—65-70°—Sow seeds now, of an outstanding strain like Super Giant Hybrids Mixed, for flowers next fall. Once germinated no extra warmth is needed —they'll do better in a range of 50-60°. Move outdoors for the summer, but provide plenty of water and fertilize every other week. Bring inside in September.

GERBERA—70°—Sow seeds now in warmth in order to have vigorous, young, flowering plants for next fall. Thompson and Morgan's Florists Strain Mixed will open flowers measuring to 5 inches in diameter with broad, stiff petals, and long, strong stems.

LANTANA—55°—Make 3-inch cuttings of older plants in order to have plenty of material for planting-out next spring.

TUBEROUS BEGONIA—65°—Start tubers now in order to have flowering plants by early summer. They need a warm, moist situation. Moist, shredded redwood bark makes an excellent starting medium, or you can use the time-honored vermiculite, or 50-50 mixture of peat moss and sand.

TULBAGHIA—50°—Now is the time to divide and repot this intermittent-blooming bulbous plant. It's always nice to propagate an unusual but easy-to-grow plant like tulbaghia in order to have extra plants to pass along to gardening friends.

VERBENA—50°—Start seeds now in order to have flowering plants by planting-out time this spring. This tender perennial, which we cultivate as a hardy annual, doesn't bloom as quickly from seed as some common annuals, and your garden will benefit from giving it an early start in the greenhouse.

March

ALLAMANDA—60°—Take cuttings of last year's growth and root in a warm, moist, shaded place. Vermiculite makes an excellent rooting medium.

APHELANDRA — 55° — Now is the time to take tip cuttings of this handsome foliage plant. Root as described for allamanda. Young plants are compact and usually attractive—nice to present as gifts.

ARDISIA—60°—The coralberry comes in for all kinds of attention this month: established plants may be repotted. It's also the time to sow seeds or plant cuttings in moist soil and warmth.

AZALEA—55°—On the surface of a mixture of peat moss and sand, sow seeds of a good hybrid strain of azaleas this month. Be sure the medium never dries out. If water in your area is on the alkaline side, water from time to time with an acid-type fertilizer of special azalea food.

BELOPERONE—55°—There's still time to take tip cuttings of the shrimp plant and place in individual small pots of moist rooting medium in order to have plenty for outdoor planting this summer.

BOUVARDIA—60°—Plant tip cuttings now in moist rooting medium in order to have vigorous, young plants next fall.

FREESIA—45°—For real abundance, sow

hybrid seeds now. Plant in a wooden flat at least 6 inches deep. Keep in constant growth, right through the usual dormant time of summer and early fall. This means the soil should never dry out and that feeding needs to be kept up until blooming begins around Christmas.

GYPSOPHILA—60°—To catch a quick crop of annual baby's-breath before summer, sow seeds now. You will have cutting material in about eight weeks, perfect filler for early spring bouquets, not to mention the pleasure of the flowers for your container garden.

KAEMPFERIA—60°—If you want flowers indoors this summer, start some kaempferias or ginger-lilies now. Mail-order specialists stock them.

PRIMULA—45-50°—Now is the time to start seeds of the showy frost-tender primroses—*P. sinensis, P. malacoides* and *P. obconica*—in order to have flowering specimens of outstanding size next winter and spring. Seeds germinate well at 60 degrees. When large enough to transplant, move to community pots or flats, transplanting later to individual 4's or 5's, finally to 6- and 7-inch pots in early fall.

ZANTEDESCHIA—55°—Now is the time to plant tubers of pink and yellow calla-lilies, as well as the newer Sunrise Hybrids which come in many interesting shades. Three tubers to a 10-inch pot will provide quite an attractive specimen by midsummer. Keep warm and just moist until growth begins, then pour on the water and begin bi-weekly feeding after foliage growth is apparent.

April

BEGONIA, TUBEROUS—65°—Plant dormant tubers now, keeping barely moist, but nicely warm, until root growth is apparent, then provide more moisture as leaves begin to grow.

BOUGAINVILLEA—55°—Make tip cuttings 3 or 4 inches long and root in a warm, moist, shaded place. As new growth begins to be vigorous, pinch out the growing tips to induce branching. Continue this practice through summer and early fall. Once well-rooted, new plants can take full sun. The effects of this baking through the summer season seem to bring on all the more bloom the following fall and winter.

CHRYSANTHEMUM—60°—If mums are in your plans for late summer, fall and early winter color in containers, begin today by writing for catalogs from specialists. There isn't a day to waste if you are to have time to study lists and descriptions before sending your order for rooted cuttings. In the best catalogs you will find French imports, anemone and spoon types, spider and threadlike varieties, cushions, pompons, buttons, tree-forming, cascades and football types.

CROTON—Tip cuttings 5 or 6 inches long may be rooted now in warmth (75-80°) and high humidity, using a porous rooting medium kept moist (equal parts vermiculite and peat moss may be used). Today's croton varieties make unusually showy foliage plants indoors and out. Direct sun is not needed—only bright diffused light will bring on the characteristic foliage coloration.

HIBISCUS, CHINESE—65°—Now is the time to take 4-inch stem cuttings in order to have plenty of vigorous, young plants coming on. Since these bloom on new wood, it is not unusual for cuttings in the rooting medium to provide an occasional bloom.

MARGUERITE—50°—Boston or Paris daisies known botanically as *Chrysanthemum frutescens,* are great to have, both in the house or greenhouse and later outdoors in the summer. Now is the time to start 3-inch tip cuttings in order to have bushy, well-formed plants for flowering next winter and spring. You can buy pink, white or yellow varieties. For best effect, plant three or four rooted cuttings of each color to an 8-inch pot.

PENTAS—50°—This everblooming plant is useful not only in the house (stake for upright growth, or let it billow out of a basket) but also for bedding outdoors in the summer. Before you put stock plants outdoors, take 3-inch tip cuttings. Root in moist vermiculite at about 70° in a humid, shady place. These young plants, if kept pinched during the summer, will be ready to put on a real flower show indoors next fall.

May

AFRICAN VIOLET—65°—Sow seeds now in order to have flowering-size plants next winter and spring. Park's Sure-Fire starting mix makes an excellent medium on which to sow the fine seeds (they need not be covered with it, but merely pressed lightly into the surface), or you can use finely milled sphagnum moss. This is also the season to divide multiple-crowned plants, and an excellent time to order new kinds.

ANEMONE — 40° — Plant seeds of hybrid strains now for flowers of unusually good quality next winter. Protection from burning sun, evenly moist soil, and as much coolness as possible are the rules for taking the seedlings through summer. Transplanting to 4-inch pots will need to be done by September.

CINERARIA—45°—Sow seeds now in order to have plants of specimen size that bloom next winter and spring. It's important with cinerarias to keep the seedlings growing without check. This means transplanting regularly so that roots do not become potpound; feeding biweekly; keeping the soil moist at all times; and spraying as necessary to prevent aphids from damaging new growth.

CITRUS—50°—If you have any of the dwarf citrus in your collection, now is the time to make tip cuttings of half-ripened wood. Once rooted these young plants will begin to bloom and bear fruit; these make excellent gifts. Cuttings need shade and high humidity while roots form.

FELICIA—50°—Sow seeds now of this blue-flowered daisy, often called "agathea." Flowers will come next winter and spring. Seedlings need lots of fresh air in the summer, and plenty of sunlight, combined with regular pinching of tip growth. If you have established plants, now is the time to root tip cuttings in moist vermiculite.

GERANIUM—55°—Take cuttings now in order to have plenty of pot-size flowering specimens for next winter and spring indoors. This is also the time to start training a strongly upright-growing geranium to standard or tree form. Pinch or rub out all sideshoots as quickly as they can be seen. Provide a sturdy stake at the beginning, one of the height you wish the tree to be. When the tip of the geranium reaches this height, pinch it out to start the branching process. As each new branch reaches a length of 2 to 3 inches, pinch out the tip until a well-branched head is achieved.

HOYA—60°—Now is the time to root cuttings of the wax plant in moist vermiculite; provide warmth, humidity and shade until rooting occurs. Look in catalogs of houseplant specialists for new and unusual kinds of hoyas.

TIBOUCHINA—55°—This purple-flowered plant makes an excellent container subject for spring-to-fall bloom. Now is

the time to make 3-inch tip cuttings; root in moist vermiculite in a shaded, moist and warm situation. If you want the cutting to grow into a bushy, compact plant, pinch out growing tips several times, up to September. If you want to develop a tree or standard shape, follow instructions given this month for geraniums.

June

ACACIA—40°—If you have a cool greenhouse or sun porch in winter and spring, acacias should play a big role in the February-to-April flower show. Cuttings made now will root in a mixture of peat moss and sand; keep evenly moist. Acacias need to be summered outdoors in a cool, partially shaded situation. Avoid dry heat at any time.

ACALYPHA—60°—The popular "chenille plant," "copper leaf" and other acalyphas make showy plants for any container garden. There are new kinds coming onto the market, especially through commercial greenhouses; keep an eye out for these when you visit your florist. Four-inch tip cuttings root readily now in moist vermiculite; provide a humid, shaded, warm place. The chenille plant (*A. hispida*) is especially valuable for fall-to-spring flowers which may vary from rosy to rusty red, to the pinkish hues of *A. h. alba* strains.

AZALEA—55°—For fall and winter flowers in a moderately cool place, hardly any plant rivals today's azaleas. It's always a wise investment to buy a heavily budded plant at your local florists in November, but you can also have fun propagating favorite plants from 3-inch tip cuttings made in the summer; root in an evenly moist mixture of peat moss and sand in a situation that has good light (but no direct sun) and high humidity.

CALCEOLARIA—45°—Start seeds now as cool as possible (50° is ideal) in order to have flower-covered plants next winter and spring. Calceolarias need a sunny, moist, airy and cool atmosphere —a combination difficult to provide in many areas during the summer. Protection from midday summer sun is a necessity. Routine care is very much like that for cinerarias (see under May notes).

CYCLAMEN—50°—Now is the time to start seeds in a moist mixture of peat moss and sand in order to have flowering-size seedlings about 18 months from now. Nearly every gardener knows what a pleasure it is to have a flower-covered and bud-filled cyclamen from the florist, but real happiness to anyone who admires these plants is to grow a quantity from seeds.

EXACUM—50°—Start seeds now of this lavender-blue, starry flower for a showing this coming winter. It's important to keep the seedlings evenly moist at all times and to provide protection from burning summer sun. Otherwise this biennial is easily cultivated and worth starting each June.

MYOSOTIS—50°—Start seeds now of 'Blue Bird' or 'Christmas Bouquet' for forget-me-nots beginning this December and continuing into next spring. This summer it will be necessary to provide a place that's moist, as cool as possible, and partially shaded. By autumn transplant to individual 5-inch pots, or three to an 8-inch container.

PASSIFLORA—50°—Tip cuttings 4 to 6 inches long root easily now in moist vermiculite; keep warm and shaded. Kinds recommended for containers include *P. alato-caerulea* (unusual flowers combining the colors blue, pink, purple and white) and scarlet-flowered *P. coccinea.* Either type can be trained upward on a small trellis.

PRIMULA—45°—Sow seeds now of *P. malacoides* and *P. obconica.* The rule for success is to provide 60-degree temperatures during the germination period, and then ample shading and cooling through hot weather. By early fall individual seedlings will need 5-inch pots, and later the largest ones can be put into 7- or 8-inch pots.

PUNICA — 55° — The dwarf pomegranate makes an excellent houseplant, and now is the time to root cuttings of half-ripened wood. Plant in moist vermiculite and keep shaded and moist. This is one plant that doesn't mind summertime sun and warmth, provided the soil is kept moist. If you enjoy training plants, here's an excellent subject for bonsai work.

July

CELOSIA—55-60°—*C. plumosa,* the plume cockscomb, has been vastly improved in recent years. Heights range from 8 inches to several feet; colors have all the brilliancy of autumn leaves. For pots of this color indoors in autumn, select types that grow not more than 15 inches tall. Sow seeds now on the surface of a pot of moist vermiculite. Cover lightly. Keep moist. After germination, feed lightly with every watering. Transplant to 3-inch pots of soil (equal parts peat, garden loam, sand). Keep seedlings outdoors until late August or early September. Move to 5- or 6-inch pots when roots begin to fill the 3's. Continue feeding. By October these July-started seeds will have turned into striking specimens, a marvelous foil for any chrysanthemum show. They'll remain attractive at least until after the holidays.

CROSSANDRA—55-68°—Three-inch tip cuttings root easily now in moist potting soil, warmth and high humidity. It's a small-growing plant with glossy, dark green leaves and a nearly endless show of salmon-orange flowers. Great to grow in a fluorescent-light garden.

DIMORPHOTHECA—50-65°—This low-growing African daisy flower needs all the sun you can provide in winter. Sow seeds now for blooms beginning in four to five months.

FUCHSIA—55-60°—Root cuttings now to have vigorous young plants for next spring and summer. These will be ready for 5-inch pots next March.

HELIOTROPE — 60° — Make cuttings now from selected specimens growing outdoors.

NERIUM—45-55°—Root cuttings now for vigorous young plants next year of oleander. 'Mrs. Roeding' blooms longest.

NICOTIANA—50-60°—Sow seeds now for winter and spring blooms from the flowering tobacco. Old-fashioned white has fragrance at night. Compact 'White Bedder' is best for potting.

OSMANTHUS—50°—Insert 3-inch tip cuttings in moist peat and sand; provide shade and high humidity. The white, wonderfully fragrant flowers appear almost year round.

PANSY—40-50°—Sow seeds of a winter-blooming type now. Keep constantly moist and as cool as possible.

SNAPDRAGON—45-60°—Sow seeds now for December bloom. Grow single stem for earlier bloom; or, at 6- to 8-inch height, pinch back to three sets of leaves, to obtain more but later bloom.

August

AGERATUM—55°—Sow seeds now for winter-spring bloom. New 'Blue Blazer' is highly recommended. Cuttings made now of plants growing in the garden will bloom indoors beginning in autumn.

BELLIS—45-50°—Sow seeds now for English daisy flowers of pink, rose or white next winter and spring. Provide sunny, airy, moist atmosphere.

CALENDULA—45-55°—Sow seeds now for October to January bloom in various shades of orange to yellow to palest cream. Best for pot culture: 'Sensation,' 'Lemon King Select,' 'Ball Orange Improved' and 'Ball Gold.'

CALLA, WHITE — 60-65° — Plant roots now for white, fragrant flowers next winter and spring; one to a 6-inch pot, three to a 10-inch tub.

CAMELLIA—45-65°—Now is the time to make tip cuttings of half-ripened wood. Insert in mixture of moist peat and sand. Provide shade and high humidity.

CENTAUREA—45-55°—Seeds of bachelor's-buttons sown now will give welcome winter flowers. 'Dwarf Blue Boy' is a good choice, although hybrid mixtures offer an interesting color range. A cool, moist, airy atmosphere during fall and winter will help prevent red spider-mite attacks.

CINERARIA—45-55°—Sow seeds in a cool, moist, shaded place early this month for blooms next spring. In autumn transplant to small pots. Keep moist at all times. Move on to 5- or 6-inch pots by January. Spray to control aphids.

CYRTANTHUS—50-65°—Now is the time to order and plant bulbs of this easily grown little amaryllid for fall and winter blooms. Amaryllis culture.

FREESIA—50°—Make first planting of these corms (six to a 6-inch pot) by the end of the month. Continue planting every two or three weeks until December 1. Corms planted now will yield late December and January bloom.

LACHENALIA—50°—Freesia culture will do nicely for the Cape cowslip which yields red or yellow flowers from early winter until spring. Plant six corms to a 6-inch pot in August.

MARIGOLD—50-60°—Sow seeds now for winter and spring bloom. Dwarf French types will do nicely in 3- and 4-inch pots; American hybrids may be finished in 6's. Large hybrids like 'Toreador' bloom in about three months from seed at 60-degree nighttime temperature.

NASTURTIUM—50°—For winter flowers, sow seeds now. The Gleam Hybrids are recommended; also some of the new dwarf hybrids. Try as basket plants for a refreshing change.

NEMESIA—45-50°—This cool-loving annual with brilliant flowers of blue, pink, red, rose, scarlet, orange and yellow, will give winter bloom from seeds started now. A cool, moist, airy atmosphere is the key to success.

September

AMARYLLIS — 60° — Order bulbs now of named Dutch, South African and American hybrids. There's much excitement to be found in hybrid amaryllis these days. Each bulb is a longtime investment in pleasure. Pot up with neck of the bulb exposed; keep moist and on the cool side while roots form.

ANEMONE—50°—Now is the time to order, and plant as quickly as possible, the clawlike roots of *Anemone coronaria* types. Instructions that come with them may advise to soak the roots 24 hours in water before planting. Unless you have been successful with this method in the past, we recommend that the roots simply be planted "claws" down, slightly covered and then that they be kept evenly moist in coolness (40-50°). Once well rooted, the pots of anemones can then be moved to the light for growing on. Be sure that anemones do not dry out severely at any time after growth begins. Also, keep an eye out for green aphids; they often cluster on new leaves and buds.

GLOXINIA—60°—Sow seeds now of hybrid strains, such as Buell, in order to have a glorious showing of flowering plants next March, April and May. The seeds

need a warm, moist, humid place in which to start. Seedlings started now will have nice-sized tubers formed by next summer, at which time the plants may be dried off and rested. Start the year-old tubers into new growth in October for another spring flower show the following year. Repeat this cycle over and over.

IXIA—55°—This member of the iris family, and the similar sparaxis, should be much more commonly cultivated. Pot six corms to a 6-inch pot. Keep around 40 to 50 degrees and evenly moist until rooting is well along. Then begin forcing in a sunny, airy, moist environment.

LACHENALIA — 50° — This bulb flower is commonly known as the Cape cowslip. Culture is practically identical to that described this month for ixia. After flowering, the rule is to rest the bulbs nearly dry and moderately warm until replanting time in early fall.

ORNITHOGALUM—55°—Essentially, culture for this bulb flower is the same as that outlined here for ixia and lachenalia, except you will need only three bulbs for a 6-inch pot. These plants need some staking as growth progresses.

SCHIZANTHUS — 55° — The poor-man's orchid, or butterfly flower, is an easily cultivated annual that gives a lot of color from airy, graceful flowers in spring. Seeds sown now will yield late winter and spring blooms. Pinch once or twice to encourage bushiness.

October

ASTER, CHINA—55°—Seeds started now will provide welcome flowers from winter until mid-spring. The seedlings will need four hours supplementary light every evening from the time they are in seedflats until buds are beginning to open.

CALENDULA—50°—Sow seeds now for these pot-marigold flowers beginning in January. You may select from several flower colors and types. Colors are welcome and cheerful in the winter: lemony yellow, golden yellow and glowing gold. Abundant sunlight in an airy, cool, moist atmosphere keeps calendula growth compact; keep soil evenly moist at all times.

CROCUS—50°—Pot up several containers of crocus corms now to force into bloom beginning after the holidays. Keep moist, cool and dark while roots form. Then, bring to a light spot for forcing. Other "little" bulbs are equally interesting as forcing material: muscari, chionodoxa, scilla and eranthis.

CYRTANTHUS — 55° — This small-growing relative of the amaryllis makes a delightful addition to any collection. The flowers come off and on over a long period beginning at the holidays and continuing until spring. Culture is the same as for hybrid amaryllis: start into growth in autumn, water and feed through winter, spring and early summer, then dry off and rest in late summer and early fall.

DAFFODIL—50°—If you follow some very simple rules, the only mistake you can make with daffodils is to not force enough. Pot up as early as you can get the bulbs, grouping them in pots of a size that will be convenient for you to handle. Personally I prefer large bulb pans that will accommodate at least six, and preferably a dozen bulbs. Keep moist, cool and dark while roots form. After eight weeks, you may check for root growth, and if found to be extensive, forcing may begin in an airy, moist, light atmosphere.

HYACINTH—50°—Forcing is virtually the same as for daffodils, except hyacinths tend to be easier and more tolerant of varied temperatures. Even one bulb forced in a 3-inch pot makes quite a fragrant display. The Roman types planted now will give bloom for the holi-

days. The Dutch hybrids started now may be forced into bloom as early as January.

PAPERWHITE NARCISSUS—55°—These popular bulbs are probably the easiest of all bulb flowers for forcing into bloom. Buy as many as you can possibly afford because there never seem to be enough pots. I force one pot a week as long as they last. The fragrant white or golden blooms are tremendously welcome in the middle of winter. Nestle the bulbs in moist soil; keep cool, moist and dark while roots form. Then bring to light for forcing, which takes about four weeks.

STOCK—55°—These fragrant flowers are among the most easily cultivated of all container annuals. Sow seeds now for late winter and spring bloom. Provide ample room for the roots to grow, and feed biweekly after New Year's. A sunny, airy, moist, cool atmosphere is the key to large flower spikes; staking may be needed, also.

SWEET PEA—45°—Sow seeds now for midwinter to spring flowers. The All-America Selections winner Knee-Hi 'San Francisco' makes an excellent choice. 'Bijou' is also a well-behaved type for container culture.

TULIP—50°—Forcing of these bulb flowers is about the same as for daffodils, except they often get a severe attack of bulb aphids, and require careful spraying or dipping with a pesticide to prevent damage to the flowers. The single- and double-flowered early types are by far the best for forcing.

November

CHRISTMAS CACTUS—60°—Remember that this is a short-day plant which needs the naturally short days of autumn in order to bloom. If you work in the same room at night, turn a cardboard carton over your Christmas cactus before you turn the lights on. It is important also to keep the soil a little less moist at this time of the year; increase the water supply in late winter or early spring.

CLEMATIS—55°—Now's the time to buy hybrid clematis, in dormancy, and start them into growth for winter-spring bloom. Pot up in a 6- to 8-inch container, depending on the size of the root ball. Use a mixture of equal parts garden loam, peat moss and sand, adding a tablespoon of ground limestone to each pot. A sunny, airy atmosphere will help bring on lush growth and the much-admired flowers.

POINSETTIA—60°—Here's another plant that needs short days in order to flower. Actually, the Christmas flower show traces back to late September and the month of October when short days are needed, but don't upset what has been started already by burning lights on your plants at night this month.

ROSES—55°—Dormant bushes available now offer all kinds of opportunity to the container gardener. Any hybrid tea, floribunda or grandiflora is worth trying for a season. You can transplant it later to the outdoor garden. Pot up dormant bushes now in a 12- to 18-inch container. Use a mixture of two parts garden loam, one part peat moss and one part sand. You can avoid problems of pest and disease by spraying on a regular basis with a rose pesticide. Another possibility for roses in containers lies in the miniatures—both bush and tree types.

December

CENTAUREA—50°—Of all the colorful annual flowers cultivated in pots, this is one of the easiest. Sow seeds now for spring flowers. Plenty of root-spreading room in evenly moist soil will keep the buds coming; and the more you cut, the more they'll bloom. Choose from the marvelous blues, or be adventuresome with the maroons, lavenders, rose-pinks and near-whites.

GLORIOSA-LILY — 60° — This climbing lily makes a spectacular showing for springtime, and now's the time to start the tubers. These may be 6 to 8 inches long, so that a sizable bulb pan is likely to be needed for planting. Provide a sunny, airy, moist atmosphere and something on which the tendril-tipped leaves can climb.

LOBELIA—60°—Now's the time to start seeds of this attractive plant for borders, baskets, benches and tubs. There are kingly purples, electric blues and snowy whites. This small-growing, tender perennial thrives in a sunny, airy, cool atmosphere.

NIEREMBERGIA—50°—Better known as cup flower, here's another subject for basketry and shelf work. It's a tender perennial that can be kept over year to year; the technique is to shear back to 3 or 4 inches after a period of heavy flowering. Seeds started now will give spring flowers.

PETUNIA—55°—For April flowers, now is the time to sow seeds of the fancy double grandifloras. The single types, too, offer a splash of color in return for very little trouble. They're especially enjoyable in baskets, or cascading from shelves. Plant breeders have spent as much time in recent years on the petunia as any other type plant; it's a good idea to cash in on the tremendous array of colors and forms available.

TUBEROUS BEGONIA—70°—These beautiful flowers are always photogenic, but they really have to be seen to be appreciated. There's no better way to see an abundance of them than to start hybrid seeds now. They're minute seeds, almost like a particle of dust, but growing them is fairly easy if you sow them on the surface of a moist, sterile medium such as Jiffy Mix or milled sphagnum moss. Seeds started now will yield flowering-size plants for next season.

33
Propagating Plants

Being a successful container gardener requires considerable experience, but the basics are quite simple. Each plant needs a suitable container and growing medium and thereafter light and water. Such amenities as feeding, providing more humidity in the atmosphere, and grooming can be developed as the need arises.

The essentials of potting and repotting, and starting container plants from seeds, cuttings, bulbs and transplants are covered in this chapter by photographs and captions. Study each set of these and you will be well on your way to understanding how all of these basics work together to make a successful container garden—and gardener.

Supplies needed for starting all kinds of seeds include, clockwise from upper left, milled sphagnum moss, vermiculite, charcoal chips, fiber flats, peat pots. Available locally and by mail from plant specialists.

ABOVE: Fill fiber flat with vermiculite.

ABOVE: Sow seeds in shallow drills; label each row.

ABOVE: Cover seeds lightly if packet so directs.

ABOVE: Moisten well with a gentle stream of water.

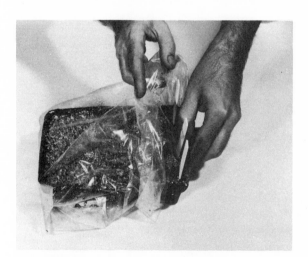

ABOVE: Enclose planting in plastic bag to keep moist.
BELOW: Transplant each seedling to a peat pot.

ABOVE: Transplant early before seedlings crowd.
BELOW: Healthy seedling ready for a larger pot.

ABOVE: Overgrown African violet ready for repotting.

ABOVE: Remove from pot; cut apart with a knife.

ABOVE: Plant yielded three divisions plus leaves.

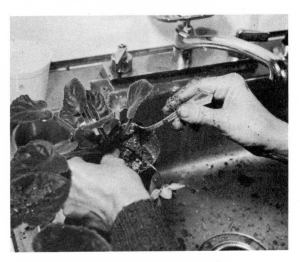

ABOVE: Sink is convenient place for potting.

ABOVE: Transplants need to be well moistened.
BELOW: Root leaves in soil or water.

ABOVE: African violet leaves prepared for rooting.
BELOW: Some begonia leaves will also root.

ABOVE: Tuberous begonia seedlings growing under lights.

ABOVE: Three-month-old tuberous begonia seedlings.

ABOVE: Gently firm soil about the roots of seedlings.

ABOVE: Planting tulip bulbs preparatory to forcing.

ABOVE: Leave neck of amaryllis bulb exposed.
BELOW: Surface roots indicate need for a larger pot.

ABOVE: Steven McDonald adds label to amaryllis.
BELOW: Using tepid, sudsy water to remove insects.

34
Soils and Other Growing Media

Container plants are presently cultivated in two basic growing mediums: (1) soil-based and (2) soil-less.

Soils

Soil-based planting mediums are mixed according to recipes. There are almost as many recipes for potted plants as there are pot gardeners. The basic, general-purpose potting soil is usually comprised of equal parts garden loam, sphagnum peat moss and clean sand (*not* sand from the beach). To amend this for desert cacti and other succulents you might mix one part garden loam, one part sphagnum peat moss and two parts clean sand. If you want to grow a jungle plant that needs lots of humus (for example, a philodendron or rex begonia) you could mix one part garden loam, one part clean sand and two parts sphagnum peat moss.

Where to obtain good garden loam can be quite a problem, especially if you live in a city apartment. Even if you have a vegetable or flower garden, the soil may not be all that good for container gardening. For one thing, soil used for pot plants ideally should be pasteurized first. This can be done by baking a container of soil for an hour at 150 to 180 degrees F.; moisten the soil well before baking; allow it to cool overnight before using in a planting mixture.

Packaged prepared potting soils are available wherever plants are sold. In my experience all of these are too heavy in texture. They should be mixed with peat moss, sand (or perlite, a sterile substitute for sand) or vermiculite (also a sterile medium which can be used in place of well-rotted leaf mold, an ingredient you may find listed in some potting-soil recipes). To mix a good general-purpose potting medium based on a packaged prepared potting soil, try combining equal parts of the soil, perlite, vermiculite and peat moss. This mixture will grow almost any container plant, indoors or outdoors.

Growing mediums based on soil will grow excellent plants in combination with normal feeding practices. On any container of garden fertilizer you will find instructions for how much and how often to feed. Follow these—but if you deviate, feed less, not more than the container recommends.

Soil-less

Soil-less growing mediums are based mostly on formulas perfected at Cornell University and the University of California. They are comprised of more or less sterile ingredients and require constant feeding for uniform growth. Most soil-less growers use a combination of organic fertilizers (fish emulsion, for example) and chemical fertilizers, feeding one time with one, the next with the other. For best results a little fertilizer should be applied every time the plant is watered. By a "little," I mean one-fourth to one-fifth the amount recommended on the fertilizer container for standard soil-grown pot plants. If the fertilizer manufacturer recommends the use of one teaspoon fertilizer to one quart of water, you would use a fourth of a teaspoon of fertilizer to one quart of water and apply this solution every time you water the plant growing in soil-less.

Soil-less planting mediums are sold under various trade names. These in-

Soil-less mixes are lightweight, even when moist.

clude Jiffy Mix, Redi-earth, Supersoil, Pro-mix, Vita-Bark University Mix and others.

Solving Plant Problems

There are almost countless problems that may be encountered in container gardening, yet almost all of them pertain to the simple basics of light, temperature, humidity, watering, feeding and a few pests. Diseases, for example, fungus or virus, are of no great threat to most container gardens. Symptoms and solutions for the most frequent problems follow.

Leaf tips and edges dry, brown, dead. Plant is too hot and dry at the same time. Keep soil evenly moist. Avoid drafts of hot, dry air from artificial heat. The plant may be receiving too much direct sun. Too much fertilizer might also cause this symptom.

Many leaves turn yellow and fall off within a short period of time. Change in environment. Lack of sufficient light. Overfeeding. Too hot and dry or too cold and wet at the same time. If leaves are yellow-flecked and tiny cobwebbing is found between leaf stems and main stalk, red spider-mites are probably present (see following paragraph).

Leaves yellow-flecked; cobwebs between leaf stems and main stalks. Red spider-mite is probably present. This pest thrives in stale, hot, dry air. Rinse the plant thoroughly in water of room temperature. Lower temperatures. Increase humidity. Add fresh air circulating among plants. Spray alternately, once a week, using Kelthane one week, Dimite the next, until no traces of red spider-mite can be seen when you examine growth through a magnifying glass.

New growth pale and weak. Lack of light. Temperatures too hot or too cold. The plant may also need to be fed.

No flowers. Lack of light. Too hot and

dry or too cold and wet at the same time. Too much nitrogen in the soil; change to a blossom-booster type fertilizer, commonly marketed specifically for African violets but also useful for promoting bloom on any indoor plant. If nonbloomer in question is sensitive to long or short days, this could be the problem. For example, chrysanthemums, Christmas cactus, poinsettias and kalanchoes bloom when the days are naturally short in autumn and early winter. If they receive any artificial light in the period between sundown and sunup in September and October, they will not bloom for the holidays. By contrast, long-day plants such as summer-flowering tuberous begonias and gloxinias will not bloom unless they have approximately 16 hours illumination in every 24. In the summertime this is no problem, but if you want winter bloom, supplementary fluorescent light will be required.

Plant parts coated with cottony white insects and matter. Mealybugs are present. Use spray or dip of malathion, having first washed off as much of the cottony residue as possible in tepid water to which a little household detergent has been added. A Shell No-Pest Strip placed in a room with houseplants will eradicate mealybugs, red spider-mites and other common pests. Each Strip is efficacious for up to four months and only one is needed in an average room.

Healthy plant suddenly wilts even though soil is moist. Overwatering or lack of drainage has caused roots to suffocate and rot. Take tip cuttings of remaining healthy growth; discard old plant.

Small brown "bumps" on leaves and stems. Brown scale is present. Remove each with tip of a pocketknife or with your fingernails. Use soft cotton cloth moistened in water to which a little household detergent has been added and wipe leaves and stems clean of all sticky residue left by the scale. If plant is too large to deal with by hand, spray with malathion or use a Shell No-Pest Strip in the same room.

Little white insects fly around plant when it is disturbed. White flies are the culprits. You'll find them clustered under the leaves. Frequent pest of container tomatoes, fuchsias and lantanas. If present on any vegetable or herb, use only a pesticide recommended for food crops (check labels at your local garden center; no recommendation is made here, since the life of books often exceeds the life of pesticides considered to be safe). Generally speaking, malathion sprays will control white flies.

New growth and flowers malformed. The effect of microscopic cyclamen mites. Spray or dip plant, using a miticide (available at garden-supply centers). Shell No-Pest Strips are also effective when placed in the same room with mite-infested plants. Cyclamen mite most often attacks cyclamen, African violets and any African violet relative known as a gesneriad, for example, columnea, episcia and gloxinia.

All growth weak, spindly, pale. Lack of light, lack of fertilizer, or both. Plants that are light-starved in an atmosphere that is too hot and too dry often display these symptoms.

Green insects clustered on new growth. A common symptom of outdoor container plants. Aphids are present. Mostly these are not difficult to control—in fact, in the outdoor garden they tend to go away in time whether or not you spray them. However, malathion will take care of them easily.

Silvery, blistered areas in leaves and on flower petals. Thrips are the cause, a tiny, threadlike, black insect that rasps away at tender plant tissue. Outdoors or indoors a spray or dip of malathion will eradicate thrips. Inside a Shell No-Pest Strip placed in the same room with infected plants will stop thrips.

Index

Appendix I

Mail-Order Sources for Plants

Note: When ordering plants or seeds, use the Latin Name to assure getting the right ones.

Abbey Garden, Box 30331, Santa Barbara, Calif. 93105—Cacti and other succulents; catalog 25¢.

Abbot's Nursery, Route 4, Box 482, Mobile, Ala. 36609—Camellias.

Alberts & Merkel Bros., Inc., P.O. Box 537, Boynton Beach, Fla. 33435 —Orchids, bromeliads, many other rare and choice tropicals; catalog 50¢.

Alpenglow Gardens, 13328 King George Highway, Surrey, B.C. V3T236 Canada—Alpines, evergreens, shrubs; catalog 25¢.

Annalee Violetry, 29-50 214th Place, Bayside, N.Y. 11360—Miniature African violets.

Antonelli Bros., 2545 Capitola Rd., Santa Cruz, Calif. 95060—Tuberous begonias, gloxinias, achimenes.

Armstrong Associates Inc., P.O. Box 127, Basking Ridge, N.J. 07920 —Carnivorous plants and terrarium kits; catalog 25¢.

Arthur Eames Allgrove, North Wilmington, Mass. 01887 —Woodland plants and tropicals for terrariums; catalog 50¢.

Louise Barnaby, 12178 Highview St., Vicksburg, Mich. 49097—African violets; send stamp for list.

Mrs. Mary V. Boose, 9 Turney Place, Trumbull, Conn. 06611—African violets and episcias; 15¢ for list.

John Brudy's Rare Plant House, P.O. Box 1348, Cocoa Beach, Fla. 32931—Unusual seeds.

Buell's Greenhouses, Eastford, Conn. 06242—Gesneriads; catalog 50¢.

Burgess Seed & Plant Co., 67 E. Battle Creek, Galesburg, Mich. 49053 —Houseplants, vegetables, herbs, bulbs.

W. Atlee Burpee Co., Box 6929, Philadelphia, Pa. 19132—Seeds, terrarium kits, supplies.

Thomas Butcher, Ltd., 60 Wickham Road, Shirley, Croydon, Surrey CR98AG, England—Seeds of exceptional house plants and alpines.

David Buttram, P.O. Box 193, Independence, Mo. 64051—African violets; send 10¢ for list.

Cactus Gem Nursery, 10092 Mann Dr., Cupertino, Calif. (visit Thurs.–Sun.); by mail write P.O. Box 327, Aromas, Calif., 95004 —Rare cacti.

Castle Violets, 614 Castle Rd., Colorado Springs, Colo. 80904 —African violets.

Champion's African Violets, 8848 Van Hoesen Road, Clay, N.Y. 13041 —Miniature African violets.

Conrard-Pyle Star Roses, West Grove, Pa. 19390—Miniature roses.

Victor Constantinou, 3321 21st St., Apt. 7, San Francisco, Calif. 94110 —African violets, columneas and episcias; send stamp for list.

Cook's Geranium Nursery, 714 N. Grand, Lyons, Kans. 67544 —Geraniums; send 25¢ for catalog.

Davis Cactus Garden, 1522 Jefferson St., Kerrville, Tex. 78028—Send 25¢ for catalog.

DeGiorgi Bros., Inc., Council Bluffs, Iowa 51501—Seeds of all kinds for container gardens.

L. Easterbrook Greenhouses, 10 Craig St., Butler, Ohio 44822 —Terrariums, accessories, plants; catalog 25¢.

Edelweiss Gardens, 54 Robbinsville-Allentown Rd.,

Robbinsville, N.J. 08691—Tropicals and ferns for terrariums; list 35¢.

Electric Farm, 104 B Lee Rd., Oak Hill, N.Y. 12460—Gesneriads; send self-addressed stamped envelope for list.

Farmer Seed and Nursery Co., Faribault, Minn. 55021—Flowers, bulbs, vegetables, herbs, fruit for container gardens.

Fennell Orchid Co., 26715 S. W. 157th Ave., Homestead, Fla. 33030 —Miniature orchids; catalog $1.

Fernwood Plants, 1311 Fernwood Pacific Dr., Topanga, Calif. 90290 —Rare and unusual cacti.

Ffoulkes, 610 Bryan St., Jacksonville, Fla. 32202—African violets; send 25¢ for list.

Henry Field Seed & Nursery Co., 407 Sycamore, Shenandoah, Iowa 51601—Flowers, bulbs, vegetables, herbs, fruit for container gardens.

Fischer Greenhouses, Linwood, N.J. 08221—Gesneriads; catalog 25¢.

Fox Orchids, 6615 W. Markham, Little Rock, Ark. 72205—Orchids and supplies for growing them at home.

Arthur Freed Orchids, Inc., 5731 S. Bonsall Dr., Malibu, Calif. 90265 —Orchids and supplies for growing them.

French J. Howard, Baltimore Pike, Lima, Pa. 19060—Bulbs for forcing.

Girard Nurseries, P.O. Box 428, Geneva, Ohio 44041—Trees for bonsai work and containers.

Grisby Cactus Gardens, 2354 Bella Vista Dr., Vista, Calif. 92083 —Catalog 50¢.

Gurney Seed and Nursery Co., Yankton, S. Dak. 57078

—Houseplants, flowers, vegetables, herbs, fruits for container gardens.

Orchids by Hausermann, Inc., P.O. Box 363, Elmhurst, Ill. 60126 —Complete array of orchids and supplies for growing them.

Helen's Cactus, 2205 Mirasol, Brownsville, Tex. 78520—Unusual cacti; send stamp for price list.

Henrietta's Nursery, 1345 N. Brawley Ave., Fresno, Calif. 93705—Cacti and other succulents; catalog 25¢.

Hillier and Sons, Winchester, England—Alpines.

Hilltop Farm, Route 3, Box 216, Cleveland, Tex. 77327—Geraniums and herbs.

Sim T. Holmes, 100 Tustarawas Rd., Beaver, Pa. 15009—African violets, miniature and regular; all grown under fluorescent lights.

House Plant Corner, P.O. Box 810, Oxford, Md. 21654—Terrariums and supplies; catalog, 25¢.

Spencer M. Howard Orchid Imports, 11802 Huston St., N. Hollywood, Calif. 91607—Species and unusual orchids; free list.

Gordon M. Hoyt Orchids, Seattle Heights, Wash. 98036—Complete listing of interesting orchids for the home grower.

Margaret Ilgenfritz Orchids, Box 665, Monroe, Mich. 48161—Miniature orchids; catalog $2.

P. deJager & Sons, Inc., 188 Asbury St., South Hamilton, Mass. 01982 —Unusual bulbs.

J & L Orchids, 20 Sherwood Rd., Easton, Conn. 06612—Unusual orchids.

Jones & Scully, Inc., 2200 N. W. 33rd Ave., Miami, Fla. 33142—Many unusual and miniature orchids; catalog $3.

Kartuz Greenhouses, 92 Chestnut St., Wilmington, Mass. 01887 —Miniature begonias, gesneriads, and other terrarium plants; catalog 50¢.

Wm. Kirch—Orchids, Ltd., 2630 Waiomao Rd., Honolulu, Hawaii 96816—Orchids.

Kirkpatrick's, 27785 De Anza St., Barstow, Calif. 92311 —Cacti/succulents; send 10¢ for list.

Kolb's Greenhouses, 725 Belvidere Rd., Phillipsburg, N.J. 08865 —African violets; send stamp for list.

Lauray of Salisbury, Undermountain Rd., Salisbury, Conn. 06068 —Miniature begonias, gesneriads, succulents; catalog 50¢.

Logee's Greenhouses, Danielson, Conn. 06239—Unusual tropicals, many of them suited to terrarium

culture; catalog $1.

Lyndon Lyon, Dolgeville, N.Y. 13329—Miniature African violets, other gesneriads.

Rod McLellan Co., 1450 El Camino Real, South San Francisco, Calif. 94080—Miniature orchids, supplies; catalog $1.

Mary-Ray Violets, 5007 Terry Dr., Alton, Ill. 62002—Miniature African Violets.

Earl May Seed & Nursery Co., Shenandoah, Iowa 51603—Flowers, vegetables, herbs, trees, shrubs, fruit to grow in containers.

Merry Gardens, Camden, Maine 04843—Miniature plants; catalog $1.

Mini-Roses, P.O. Box 245 Sta. A., Dallas, Tex. 75208—Miniature roses.

Modlins Cactus Gardens, 2416 El Corto, Vista, Calif. 92083—Catalog 25¢.

Moore Miniature Roses, 2519 E. Noble, Visalia, Calif. 93277 —Miniature roses.

Cactus by Mueller, 10411 Rosedale Highway, Bakersfield, Calif. 93308—Send stamp for list.

Nichols Garden Nursery, 1190 N. Pacific Highway, Albany, Ore. 97321—Unusual vegetables; herbs.

Nor East Miniature Roses, Box 852, Gloucester, Maine 01930 —Miniature roses.

Norvell Greenhouses, 318 S. Greenacres Rd., Greenacres, Wash. 99016—Houseplants.

George W. Park Seed Co., Inc., Greenwood. S.C. 29646—Large catalog of seeds, bulbs, plants and supplies for indoor gardening; also fluorescent-light gardening equipment.

Penn Valley Orchids, 239 Old Gulph Rd., Wynnewood, Pa. 19096 —Orchids.

Frank Peterson, 761 Hialeah Dr., Hialeah, Fla. 33010—Bromeliad specialist.

Plantation Garden Products, P.O. Box 127, Boynton Beach, Fla. 33435 —Orchids, bromeliads; catalog 25¢.

Roehrs Exotic Nurseries, RFD 2, Box 144, Farmingdale, N.J. 07727 —Extensive listings of tropicals.

John Scheepers, Inc., 63 Wall St., New York, N.Y. 10005—Bulbs for forcing, including lily-of-the-valley pips.

Schmelling's African Violets, 5133 Peck Hill Rd., Jamesville, N.Y. 13078—African violets; catalog 20¢.

Seaborn Del Dios Nursery, Box 455, Escondido, Calif. 92025

—Bromeliads.

Sequoia Nursery, 2519 E. Noble, Visalia, Calif. 93277—Miniature roses.

Shaffer's Tropical Gardens, 1220 41st Ave., Santa Cruz, Calif. 95060 —Growth chambers and outstanding orchids.

P. R. Sharp, 104 N. Chapel Ave., #3, Alhambra, Calif. 91801—South American and Mexican cacti.

R. H. Shumway Seedsman, Rockford, Ill. 61101—Flowers, vegetables, herbs, bulbs, fruit, trees, shrubs for container gardening.

Singer's Growing Things, 6385 Enfield Ave., Reseda, Calif 91335 —Succulents for container gardens.

Sky-Cleft Gardens, Camp Street Ext., Barre, Vt. 05641—Alpines.

Smith's Cactus Garden, P.O. Box 871, Paramount, Calif. 90723—Send 30¢ for list.

Star Roses, Box 203, West Grove, Pa. 19390—Miniature roses, other woody plants for container gardening.

Fred A. Stewart Co., 1212 E. Las Tunas Dr., San Gabriel, Calif. 91778—Miniature orchids.

Ed Storms, 4223 Pershing, Ft. Worth, Tex. 76107—Specialist in lithops and other succulents.

Sunnybrook Farms, 9448 Mayfield Rd., Chesterland, Ohio 44026 —Herbs; scented geraniums; source for *Aloe vera,* the "inguentine plant."

Sutton and Sons, Ltd., Reading, RG 6 1AB England—Outstanding seeds.

Thompson & Morgan, Ltd. (England) U.S. Address: Box 24, Somerdale, N.J. 08083—Wide array of outstanding seeds.

Three Springs Fisheries, Inc., Lilypons, Md. 21717—Aquarium plants.

Tinari Greenhouses, 2325 Valley Rd., Huntingdon Valley, Pa. 19006 —African violets and other gesneriads; 25¢.

William Tricker, Inc., Allendale Ave., Saddle River, N.J. 07458 —Aquarium plants.

W. J. Unwin, Ltd., Southampton, England—Extensive listing of seeds, some alpines.

Van Ness Water Gardens, 2460 N. Euclid Ave., Upland, Calif. 91786 —Aquarium plants.

Visual Design Mfg. Co., 6335 Skyline Dr., Houston, Tex. 77027 —Terrariums (unplanted).

Volkmann Bros. Greenhouses, 2714 Minert St., Dallas, Tex. 75219 —Send stamped, self-addressed long envelope for catalog of African violets and supplies, including the Reservoir Wick Pot.

West Coast Gesneriads, 2179 44th Ave., San Francisco, Calif. 94116 —Unusual gesneriads.

Whistling Hill, Box 27, Hamburg, N.Y. 14075—Miniature gesneriads; list 25¢.

Wilson Brothers, Roachdale, Ind. 47121—Geraniums, begonias, many other flowering plants for container gardens.

H. E. Wise, 3710 June St., San Bernardino, Calif. 92405—Cacti; send stamp for list.

Mrs. Ernie Wurster, Route 1, Box 156, Elizabeth, Ill. 61028—African violets; send 15¢ for list.

Appendix II

Where to Buy Supplies and Equipment

A & N Terrarium Co., 5979 Hosta Lane, San Jose. Calif. 95124—Tools for terrarium and bottle gardening.

Aladdin Industries, Inc., Nashville, Tenn. 37210—Manufacturers of growth chambers and fluorescent-light gardening equipment.

Aluminum Greenhouses, Inc., 14615 Lorain Ave., Cleveland, Ohio 44111—Prefabricated home greenhouses.

Armstrong Associates, Inc., P.O. Box 127, Basking Ridge, N.J. 07920 —Carnivorous plants and terrarium kits.

Charles Bateman, Box 25, Thornhill, Ontario, Canada—Liquid whale organic fertilizer.

Brookstone Co., Peterborough, N.H. 03458—Unusual tools for terrarium and bottle gardening.

W. Atlee Burpee Co., Box 6929, Philadelphia, Pa. 19132—Seeds, terrarium kits, supplies.

Dome Enterprises, Inc., P.O. Box 35642, Dallas, Tex. 75325 —Glass-top tables for terrariums.

Dover Scientific, Box 6011 C, Long Island City, N.Y. 11106—Unusual terrarium accessories; catalog 50¢.

L. Easterbrook Greenhouses, 10 Craig Street, Butler, Ohio 44822 —Terrariums, accessories, plants; catalog 25¢.

Fleco Industries, 3347 Halifax St., Dallas, Tex. 75247—Attractive fluorescent lighted shelves for plants.

Floralite Co., 4124 E. Oakwood Rd., Oak Creek, Wis. 53154 —Fluorescent-light gardening equipment and supplies.

Fox Orchids, 6615 W. Markham, Little Rock, Ark. 72205—Orchids and supplies for growing them at home.

Arthur Freed Orchids, Inc., 5731 S. Bonsall Dr., Malibu, Calif. 90265 —Orchids and supplies for growing them.

The Greenhouse, 9515 Flower St., Bellflower, Calif. 90706 —Fluorescent-light gardening equipment.

Bernard D. Greeson, 3548 N. Cramer, Milwaukee, Wis. 53211—Indoor gardening supplies; list 25¢.

The House of Violets, 936 Garland St. S. W., Camden, Ark. 71701—Self-watering African violet planters.

House Plant Corner, P.O. Box 810, Oxford, Md. 21654—Terrariums and supplies; catalog 25¢.

Hydroponic Chemical Co., Copley, Ohio 44321—Special fertilizers for container gardening.

Hyponex Co., Copley, Ohio 44321 —Fertilizers and supplies.

Indoor Gardening Supplies, P.O. Box 40551, Detroit, Mich. 48240 —Fluorescent-light gardening equipment.

J & D Lamps, 245 S. Broadway, Yonkers, N.Y. 10705 —Fluorescent-light gardening equipment.

Lord and Burnham, Irvington, N.Y. 10533—Home greenhouses, window greenhouses.

Rod McLennan Co., 1450 El Camino Real, South San Francisco, Calif. 94080—Miniature orchids, supplies; catalog $1.

Mary's African Violets, 19788 San Juan, Detroit, Mich. 48221 —Supplies and lighting equipment.

Nature's Way Products, 3505 Mozart Ave., Cincinnati, Ohio 45211 —Supplies.

J. A. Nearing Co., 10788 Tucker St., Beltsville, Md. 20705 —Prefabricated home greenhouses.

New Renaissance Glass Works, 5636 College Ave., Oakland, Calif. 94618—Leaded glass terrarium kits.

Walter F. Nicke, Hudson, N.Y. 12534—Useful as well as unusual gardening supplies and equipment, much of it made in England.

George W. Park Seed Co., Inc., Greenwood, S.C. 29646—Large catalog of seeds, bulbs, plants, and supplies for indoor gardening; also fluorescent-light gardening equipment.

Robert B. Peters Co., Inc., 2833 Pennsylvania St., Allentown, Pa. 18104—Peters fertilizers, available in several formulations designed for specific growth responses.

Raja Toy Company, 1206 LaJolla Ave., Los Angeles, Calif. 90035—Plastic terrarium domes and kits.

Ra-Pid-Gro Corp., 88 Ossian, Dansville, N.Y. 14437 —Manufacturers of Ra-Pid-Gro, root and foliar fertilizer.

Redfern's Prefab Greenhouses, 55 Mt. Hermon Rd., Scotts Valley, Calif. 95060.

Redwood Domes, 2664 Highway 1, Aptos, Calif. 95003—Prefabricated home greenhouses.

Schultz Co., 11730 Northline, St. Louis, Mo. 63043—Manufacturers of excellent container garden fertilizer.

Shaffer's Tropical Gardens, 1220 41st Ave., Santa Cruz, Calif. 95060 —Growth chambers and outstanding orchids.

Shoplite Co., Inc., 566 Franklin Ave., Nutley, N.J. 07110 —Fluorescent-light gardening equipment; catalog 25¢.

Sturdi Built Manufacturing Co., 11304 S. W. Boones Ferry Rd., Portland, Ore. 97219—Prefabricated home greenhouses.

Texas Greenhouse Co., Inc., 2717 St. Louis Ave., Ft. Worth, Tex. 76110 —Prefabricated home greenhouses.

Tube Craft, Inc., 1331 W. 80th St., Cleveland, Ohio 44102 —Fluorescent-light gardening equipment.

Turner Greenhouses, P.O. Box 1260, Goldsboro, N.C. 27530 —Prefabricated home greenhouses.

Verilux TruBloom, 35 Mason St., Greenwich, Conn. 06830
—Manufacturers of TruBloom

fluorescents for plants.
Volkmann Bros. Greenhouses, 2714 Minert St., Dallas, Tex. 75219

—Send stamped, self-addressed long envelope for catalog of African violets and supplies, including the Reservoir Wick Pot.

Appendix III

Plant Societies

African Violet Society of America, Inc., P.O. Box 1326, Knoxville, Tenn. 37901.

American Begonia Society, 14050 Ramona Dr., Whittier, Calif. 90605.

American Fern Society, Department of Botany, University of Tennessee, Knoxville, Tenn. 37916.

American Gloxinia and Gesneriad Society, P.O. Box 174, New Milford, Conn, 06776.

American Orchid Society, Botanical Museum of Harvard University, Cambridge, Mass. 02138.

Bromeliad Society, P.O. Box 3279, Santa Monica, Calif. 90403.

Cactus and Succulent Society of America, Box 167, Reseda, Calif. 91335. Members receive the excellent bimonthly magazine called the *Cactus and Succulent Journal.*

Indoor Light Gardening Society of America, 128 W. 58th St., New York, N.Y. 10019.

International Fern Society, 2423 Burritt Ave., Redondo Beach, Calif. 90278.

Saintpaulia International, Box 10604, Knoxville, Tenn. 37919.

The Terrarium Association, 57 Wolfpit Ave., Norwalk, Conn. 06851.

Appendix IV

Plant Periodicals

African Violet Magazine, bimonthly publication of the African Violet Society of America, Inc., Box 1326, Knoxville, Tenn. 37901.

American Fern Journal, quarterly publication of the American Fern Society, Biological Sciences Group, University of Connecticut, Storrs, Conn. 06268.

American Horticulturist, bimonthly publication of the American Horticultural Society, Mount Vernon, Va. 22121.

American Ivy Society Bulletin, periodical of the American Ivy Society. 128 W. 58th St., New York, N.Y. 10019.

American Orchid Society Bulletin, monthly publication of the American Orchid Society, Inc., Botanical Museum of Harvard University, Cambridge, Mass. 02138.

The Begonian, monthly of the American Begonia Society, Inc., 139 N. Ledoux Rd., Beverly Hills, Calif. 90211.

Bonsai (quarterly) and ABStracts (monthly newsletter), publications of the American Bonsai Society, 953 S. Shore Dr., Lake Waukomis, Parkville, Mo. 64151.

Bonsai Magazine, ten times a year, publication of Bonsai Clubs International, 445 Blake St., Menlo Park, Calif. 94025

The Bromeliad Journal, bimonthly publication of the Bromeliad Society, Inc., P.O. Box 3279, Santa Monica, Calif. 90403

Cactus and Succulent Journal, bimonthly publication of the Cactus and Succulent Society of America, Inc., Box 167, Reseda, Calif. 91335

The Camellia Journal, quarterly publication of the American Camellia Society, Box 212, Fort Valley, Ga. 31030.

Cymbidium Society News, monthly publication of the Cymbidium Society of America, Inc., 6787 Worsham Dr., Whittier Calif. 90602

Epiphyllum Bulletin, publication of the Epiphyllum Society of America, Inc., 218 E. Greystone Ave., Monrovia, Calif. 91016.

Geraniums Around the World, quarterly publication of the International Geranium Society, 11960 Pascal Ave., Colton, Calif. 92394

Gesneriad Saintpaulia News, bimonthly publication of the American Gesneriad Society, 11983 Darlington Ave., Los Angeles, Calif. 90049.

Gesneriad Saintpaulia News, bimonthly publication of Saintpaulia International, P.O. Box 10604, Knoxville, Tenn. 37919.

The Gloxinian, bimonthly publication of the American Gloxinia Gesneriad Society, Inc., P.O. Box 174, New Milford, Conn. 06776.

Light Garden, bimonthly publication of the Indoor Light Gardening Society of America, Inc., 128 W. 58th St., New York, N.Y. 10019.

Monthly Fern Lessons, with newsletter and annual magazine, publications of the Los Angeles International Fern Society, 2423 Burritt Ave., Redondo Beach, Calif. 90278.

The National Fuchsia Fan, monthly publication of the National Fuchsia Society, 10934 E. Flory St., Whittier, Calif. 90606.

The Orchid Digest, 25 Ash Ave., Corte Madera, Calif 94925.

Plantlife-Amaryllis Yearbook, bulletin of the American Plant Life Society, Box 150, La Jolla, Calif. 92037.

Plants Alive, monthly magazine about indoor gardening, 2100 N. 45th, Seattle, Wash. 98103.

Princepes, quarterly publication of the

Palm Society, 1320 S. Venetian Way, Miami, Fla. 33139.

Seed Pod, quarterly publication of the American Hibiscus Society, Box 98, Eagle Lake, Fla. 33139.

Terrarium Topics, published by The Terrarium Association, 57 Wolfpit Ave., Norwalk, Conn. 06851.

Under Glass, bimonthly devoted to home greenhouse growing; c/o Lord and Burnham, Irvington, N.Y. 10533.

Appendix V

Important Cacti/Succulents Collections to Visit

Arizona: Boyce Thompson Southwestern Arboretum, Superior. Desert Botanical Garden, Phoenix.

California: Huntington Gardens, San Marino. Lotusland (estate of Mme Ganna Walska), by appointment only, Santa Barbara. Rancho Santa Ana Botanic Garden, Claremont University of California Botanical Garden, Berkeley.

Hawaii: Pa'u-a-Laka Gardens, Koloa, Poipu, Kauai.

Michigan: University of Michigan, Ann Arbor.

Missouri: Missouri Botanical Garden, St. Louis.

New York: Brooklyn Botanic Garden, Brooklyn. New York Botanical Garden, Bronx Park.

Pennsylvania: Longwood Gardens, Kennett Square.

Canada: Montreal Botanical Garden, Montreal.

Acknowledgments

The authors wish to express their appreciation to the following for permission to use their illustrations in this book: A & N Terrarium Company: p. 178, p. 179; Abbey Garden: p. 95 left, p. 98 top right, p. 102 right, p. 112 bottom right, p. 113 top, p. 114 top, p. 117, p. 119 bottom, p. 120 top, p. 129 bottom right, p. 129 top right, p. 136 top, p. 136 bottom left, p. 136 bottom right, p. 147 bottom right, p. 148 left, p. 148 bottom right, p. 149 bottom, p. 149 top right, p. 150 bottom right, p. 150 top right; Alladin Industries: p. 236 right, p. 249 top; Arthur E. Allgrove: p. 153; Anchor Hocking: p. 206, p. 216; Armstrong Nurseries: p. 306 middle top left; W. Atlee Burpee Co.: p. 84; Ralph Bailey: p. 201 bottom right, p. 223, p. 266 bottom right; Geo. J. Ball, Inc.: p. 85; Morley Baer: p. 256; B E H Housewares Corporation: p. 241 top; John Benetos and Robert Gregoretti: all drawn illustrations on pp. 7–89; California Redwood Association: p. 237 top, p. 254 top, p. 254 bottom, p. 255 top, p. 255 bottom; Casa-Planta, Inc.: p. 225; Christen, Inc.: p. 192, p. 196; Fred R. Dapprich: p. 272; George Elbert: p. 228 top left, p. 228 bottom right; T. H. Everett: p. 37, p. 38, p. 39, p. 40, p. 41, p. 48, p. 50, p. 51, p. 52, p. 54, p. 55, p. 56, p. 57, p. 58, p. 59, p. 60, p. 61, p. 62, p. 63, p. 64, p. 65, p. 67, p. 68, p. 70, p. 71, p. 72, p. 73, p. 76, p. 77, p. 78, p. 79, p. 88, p. 91; Phil Fein: p. 102 top left; Fernwood Plants: p. 148 top right, p. 208 top, p. 211 bottom, p. 212 bottom right; Fleco Industries: p. 247 bottom, p. 224 bottom; George W. Park Seed Co.: p. 111 right, p. 182 top, p. 188 top, p. 218 bottom, p. 218 top, p. 258 middle left, p. 258 middle right, p. 258 bottom, p. 259 top, p. 259 middle, p. 259 bottom, p. 268 top; W. R. Grace & Co.: p. 308; Howard Graf: p. 100 right, p. 101 bottom right; The Greenhouse: p. 236 left; Grisby Cactus Gardens: p. 120 bottom, p. 121 top, p. 121 bottom, p. 125 bottom left, p. 125 top right, p. 127 top right, p. 128 bottom right, p. 128 top right, p. 130 bottom right, p. 130 middle right, p. 130 top right, p. 147 top left, p. 147 bottom left, p. 147 top right, p. 150 top left, p. 214 right; Henrietta's Nursery: p. 124 bottom right, p. 124 bottom left, p. 124 top left, p. 125 bottom right, p. 125 top left, p. 126 bottom left, p. 126 bottom right, p. 126 top left, p. 126 top right, p. 127 bottom left, p. 127 top left, p. 128 top left, p. 128 bottom left, p. 129 left, p. 130 top left, p. 150 bottom left, p. 210 top, p. 211 top left, p. 211 top right, p. 211 middle right, p. 211 bottom right, p. 212 bottom left, p. 213 top, p. 213 middle, p. 214 left; Hort-Pix: p. 95 top right, p. 95 bottom right, p. 96 bottom, p. 97 top left, p. 97 top right, p. 97 bottom left, p. 97 bottom right, p. 98 bottom right, p. 98 top left, p. 99 top right, p. 99 bottom right, p. 101 top left, p. 101 top right, p. 102 bottom left, p. 111 left, p. 112 top right, p. 113 bottom, p. 116, p. 118 left, p. 123 bottom right, p. 133 top, p. 135 top, p. 135 bottom, p. 137 top, p. 137 bottom, p. 138, p. 139 bottom, p. 205 top, p. 229, p. 238 top, p. 241 bottom, p. 271 top right, p. 274 left, p. 274 right, p. 275 right, p. 282, p. 284, p. 288 top, p. 288 bottom, p. 290, p. 291 right; House Beautiful: p. 245 bottom; The Howland Associates: p. 99 left; Jackson & Perkins: p. 114 bottom, p. 206, p. 235 left, p. 252 right, p. 270, p. 278; Peter Kalberkamp: p. 141, p. 142, p. 221; Leaf Fiberglass: p. 253 right, p. 271 bottom right, p. 273 top, p. 273 bottom; Ward Linton: p. 96 top, p. 118 bottom right, p. 130 bottom left, p. 200, p. 238 bottom left, p. 262, p. 268 middle; Lord & Burnham Greenhouses: p. 226 top, p. 226 bottom, p. 227, p. 249 bottom; Frank Lusk: p. 106, p. 107, p. 108; Elvin McDonald: p. 101 bottom left, p. 118 top right, p. 119 top, p. 133 bottom, p. 134 top, p. 134 bottom, p. 156, p. 157, p. 164 top, p. 164 bottom, p. 165 top, p. 165 bottom, p. 166 top left, p. 166 top right, p. 166 bottom left, p. 166 bottom right, p. 176 top left, p. 176 top right, p. 176 bottom left, p. 182 middle, p. 182 bottom, p. 184 top, p. 184 middle, p. 184 bottom, p. 187, p. 188 bottom, p. 189 top, p. 189 middle, p. 189 bottom, p. 190 top, p. 190 middle, p. 190 bottom, p. 193 top, p. 193 middle, p. 193 bottom, p. 194 top, p. 194 middle, p. 194 bottom, p. 195, p. 197 bottom, p. 198 middle, p. 198 bottom, p. 199 bottom, p. 201 bottom left, p. 201 top right, p. 202 top, p. 202 middle, p. 202 bottom, p. 203 top, p. 203 middle, p. 203 bottom, p. 204 top, p. 204 middle, p. 204 bottom, p. 205 middle, p. 205 bottom, p. 208 middle, p. 208 bottom, p. 210 bottom, p. 212 top, p. 213 bottom, p. 215, p. 219, p. 224 top, p. 228 bottom left, p. 230 top, p. 230 bottom, p. 232 top left, p. 232 bottom left, p. 232 bottom right, p. 235 right, p. 238 bottom right, p. 244 top, p. 244 bottom, p. 246, p. 247 bottom, p. 252 left, p. 253 left, p. 260, p. 263 top, p. 263 middle left, p. 263 middle right, p. 263 bottom, p. 264, p. 267, p. 275 left, p. 285, p. 291 left, p. 305 top left, p. 305 top right, p. 305 middle top right, p. 305 middle bottom left, p. 305 middle bottom right, p. 305 bottom left, p. 305 bottom right, p. 306 top left, p. 306 top right, p. 306 middle top right, p. 306 middle bottom left, p. 306 middle bottom right, p. 306 bottom left, p. 306 bottom right; J. Horace McFarland Company: p. 268 bottom; John Marmarus: p. 4, p. 13, p. 44, p. 45, p. 46; Hamilton Mason: p. 266 top left; O'Dell Manufacturing Company: p. 162 top right, p. 220; Arthur Norman Orans: p. 286; The Orchid Digest: p. 197 top; Pan-American Seed Company: p. 279 bottom; Maynard L. Parker Modern Photography: p. 98 bottom left, p. 100 top left, p. 122, p. 237 bottom left, p. 240, p. 271 left, p. 276, p. 281; Paul J. Pearl: p. 242 top, p. 266 bottom left; Riekes Crisa Corporation: p. 154 top, p. 154 bottom, p. 160, p. 161, p. 162 bottom left, p. 167, p. 168, p. 169 top, p. 170 top, p. 170 bottom, p. 171, p. 172, p. 174, p. 177, p. 180 top, p. 180 bottom; Rohm and Haas Company: p. 155, p. 158, p. 162 top left; Ross Photos: p. 27; Peto Seed Company, Inc.: p. 279 top; Ed Sievers: p. 100 bottom left; Star Roses: p. 237 bottom right; Fred A. Stewart, Inc.: p. 198 top; Ezra Stoller Associates: p. 139 top; Sturdi-Built Manufacturing Company: p. 250; George R. Szanik: p. 242 bottom; Terrestrial Terrariums, p. 173, p. 186, p. 191; U.S. Department of Agriculture: p. 25, p. 31, p. 74; U.S. Forest Service: p. 92; U.S. Soil Conservation Service: p. 94; Vanguarde, Inc.: p. 199 top; Verilux TruBloom, Inc.: p. 248 top.